Economics for Financial Markets

Butterworth-Heinemann Finance

QUANTITATIVE
FINANCE SERIES

Aims and Objectives

- books based on the work of financial market practitioners, and academics
- presenting cutting edge research to the professional/practitioner market
- combining intellectual rigour and practical application
- covering the interaction between mathematical theory and financial practice
- to improve portfolio performance, risk management and trading book performance
- covering quantitative techniques

Market

Brokers/Traders; Actuaries; Consultants; Asset Managers; Fund Managers; Regulators; Central Bankers; Treasury Officials; Technical Analysts; and Academics for Masters in Finance and MBA market.

Series titles

Return Distributions in Finance
Derivative Instruments: theory, valuation, analysis
Managing Downside Risk in Financial Markets: theory, practice, and
  implementation
Economics for Financial Markets
Global Tactical Asset Allocation: theory and practice
Performance Measurement in Finance: firms, funds and managers
Real R&D Options

Series Editor

Dr Stephen Satchell

Dr Satchell is Reader in Financial Econometrics at Trinity College, Cambridge, Visiting Professor at Birkbeck College, City University Business School and University of Technology, Sydney. He also works in a consultative capacity to many firms, and edits the journal *Derivatives: use, trading and regulations*.

Economics for Financial Markets

Brian Kettell

OXFORD   AUCKLAND   BOSTON   JOHANNESBURG   MELBOURNE   NEW DELHI

332.4
K43e

This book is dedicated to my wife Nadia without whose support it
would not have been written and to my sister Pat without whom it
would not have been typed.

Butterworth-Heinemann
Linacre House, Jordan Hill, Oxford OX2 8DP
225 Wildwood Avenue, Woburn, MA 01801-2041
A division of Reed Educational and Professional Publishing Ltd

A member of the Reed Elsevier plc group

First published 2002

AH

British Library Cataloguing in Publication Data
Kettell, Brian
    Economics for financial markets. – (Quantitative finance
    series)
    1. Money market
    I. Title
    332.4

Library of Congress Cataloguing in Publication Data
A catalogue record for this book is available from the Library of Congress

ISBN 0 7506 5384 1

For information on all Butterworth-Heinemann publications visit
our website at www.bh.com and for finance titles in particular go
to www.bh.com/finance

Composition by Genesis Typesetting, Laser Quay, Rochester, Kent
Printed and bound in Great Britain by Biddles Ltd, *www.biddles.co.uk*

FOR EVERY TITLE THAT WE PUBLISH, BUTTERWORTH-HEINEMANN
WILL PAY FOR BTCV TO PLANT AND CARE FOR A TREE.

Contents

Preface

This book is about what aspects of economics it is necessary to
know about to understand why financial markets are so
volatile. It is designed to demonstrate that behind all the jargon
associated with the financial markets there are some basic
economic ideas operating. What these basic ideas are is not
evident from either existing textbooks nor from reading the
financial press. The text is not designed as a standard
economics textbook as the market place is full of excellent
textbooks for anyone seeking to understand basic economic
ideas.

Prior to the publication of this text readers seeking to
understand how the economics world and the real financial
market place interact have had a problem. The financial
markets are unundated with information. From all this information how can one make sense of this to see the big financial
market picture? Certainly not by reading standard economics
textbooks.

The text is designed for a broad readership including students, both undergraduate or postgraduate majoring in economics of finance, practitioners in the markets seeking a fresh
insight into what is going on around them every day, and for
newcomers to the financial markets who need a clear perspective on all the daily ups and downs in the markets. To repeat,
these objectives are not achieved by reading the existing
literature.

The text takes the US economy as its frame of reference. This
is based on the fact that the sheer size of the US economy in the
world financial markets is so large that it dwarfs most other
financial market places. Also the domination of the US dollar as
the world's global currency means that what moves the dollar

basically moves all the other financial markets, and clearly whatever can move the value of the dollar has to be understood. However the text is just as relevant to readers operating in other financial markets, as once they understand the economic implications of changes in the US financial market place they can easily see the implications for their own domestic economy.

What do you need to know about macroeconomics to make sense of financial market volatility?

In order to appreciate the impact of economic activity on the financial markets it is essential to first appreciate what are the major constituent items that drive the economy. These items are best understood by examining what is referred to as the standard macroeconomic model.

Macroeconomics concentrates on the behaviour of entire economies. Rather than looking at the price and output decisions of a single company, macroeconomists study overall economic activity, the unemployment rate, the price level, and other broad economic categories. These are referred to as economic aggregates. An 'economic aggregate' is nothing but an abstraction that people find convenient in describing some salient feature of economic life. Among the most important of these abstract notions is the concept of national product, which represents the total production of a nation's economy. The process by which real objects, such as cars, tickets to football matches and laptop computers, get combined into an abstraction called the national product is one of the foundations of macroeconomics. We can illustrate this by a simple example.

Imagine a nation called Titanica whose economy is far simpler than the more developed economies of the West. Business firms in Titanica produce nothing but food to sell to consumers. Rather than deal separately with all the markets for hamburgers, ice cream, automobiles and so on, macroeconomists group them all into a single abstract 'market for output'. Thus when macroeconomists in Titanica announce that output in Titanica rose 10 per cent this year, are they referring to more potatoes, hamburgers or onions? The answer is: They do not care. They simply aggregate them all together.

During economic fluctuations, markets tend to move in unison. When demand in the economy rises, there is more demand for potatoes and tomatoes, more demand for artichokes and apples, more demand for spaghetti and pizzas. And vice versa when the economy slows down.

There are several ways to measure the economy's total output, the most popular being the gross national product, or GNP for short. The GNP is the most comprehensive measure of the output of all the factories, offices and shops in the economy. Specifically it is the sum of the money values of all final goods and services produced within the year. This is often referred to as nominal GNP.

Aggregate demand within the economy, another application of the aggregation principle, refers to the total amount that all consumers, business firms, government agencies, and foreigners wish to spend on all domestically produced goods and services. The level of aggregate demand depends on a variety of factors, for example, consumer incomes, the price level, government economic policies, and events in foreign countries.

The big picture

The nature of aggregate demand can be understood best if we break it up into its major components. These are Consumer Expenditure (C), Investment Spending (I), Government Spending (G), and the level of Exports (X) minus the level of Imports (M). This gives us the following familiar relationship:

Aggregate Demand (GNP) = C + I + G + (X – M)

- Consumer Expenditure (C) is the total amount spent by consumers on newly produced goods and services (excluding purchases of new homes, which are considered investment goods).
- Investment Expenditure (I) is the sum of the expenditure of business firms on new plant and equipment, plus the expenditures of households on new homes. Financial 'investments', such as bonds or stocks, are not included in this category.

- Government Spending refers to all the goods (such as aeroplanes and pencils) and services (such as school teaching and police protection) purchased by all levels of government. It does not include government transfer payments, such as social security and unemployment benefits.
- Net exports (X – M) is the difference between exports (X) and imports (M). It indicates the difference between what a country sells abroad and what it buys from abroad.
- National Income is the sum of the incomes of all the individuals in the economy, earned in the form of wages, interest, rents, and profits. It excludes transfer payments and is calculated before any deductions are taken for income taxes.
- Disposable Income (DI) is the sum of the incomes of all the individuals in the economy after taxes have been deducted and all transfer payments have been added.

Having introduced the concepts of national product, aggregate demand and national income we must illustrate how they interact in the market economy. We can best do this with reference to Figure 1.1, which is not as complex as it may initially appear.

Figure 1.1 is called a circular flow diagram. It depicts a large circular tube in which a fluid is circulating in a clockwise direction. There are several breaks in the tube where either

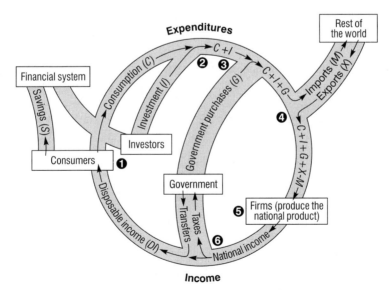

Figure 1.1 The circular flow of expenditure and income (adapted from Baumol and Blinder: *Economics*).

some of the fluid leaks out, or additional fluid is injected in. At point 1 on the circle there are consumers. Disposable Income (DI) flows into them, and two things flow out: consumption (C), which stays in the circular flow, and savings (S), which 'leak out'. This just means that consumers normally spend less than they earn and save the balance. This 'leakage' to savings does not disappear, of course, but flows into the financial system.

The upper loop of the circular flow represents expenditure, and as we move clockwise to point 2, we encounter the first 'injection' into the flow: investment spending (I). The diagram shows this as coming from 'investors' – a group that includes both business firms investing for future production and consumers who buy new homes. As the circular flow moves beyond point 2, it is bigger than it was before. Total spending has increased from C to C + I.

At point 3 there is yet another injection. The government adds its demand for goods and services (G) to those of consumers and investors (C + I). Now aggregate demand is up to C + I + G.

The final leakage and injections comes at point 4. Here we see export spending coming into the circular flow from abroad and import spending leaking out. The net effect of these two forces, i.e., net exports, may increase or decrease the circular flow. In either case, by the time we pass point 4 we have accumulated the full amount of aggregate demand, C + I + G + (X – M).

The circular flow diagram shows this aggregate demand for goods and services arriving at the business firms, which are located at point 5 at the south-east portion of the diagram. Responding to this demand, firms produce the national product. As the circular flow emerges from the firms we have renamed it national income. National product is the sum of the money values of all the final goods and services provided by the economy during a specified period of time, usually one year.

National income and national product must be equal. Why is this the case? When a firm produces and sells $100 worth of output, it pays most of the proceeds to its workers, to people who have lent it money, and to the landlord who owns the property on which the firm is located. All of these payments are income to some individuals. But what about the rest? Suppose, for example, that the wages, interest, and rent that the firm pays add up to $90, while its output is $100. What happens to the remaining $10? The answer is that the owners of the firm receive it as profits. But these owners are also citizens of the country, so their incomes also count in the national income. Thus, when we add up all the wages, interest, rents, and profits in the economy to obtain the national income, we must arrive at the value of the national output.

The lower loop of the circular flow diagram traces the flow of income by showing national income leaving the firms and heading for consumers. But there is a detour along the way. At point 6, the government does two things. First, it siphons off a portion of the national income in the form of taxes. Second, it adds back government transfer payments, such as unemployment pay and social security benefits, which are sums of money that certain individuals receive as outright grants from the government rather than as payments for services rendered to employers. When taxes are subtracted from GNP, and transfer payments are added, we obtain disposable income.

> DI = GNP – Taxes + Transfer Payments.

Disposable income flows unimpeded to consumers at point 1, and the cycle repeats.

Financial markets and the economy

Now that we have an appreciation of how the economy works we must examine how the financial markets interrelate to the real economy. In trying to assess the significance of an economic indicator to the financial markets it is imperative to understand that each particular indicator provides a piece of information about some aspect of nominal GNP. Economic analysts are concerned about nominal GNP because there is a relationship between nominal GNP and money growth. This relationship comes about because as nominal GNP accelerates there is increased demand for transactions balances, the money we hold to spend later. Not surprisingly, therefore, the growth rate and nominal GNP are related.

What is important here is that there is an identifiable relationship between the growth rates of nominal GNP and the various monetary aggregates. Because of this long-standing historical relationship, the US Federal Reserve (the US central bank) has adopted specific growth rate targets for several of the monetary aggregates. Therefore, if something causes nominal GNP to grow more quickly, then it will translate almost assuredly into more rapid growth of the money supply. If money supply growth picks up, the Federal Reserve is likely to respond by tightening its grip on monetary policy. It does this by raising interest rates.

As interest rates rise the price of fixed income securities declines. This is discussed in Chapter 2, and later in the book, but as an example, consider a situation in which somebody holds a Treasury bond that yields 10 per cent. If the economy expands rapidly and the Federal Reserve is eventually forced to tighten so that bond rates rise to 12 per cent, the 10 per cent bond becomes less attractive and its price declines. Investors would rather own the higher yielding 12 per cent security, and they would therefore sell the lower yielding asset driving down its price and forcing up its yield. Thus, anything that causes nominal GNP to rise increases the likelihood that the Federal Reserve will tighten by raising interest rates, which in turn causes bond prices to decline.

It is also important to recognize that nominal GNP consists of two parts: real (or inflation-adjusted) GNP; and the inflation rate, which is measured by the GNP deflator, defined further in Chapter 4. When we refer specifically to growth rates, the growth rate of nominal GNP equals the sum of the growth rates of real GNP and the inflation rate. Thus, 8 per cent nominal GNP growth might consist of 4 per cent real GNP growth and 4 per cent inflation, or 2 per cent real GNP growth and 6 per cent inflation. From the market's point of view, anything that results in either more rapid GNP growth or a higher rate of inflation will cause nominal GNP to grow more rapidly. As noted earlier, this causes money growth to accelerate, increases the likelihood of a Federal Reserve tightening move, and implies higher interest rates and lower securities prices. Conversely, lower GNP growth and lower inflation imply slower GNP growth, which could cause the Federal Reserve to ease. A Federal Reserve easing move would bring about lower interest rates and higher securities prices.

While it may seem somewhat unsavoury, the fact of the matter is that the fixed income markets thrive when the economy collapses and moves into a recession, and they suffer when the economy is doing well and expanding rapidly. Therefore, when interpreting an economic indicator it is critical to determine the effect that a particular indicator will have on either GNP growth or on the inflation rate.

It is useful to carry the breakdown of real GNP one step further in order to focus on specific sectors of the economy that can at times move in several different directions. As we discussed earlier, real GNP consists of the sum of consumption expenditures (C), investment spending (I), government expenditures (G) and net exports (or exports–imports) (X – M). This equation is frequently referred to as GNP = C + I + G + (X – M). If one is looking at an economic indicator that refers to the real economy, it is extremely helpful to be able to identify the particular component of GNP that it affects. For example, when retail sales are released one should immediately recognize that retail sales provide information about consumer spending, which in turn has implications for the consumption component of GNP. Then, having determined the effect on GNP, one can say something about the likelihood of a change in Fed policy.

In Chapters 4, 5 and 6 we describe in detail the way an experienced economic analyst would use the plethora of data on the US Economy to gain a feel for the prospects for the economy and in turn the financial markets.

Having stressed the importance of determining how an economic indicator affects nominal GNP, it is also important to be aware that it is not so much the *absolute* change in an indicator that is important, but how it compares to market expectations. Indeed the critical judgement to be made when analysing market behaviour is on what the financial market is expecting and why. In financial market language, this is called knowing what has been 'discounted' by the market.

For example, if it is widely believed that the Federal Reserve is likely to cut the Fed funds rate over the next few weeks, then bond prices will reflect that belief. When the Fed funds rate is actually cut, bond prices may not move very much, because the expectation that was discounted into the market was actually realized. On the other hand, if for some reason the Federal Reserve chooses not to cut the Fed funds rate, when everyone thought it was going to, then bond prices may react quite negatively, because the expectation of a Fed funds rate cut proved to be incorrect.

What this example shows is the important function that expectations play in the timing of a price movement. Major events that are widely anticipated may have absolutely no effect on prices at the time they occur. Other, equally major, events can have a profound impact on prices if they were not anticipated. The first lesson then of market dynamics and expectations is that one must know what future events have already been discounted by the financial markets.

In Chapters 4, 5 and 6 we breakdown the components of GNP and analyse which regularly published data will best indicate the likely future trend of the US economy and their likely impact on financial markets. We will analyse economic data using the following classification system, in order that a consistent analytical approach can be applied.

- Title of the Indicator
- Definition
- Who publishes it and when?
- How do you interpret it?
- What is its impact on financial markets?

Gross national product and gross domestic product

Gross domestic product (GDP) measures the total value of US output. It is the total of all economic activity in the US, regardless of whether the owners of the means of production reside in the US. It is 'gross' because the depreciation of capital goods is not deducted.

GDP is measured in both current prices, which represent actual market prices, and constant prices, which measure changes in volume. Constant price, or real, GDP is current-price GDP adjusted for inflation. The financial markets focus on the seasonally adjusted annualized percentage change in real-expenditure based GDP in the current quarter compared to the previous quarter.

The difference between GDP and gross national product (GNP) is that GNP includes net factor income, or net earnings, from abroad. This is made up of the return on US investment abroad (profits, investment income, workers' remittances) minus the return on foreign investment in the US. It is national, because it belongs to US residents, but not domestic, since it is not derived solely from production in the US.

Monetarism and financial markets

Monetarist views gained widespread influence in the United States in the 1970s. These views have since spread to Europe with the European Central Bank now also applying monetarist principles in implementing economic stabilization policies.

The rise of monetarism as a key anti-inflation policy started in October 1979 when the new Chairman of the Federal Reserve, Paul Volcker, launched a fierce counter-attack against inflation in what has been called the monetarist experiment. In a dramatic change of its operating procedures the Federal Reserve decided to stop smoothing interest rates and instead focused on keeping bank reserves and the money supply on predetermined growth paths.

The Federal Reserve hoped that a strict quantitative approach to monetary management would accomplish two things. First, it would allow interest rates to rise sharply enough to brake the rapidly growing economy, raising unemployment and slowing wage and price growth through the Phillips-curve mechanism. Second, some believed that a tough and credible monetary policy would deflate inflationary expectations, particularly in labour contracts, and demonstrate that the high-inflation period was over. Once people's expectations were deflated, the economy could experience a relatively painless reduction in the underlying rate of inflation.

The monetarist experiment was largely successful in reducing inflation. As a result of the high interest rates induced by slow money growth, interest-sensitive spending slowed. Consequently real GNP stagnated from 1979 to 1982, and the unemployment rate rose from under 6 per cent to a peak of 10.5 per cent in late 1982. Inflation fell sharply. Any lingering doubts about the effectiveness of monetary policy were stilled and its influence on policy makers remains forefront to this day.

The quantity theory of money – the basis of monetarism

'Monetarist' economists emphasize that the government's monetary policy (i.e., controlling the supply of money in the economy) is more important for the management of the economy than fiscal policy (i.e., government policy on spending, taxation and borrowing). The fundamental idea behind 'monetarism' is that there is a close link between the amount of money in the economy and the level of prices. This relationship is based upon the quantity theory of money.

Misuse of the money supply can be illustrated by two spectacularly unstable episodes in economic history. One

involved the infamous German inflation in the years following
the First World War. In December 1919, there were about 50
billion marks in circulation in Germany. Four years later, this
figure had risen to almost 500 000 000 000 billion marks – or an
increase of 10 000 000 000 times! Money became practically
worthless and prices sky-rocketed. Indeed, money lost its value
so quickly that people were anxious to spend whatever money
they had as soon as possible, while they could still buy
something with it.

The second illustration involves the United States experience
in the Depression of the 1930s. Economists are still debating
the exact causes of that depression and their relative importance. But it can scarcely be denied that the misbehaviour of
the monetary and banking system played a role. As the
economy slid down into the depression, the quantity of money
fell from $26.2 billion in mid 1929 to $19.2 billion in mid 1933
– or by 27 per cent. By the time Franklin D. Roosevelt became
President in 1933, many banks had closed their doors and
many depositors had lost everything.

The quantity theory is essentially concerned with the demand
for a stock of money in one's portfolio. People wish to hold money
primarily to effect transactions in goods, services, and financial
assets. In a modern economy we normally use the medium of
money because it saves us the extensive costs of search and
lengthy arguments of barter transactions. But this implies that,
to avoid barter, we must maintain some quantity of money in our
portfolio, since sales of goods and purchases are not nicely
matched with one another in any given period of time.

The quantity of money we require in our portfolio will depend
on many factors. Probably the most important will be the value
of transactions concluded during a given time period. Other
things being equal, the higher the value of transactions, the
larger will be the quantity of money we shall wish to hold. The
value of transactions consists of two elements, price and
quantity; for a given quantity, the higher the price, the larger
the amount of money one would wish to hold (and vice versa).

Each of us, individually, makes a decision about the quantity
of money that we will hold in our portfolio. Each person adjusts
their stock of money according to the value of the transactions,
which they wish or expect to make during the ensuing time
period. For any given value of transactions in the economy
therefore, we could find the total demand for money by
summing the demands of individuals. This gives us the
aggregate demand for money.

Let us now assume that the aggregate amount of money demanded is greater than the supply of money that the government has made available (or printed), i.e., there is an excess demand for money. Using elementary economic analysis one would predict that as individuals desire more money in their portfolios of wealth than they currently have, they would achieve this by selling goods in exchange for money and/or forego buying goods. This will reduce the demand for goods and the price of goods will fall. If the production of physical goods does not change the only effect will be on the level of prices. As prices diminish so will the demand for money, as one's need for transactions to balance is that much lower. Thus, when prices have been reduced so that at the lower value of transactions people are, in aggregate, just willing to hold the supply of money made available by the government, the price reductions will stop. Then the demand for money will be just equal to the supply and the system is back in equilibrium at a lower level of prices. So if the demand for money is greater than the supply of money there are forces in the economy which bring the two back together.

One may trace the effects of an excess supply of money in precisely the same way. Imagine that the government prints some extra dollar bills and distributes them freely to everyone in the economy. Each of us would then find that he has too much money in his account relative to the value of his transactions. Consequently, he would reduce his money stock by buying goods. This would drive up the price of goods. Thus, the value of transactions would increase until people's demands for money were at such a level that they would be willing to hold the increased stock of money at this new high level of prices. Again there are forces bringing the demand for, and supply of, money back together.

These ideas underline the simplest version of the quantity theory. To illustrate this point further, consider the following.

PQ = national income measured in money terms, where M = quantity of money, P = average level of prices, and Q = quantity of output. It is assumed here that the quantity of output and the quantity of income are interchangeable terms on the grounds that output (i.e. producing) generates income. V = income velocity of money, that is, the average number of times that the money stock (M) is spent to buy final output during a year. Specifically, V is defined as being equal to PQ/M. An example will make the understanding of this clearer.

Suppose that the money stock is $100 million in a given year. Assume that the national income in the same year is $400 million (PQ). This means that the given money supply, $100 million, has financed spending of $400 million. How is this possible? Well, when you spend money in a shop, the owner spends it on re-stocking. His supplier in turn uses it to pay his supplier and so on. In this way the same amount of money finances expenditures of a larger amount. The extent to which money is spent in this way is measured by its velocity of circulation. In this example, velocity is equal to 4, i.e., PQ/M = $400 million/$100 million = 4. Thus, as V = PQ/M, then rearranging the terms we derive the truism that MV = PQ.

In the hands of the early classical economists, however, this truism became the basis of the quantity theory of money. The quantity theory of money is the proposition that velocity (V) is reasonably stable. Therefore, a change in the quantity of money (M) will cause the money national income (PQ) to change by approximately the same percentage. If, for example, the money stock (M) increases by 20 per cent, then classical economists argue that velocity (V) will remain reasonably stable. As a consequence nominal national income will rise by 20 per cent. In addition they argue that over longer time periods, output (Q) tends to be fairly fixed, depending on real factors such as the level of the capital stock, structure of the labour force, training and entrepreneurship rather than monetary disturbances. Therefore, the long-run effect of a change in M is on P, not on Q. So MV ($480 million) equals PQ ($480 million), i.e., a 20 per cent increase in the money supply causes prices to rise by 20 per cent.

The success of this theory in predicting economic changes, depends on the extent to which:

● the government can control the money supply;
● whether V is constant or not;
● whether Q is constant or not.

How money affects the economy – the transmission mechanism

It is not unreasonable to expect that, since one of the main functions of money is to facilitate transactions, the desired amount of money balances will vary proportionally with the level of transactions and, therefore, with the level of income. If this relationship is fairly stable, for example, one holds 10 per cent of income on the *average* of any single time period in the form of money balances as opposed to any other type of assets, then if something causes these balances to increase, one will restore that 10 per cent level by spending. As already discussed, the fact that there is a stable relationship between money balances held by people and the level of their income is one of the key assumptions of the Quantity Theory.

A different way of seeing this mechanism in action is to think of what you would do if a rich aunt left you $10 000 in her will (although a silly example, it works!). Would you keep $10 000 in the bank or as cash? Perhaps you would hold some of your legacy in one of these forms, but perhaps you would spend a part of it. And this is the point. Holding $10 000 in money balances does not provide the same pleasure or services as holding $9000 in money balances and $1000 in the form of new clothes, a new DVD and a long holiday. In other words $10 000 was too much money in the sense that it was too much of a particular asset. Now money is instantly transformed into goods and services. There is a perfect degree of substitutability between money and other things. This is another important aspect of the Quantity Theory. If money is substitutable for other goods then increases or decreases in the quantity of money are bound to be reflected in the demand for goods. Since on a quarter-to-quarter basis output of goods and services is unlikely to vary significantly, then these increases or decreases in demand will be reflected in changes in prices.

There is, however, a group of economists who argue that money has its main influence not on goods, but on financial assets only. So the monetary transmission mechanism is the same as that described for the Quantity Theory approach but with the difference that people may well 'buy' or 'sell' (hold less) of other financial assets. This approach is called the Keynesian Theory of the transmission mechanism (after the economist J.M. Keynes).

The Keynesian Theory examines what happens if we have a series of goods that are close substitutes. Under these circumstances then, increasing/decreasing the quantity of one good will affect the prices of the rest, as consumers shift their purchases from one good to the other. To appreciate this point it is important to remember that the return on an asset varies inversely with its price. (See Chapters 2 and 3 for further discussion of this principle.)

There are, of course, a lot of assets with fixed capital and interest rate values. A deposit with a bank of $100 will yield say 10 per cent p.a., and since its capital value is fixed so is the rate of return – unless of course the bank changes the interest rate it pays depositors.

Now if demand for a certain asset increases then there will be a downward pressure on the rate of return. If banks are bulging with deposits they are more likely to decrease interest rates than increase them. If on the other hand the demand for, say government bonds decreases then this will lead to an upward pressure on interest rates. So you can see what matters here is the differentials between the yields of different assets and the speed by which the interest rates (i.e., the rates of return) are adjusted. But interest rates are not only returns for investors, they are also costs for borrowers. So increases in the supply of money (the bank example) leading to a shift to other financial assets will also lead to a downward pressure on interest rates.

Certain classes of expenditure, such as business investment, consumer spending on durables (and especially on housing), are fairly interest-rate elastic, i.e., they respond quickly to changes in interest rates. So, the argument here is that levels of aggregate demand and expenditure can be affected by changing the quantities of money and therefore by affecting interest rates, which in their turn affect expenditures. Thus as the money supply rises, Keynesians argue, returns on financial assets alter first, before expenditures. Monetarists believe that expenditures alter first and returns on financial assets alter later.

We can crudely summarize the 'transmission mechanism' of the Keynesian and Quantity (usually called the 'Monetarist Approach') Theories as follows.

- Keynesian transmission mechanism:
  Changes in quantity of money ⇨ interest rate changes ⇨ changes in the level of expenditures which are affected by changes in the interest rate.
- Monetarist transmission mechanism:
  changes in the quantity of money ⇨ changes in expenditures (with likely effects on the price level, especially in the short run).

You can see that there is an extra 'link' in the Keynesian mechanism. If interest rates do not respond to changes in the quantity of money or if aggregate demand does not respond to changes in interest rates then varying the quantity of money will not have much effect on either prices or the level of aggregate demand. This is a very different view from that of the monetarists.

So whether variations in the quantity of money have their effects principally upon goods or financial assets depends on the respective degrees of substitutability. Monetarists consider money to be a unique financial asset distinguished by its ability to serve as a medium of exchange. Keynesians tend to view money as just another financial asset and see the key distinction between financial assets in general and goods.

The modern quantity theory – modern monetarism

As discussed above, the Quantity Theory of money was discredited by the evidence of the great depression in the 1920s and 1930s and the subsequent ascendancy of Keynesian ideas. In the early 1950s Milton Friedman of Chicago University began to reformulate the Quantity Theory. Since then his ideas have become increasingly influential.

Friedman's basic advance was to concede many of the arguments of Keynes as descriptions of the short-run behaviour of the economy, albeit with reservations, whilst retaining the basic tenets of the quantity theory as longer-term propositions. Friedman and the monetarists retained the old quantity theory assumptions that:

- money (M) was held for transactions purposes;
- velocity (V) was constant in the longer run (or at any rate grew at a constant rate);
- output (Q) was unaffected by money in the long run.

But Friedman conceded that:

- short-term movements in velocity were possible in response to fluctuations in the money supply;
- velocity also depended on interest rates (although he asserted that the sensitivity was not great);
- short-term movements in output could be produced by varying the money supply. Indeed, Friedman argued that changes in money had powerful, albeit temporary, effects on output.

The monetarist view of the world is perhaps more easily understood by explaining how they see the effect of a rise in the money supply (the transmission mechanism). Initially a rise in M is absorbed by a fall in V, i.e., the extra money supply is hoarded. Very quickly, however, economic agents begin to run down their excess money holdings. They do this partly by increasing spending, partly by buying financial assets (such as stocks and shares) and partly by buying up physical assets (e.g. houses and paintings). This bids up the stock market and reduces interest rates, stimulating investment. Through these diverse mechanisms the rise in money feeds through to an increase in the pace of economic activity. Whilst a fall in V takes up all the slack initially, Q soon begins to increase. However, whilst an individual can replace his holding of money (by exchanging it for goods and services) this is not the case for the economy at large.

The effect of the increase in aggregate spending is to cause prices to rise. Firms initially respond to higher demand by producing more and widening mark-ups (which raises prices immediately). Extra output requires more workers and the associated tightening of the labour market pushes up wages, which raises costs and feeds through into higher prices. As prices rise the demand for money is increased and the excess money holdings that began the whole process are eroded. When prices have risen by the same proportion as the rise in the money supply, excess money balances have disappeared and V and Q return to their normal level.

The monetarists believe that changes in M have only temporary effects on output but have permanent effects on prices.

The monetarist claims revisited

As already indicated, the basic monetarist claim is that prices are determined by the supply of money. All that a government has to do, in order to control the level of price increase, is to obey a fixed monetary rule that would permit the money supply to increase by no more than the anticipated growth in output. Any departure from this rule, or any attempt to use other means, such as fiscal measures, to influence economic developments, will be self-defeating.

The basis for these claims has been fully advanced by Professor Milton Friedman in *A Monetary History of the United States 1867–1960*, written in association with Anna Jacobson Schwarz. According to Friedman, the United States' experience over this period shows that:

- changes in the behaviour of the money stock have been closely associated with changes in economic activity, money incomes and prices;
- the interrelation between monetary and economic change has been highly stable; and
- monetary changes have often had an independent origin – they have not simply been a reflection of changes in economic activity.

These three propositions, stated somewhat rigorously, have become embodied in a body of doctrine which can be summarized as follows:

- Past rates of growth in the stock of money are the major determinants (indeed, virtually the only systematic non-random determinants) of the growth of GNP in terms of current prices. It follows from this that fiscal policies do not significantly affect GNP in money terms, although they may alter its composition and also affect interest rates. It also follows that the overall impact on GNP in money terms of monetary and financial policies is, for practical purposes, summed up in the movements of a single variable, the stock of money. Consequently, the argument goes that monetary policy should be exclusively guided by this variable, without regard to interest rates, credit flows or other indicators.
- Nominal interest rates are geared to inflationary expectations and thus, with a time lag, to actual inflation. Although the immediate market impact of expansionary monetary policy may be to lower interest rates, it is fairly soon reversed when premiums for the resulting inflation are added to interest rates.
- The central bank can and should make the money stock grow at a steady rate equal to the rate of growth of potential GNP plus a target rate of inflation.
- There is no enduring trade-off between unemployment and inflation. There is instead a unique natural rate of unemployment for each economy, which allows for structural change and job search but which cannot be departed from in the long term. Government policy will produce ever-accelerating inflation if it persistently seeks a lower than natural rate of unemployment. If it seeks a higher rate, there will be an ever accelerating deflation. The natural rate of unemployment cannot be identified except through practical experience; it is the rate that will emerge if the proper steady-growth monetary policy is pursued.

The attractive simplicity of this doctrine is easily recognized. The essence of the monetarist position is that increases in prices and wages can be held in check by nothing more complicated than the apparently simple device of controlling the amount of money in circulation. Ideally, a condition of nil inflation is achieved when the increase in the money supply equals the increase in the real output of the economy. Since both wage and price increases can only occur if extra money to finance them is made available, then no increase will take place if no more money is provided. If attempts are made by firms or wage-earners to gain an advantage by putting up the cost of their goods and services on the one hand or labour rates on the other, a constant money supply will mean unsold goods and services for the firm and the loss of jobs for labour. Thus, so the argument goes, as long as the government is prepared to control the money supply, everyone will see it as being in his interest to exercise restraint, and inflation will be reduced to whatever level is deemed to be acceptable.

The practical problem of applying monetarist ideas is the subject matter of the remainder of this chapter.

Monetarism and Federal Reserve operating targets from 1970 to the present

For the Federal Reserve a monetary policy strategy is a plan for achieving its economic objectives. The Federal Reserve normally tries to implement such a plan by following an operating target that is a self-imposed guideline for conducting monetary policy over time.

In practice the Federal Reserve has varied its operating targets in recent years. Since 1970 four separate targets have been applied. These are:

- Targeting Monetary Growth and the Fed Funds Rate: 1970 to 1979
- Targeting Non-Borrowed Reserves: October 1979 to October 1982
- Targeting Borrowed Reserves: October 1982 to October 1987
- Targeting Federal Funds: October 1987 to the Present.

Changes in Operating Procedure 1979–1996 are summarized in Table 1.1. Developments after this date are discussed in the text. For readers not needing to know the intricacies of Federal Reserve operating strategies the next section can be safely skipped.

Targeting monetary growth and the Fed funds rate: 1970 to 1979

In 1970 the Federal Reserve formally adopted monetary targets with the intention of using them to reduce inflation gradually over time. The techniques for setting and pursuing monetary growth targets developed gradually, with frequent experimentation and modification of procedures taking place in the first few years of the 1970s. Nonetheless, until October 1979 the framework generally included setting a monetary objective and encouraging the Fed funds rate to move gradually up or down if monetary growth was exceeding or falling short of the objective. The Fed funds rate, as an indicator of money market conditions, became the primary guide to day-to-day open market operations.

Free reserves served as an indicator of the volume of reserves needed to keep the Fed funds rate at the desired level. The role of free reserves as indicators of the strength of monetary policy is illustrated in Table 1.2. Tight monetary policy is reflected in a fall in free reserves and an easing of monetary policy is reflected in a rise in free reserves.

Excess reserves are total reserves minus required reserves. The net difference between excess and borrowed reserves is called free reserves and/or net borrowed reserves; the latter term is sometimes used instead of referring to excess and borrowed reserves separately. The method of calculating net free reserves and net borrowed reserves is illustrated in Figure 1.2.

Table 1.3 illustrates that as easy monetary policy occurs as net free reserves rise, and a tight monetary policy occurs as free reserves fall.

The Federal Open Market Committee (FOMC) trading desk (known as the Fed open market desk) uses the forecasts of these reserve factors to gauge the appropriate direction and magnitude for open market operations, irrespective of the choice of operating target.

Under the 1970–1979 procedures, the FOMC instructed the trading desk to raise the Fed funds rate within a limited band if the monetary aggregates were significantly above the desired

Table 1.1   Changes in Operating Procedures, 1979–1996

Period	Operating Procedures		Implications	
	Key Elements	NBR Path	Fed Funds Rate	Other
1979–82	Target for NBR quantity	Based on the FOMC's desired money growth	High levels of volatility; automatic movements in the funds rate over a wide and flexible range	No significant accommodation of short-run fluctuations in reserves demand; operations could signal policy shifts
1983–87	Degree of reserve pressure; targets for borrowed reserves	Consistent with the FOMC's intended levels of discount window borrowing and the funds rate	Modest amount of volatility within and between maintenance periods	Partial accommodation of short-run fluctuations in reserves demand; operations could signal policy shifts
1989–93	Degree of reserve pressure; assumed initial borrowing allowance	Consistent with the FOMC's intended Federal funds rate	Limited variations within maintenance periods around the intended level	Nearly complete accommodation of short-run fluctuations in reserves demand; operations could signal policy shifts
1994–96	Degree of reserve pressure and associated federal funds rate target; new policy disclosure procedures	Consistent with the FOMC's intended Federal funds rate	Limited variations within maintenance periods around the intended level	Nearly complete accommodation of short-run fluctuations in reserves demand; operations do not signal policy shifts

Note: NBR = non-borrowed reserves
Source: *Understanding Open Market Operations*, M.A. Akhtar, Federal Reserve Bank of New York

Table 1.2   Free reserves: an indicator of the strength of monetary policy

---

Excess reserves (ER) – Discount window borrowing (DWB) = Free reserves

DWB > ER = Net borrowed reserves (NEBR)
ER > DWB = Net free reserves (NFR)

Tight monetary policy	Easy monetary policy
– Free reserves fall	– Free reserves rise
– Net borrowed reserves rise	– Net borrowed reserves fall

---

growth rates, or to lower the Fed funds rate within that band if the aggregates were below them. The procedure required the staff to estimate what level of Fed funds rate would achieve the desired money growth. The Fed funds rate worked by affecting the interest rates that banks both paid and charged customers and hence the demand for money.

During most of the 1970s, the FOMC was reluctant to change the funds rate by large amounts at any one time. Part of that reluctance reflected a wish to avoid short-term reversals of the rate. Keeping each rate adjustment small minimized the risk of overdoing the rate changes and then having to reverse course. These priorities meant that the FOMC was handicapped at times when it sensed a large rate move might be needed but was uncertain about its size. The adjustments in the funds rate often lagged behind market forces, allowing trends in monetary growth, the economy, and prices to get ahead of policy.

The key equations:

$$TR = RR + ER$$
$$NBR = RR + ER - DWB$$
$$NFR \text{ or } NEBR = ER - DWB$$

Example

$$40\,000 = 39\,000 + 1000$$
$$39\,700 = 39\,000 + 1000 - 300$$
$$700 = 1000 - 300$$

Where:

TR = Total reserves
RR = Required reserves
ER = Excess reserves
NBR = Non-borrowed reserves
DWB = Discount without borrowing
NFR = Net free reserves
NEBR = Net borrowed reserves

Figure 1.2   Calculating net free reserves (NFR) and net borrowed reserves (NEBR).

Table 1.3 How do you measure the strength of monetary policy?

Easy money	ER > DWB Free reserves rise Net borrowed reserves fall
Neutral monetary policy	Free reserves constant
Tight money	DWB > ER Free reserves fall Net borrowed reserves rise

So prior to October 1979, the System attempted to estimate the level of the Fed funds rate, i.e., the overnight interest rate on reserve funds in the open money market, consistent with the rate at which it wanted M1 and the other monetary aggregates to grow. It then used open market operations to hold the Fed funds rate within a narrow range around that level, in the short run.

An important disadvantage of this approach in practice was that when the public became fully aware that the Federal Reserve was using the Fed funds rate in this way, financial markets became very sensitive in the short run to even small changes in the rate, and small adjustments in the rate sometimes produced strong political reactions. Both conditions made it difficult for the Federal Reserve to adjust the rates as frequently as was necessary for effective control of the monetary aggregates.

Targeting Non-Borrowed Reserves: October 1979 to October 1982

Against this background, in October 1979 the Federal Reserve stopped using the Fed funds rate as its direct control instrument and began to focus on various reserve measures in order to improve its monetary control performance.

In October 1979, Paul Volcker, who had recently become Chairman of the Board of Governors, announced far-reaching changes in the FOMC's operating techniques for targeting the monetary aggregates. The acceleration of inflation to unacceptable rates over the preceding decade inspired a change in priorities. Chairman Volcker and other FOMC members realized that turning around these inflationary pressures, which had come to permeate economic relations, would involve costs. Interest rates would have to rise significantly beyond recent levels, although the extent of the increase could not be determined in advance. Increased rate volatility was also likely to accompany the efforts to halt inflation. The Federal Reserve's credibility with the public was low after previous efforts to slow inflation had been followed by further price acceleration. Chairman Volcker felt that only strong measures could rebuild public confidence.

From October 1979 until late 1982, the Federal Reserve used non-borrowed reserves (NBR) as its instrument. In this regime, the System set a path for non-borrowed reserves that it believed was consistent with the desired paths of the monetary aggregates. With non-borrowed reserves thus predetermined, any change in depository institution demand for total reserves, occasioned by a deviation of the monetary aggregates from their desired paths, had to be accommodated by a corresponding change in the level of borrowing at the discount window, either upwards or downwards. The change in borrowing, in turn, affected the Fed funds rate and other short-term interest rates, and hence the demand for money.

At a technical level the relationship between borrowing at the discount window and short-term rates was the central relationship in the non-borrowed reserve regime.

If the growth of the monetary aggregates began to exceed the desired paths, the demand of depository institutions for total reserves would rise, which would cause the level of borrowing at the discount window to increase. The increased borrowing would then put upward pressure on the Fed funds rate and other market rates, given the general reluctance to borrow and the Federal Reserve's administrative restrictions on borrowing. The rise in rates, finally, would reduce the demand for money and the growth of the monetary aggregates.

In implementing the policy, the Fed open market desk emphasized that it was targeting reserves and not the Fed funds rate by entering the market at about the same time each day – usually between 9:30 and 9:45 a.m. – to perform its temporary operations. It confined outright purchases or sales to estimated reserve needs or excesses extending several weeks into the future. It arranged outright operations early in the afternoon for delivery next day or two days forward. The Fed funds rate was not ignored; it was used as an indicator of the accuracy of reserve estimates.

By setting an objective for non-borrowed reserves the Federal Reserve ended up by allowing some variability in total reserves, in an attempt to dampen interest rate variability. Nevertheless interest rates were much more volatile after the Federal Reserve switched to targeting non-borrowed reserves. By allowing reserves to vary somewhat, the Federal Reserve ended up permitting the quantity of money to vary from its target level. In the end targeting non-borrowed reserves led to significant variations in both interest rates and the quantity of money.

Targeting Borrowed Reserves: October 1982 to October 1987

In October 1982 the Federal Reserve tried an operating procedure that lay between targeting reserves and targeting the Fed funds rate. It began to target the level of borrowed reserves. By targeting borrowed reserves the Federal Reserve tended to stabilize free reserves.

Changes in the behaviour of M1 had led the FOMC to abandon the non-borrowed reserves procedures and to emphasize the level of discount window borrowing as the focus of policy actions. Under the borrowed reserves procedures there was no longer an automatic response of interest rates to a monetary aggregate intermediate target. To implement a policy change the FOMC would tell the trading desk to aim for higher or lower levels of discount window borrowing.

To tighten policy the borrowing target would be raised and the Fed open market desk would use open market operations to reduce non-borrowed reserves. Decreased reserves would put upward pressure on the Fed funds rate and with an unchanged discount rate would result in a higher level of discount window borrowing.

To relax monetary policy the borrowing target would be lowered and the Fed open market desk would use open market operations to increase non-borrowed reserves. Increased reserves would put downward pressure on the Fed funds rate and with an unchanged discount rate would result in a lower level of discount window borrowing.

To be sure, the borrowed reserve procedure was implemented in a way so as not to lose control over Fed funds rate. In its day-to-day operations, the Fed open market desk considered not just the assumed level of discount window borrowing, but also the degree of uncertainty surrounding the reserve estimates, as well as other signals about reserve market conditions, including movements of the Fed funds rate. Occasionally, the Fed funds rate was given the dominant position in assessing the reserve pressures.

On average, however, the FOMC and the trading desk used the intended level of discount window borrowing as the main factor for evaluating reserve availability conditions during 1983–1987, with short-run market expectations being allowed to play a relatively modest role in determining the funds rate. In this setting, the Federal funds rate had considerable leeway to fluctuate without changes in the desired policy stance. Through much of the 1983–1987 period it was not unusual for the average effective Federal funds rate to vary by 20–40 basis points even between those maintenance periods in which the FOMC had not sought to change the degree of reserve pressure.

Targeting the Fed funds rate: 1987 to the present

The use of a borrowed reserve targeting procedure is dependent upon a stable demand for discount window borrowing. Beginning in the mid 1980s, periodic changes in banks' demand for borrowed reserves made it increasingly difficult to implement the borrowed reserves procedure, leading the FOMC to move back towards a Fed funds rate procedure.

The change in procedure was precipitated by the October 1987 stock market collapse, with many stocks falling by over one third in a single day. To help prevent a broader financial crisis the Federal Reserve announced that it stood ready to provide as much liquidity as needed. It also decided to keep interest rates stable to prevent further volatility in the prices of financial instruments. To do this, it switched to a Fed funds rate target once again.

The operating procedures that began in the late 1980s have been used throughout the subsequent period. While the FOMC continues to express its policy stance in the directive in terms of the degree of pressure on reserve positions, the Fed funds rate is now the principal guide for evaluating reserve availability conditions, and has therefore become the day-to-day policy objective for open market operations. The Fed open market desk still uses an anticipated level of discount window borrowing in constructing the non-borrowed reserves path, but it compensates for deviations from that anticipated level by modifying the non-borrowed reserves objective, formally or informally, so as to maintain the FOMC's intended Fed funds rate. On average, changes in the demand for reserves during the maintenance period are now more fully accommodated by adjusting the supply of non-borrowed reserves than was the case in the 1983–1987 period. As a result, the average level of the funds rate during the period is more closely associated with the intended degree of reserve pressures than before. The Federal funds rate does fluctuate during the maintenance period, but its average value from one period to the next remains essentially the same as long as there is no change in the intended stance of monetary policy.

Does a move to targeting Fed funds mean that the Federal Reserve no longer targets the money supply?

Traditional discussion of monetary policy focuses on the assumption that the Fed Reserve influences the economy by controlling the money supply. By contrast, when you read about Federal Reserve policy in the media, the policy instrument mentioned most often is the Fed funds rate, which is the interest rate that banks charge one another for overnight loans. What then is being targeted? Is it the money supply or is it the Fed funds rate? The answer is both.

As discussed above in recent years the Federal Reserve has used the Fed funds rate as its short-term policy instrument. This means that when the FOMC meets every six weeks to set monetary policy, it votes on a target for this interest rate that will apply until the next meeting. After the meeting is over, the Federal Reserve's bond traders in New York are told to conduct the open-market operations necessary to hit the target. These open-market operations change the money supply and move the existing Fed funds rate to the new target Fed funds rate that the FOMC has chosen.

As a result of this operating procedure, Federal Reserve policy is often discussed in terms of changing interest rates. Keep in mind, however, that behind the changes in interest rates are the necessary changes in the money supply. A newspaper might report, for instance, that 'the Fed has lowered interest rates'. To be more precise, we can translate this statement as meaning 'the Federal Open Market Committee has instructed the Federal Reserve bond traders to buy bonds in open-market operations so as to increase the money supply, and reduce the equilibrium interest rate to hit a new lower target'.

Why has the Federal Reserve chosen to use an interest rate, rather than the money supply, as its short-term policy instrument? One possible answer is that the money supply growth can be somewhat unpredictable. Targeting an unpredictable money supply can lead to perverse results. If this is such a problem then a policy of targeting the interest rate leads to greater macro-economic stability than a policy of targeting the money supply. Another possible answer is that interest rates are easier to measure than the money supply. The Federal Reserve has several different measures of money that sometimes move in different directions. Rather than deciding which measure is best, the Federal Reserve avoids the question by using the Fed funds rate as its short-term policy instrument. Whatever the reason for choosing the Fed funds rate target, a belief in the role of monetarism still lies behind current Federal Reserve operating tactics.

New FOMC disclosure procedures

Another, more recent, development that has affected the conduct of open market operations considerably was the FOMC's change in procedures, initiated in early 1994 and formalized in early 1995, for disclosing monetary policy decisions immediately after they are made. Until the end of 1993, the Committee's policy decisions were announced with a 5–8 week lag, through the release of its minutes, which contain the domestic policy directive. However, any changes in the stance of monetary policy were quickly communicated to financial markets through open market operations as the Fed open market desk implemented the policy directive. Under the new procedures, which are now standard, changes in the FOMC's stance on monetary policy, including any intermeeting changes, are announced on the day they are made. The FOMC continues to release its directive for each meeting with a delay, on the Friday after the next meeting.

Before the recent disclosure procedures for policy decisions went into effect, market participants closely watched the Fed open market desk's operations to detect policy signals. The use of open market operations to signal policy changes created, at times, considerable complications for the FOMC trading desk, especially when the funds rate and the reserve estimates gave conflicting signals. Just as importantly, the Fed open market desk also faced considerable risks that its day-to-day technical or defensive operations would be viewed as indicators of policy moves. Such risks were heightened during periods when market participants expected shifts in policy.

The recent disclosure procedures have essentially freed the Fed open market desk from the risk that its normal technical or defensive operations would be misinterpreted as policy moves. Open market operations no longer convey any new information about changes in the stance of monetary policy. In implementing the directive, the Fed open market desk carries out a policy that is already known to financial markets and the public at large, and is no longer concerned about using a particular type of operation to signal a change in policy. Of course, market partici- pants speculate, just as they always did, about possible future policy moves, especially in the period immediately leading up to the FOMC meetings. But, in general, they no longer closely watch day-to-day open market operations to detect policy signals.

On October 2, 1997 the Federal Reserve announced that the FOMC policy directive had been reworded at the Committee's meeting on August 19. The directive now specifies an explicit target for the Fed funds rate, and also expresses the bias to possible future action in terms of the rate. Previously, the operational sections of the directive had been expressed in terms of the degree of pressure on reserve positions. This is discussed further in Chapter 11.

Figure 1.3 provides a useful taxonomy of the interrelation- ship between the different components of Nominal GNP and those market-sensitive economic indicators that most closely influence it.

The Non-Accelerating Inflation Rate of Unemployment (NAIRU)

As will be discussed further in Chapter 6, on the first Friday of every month the US Bureau of Labour Statistics releases the latest data on employment and unemployment in the United States. Sharp movements in financial markets have often followed these releases. In particular, markets have taken lower-than-expected unemployment rates to mean that infla- tion is about to accelerate, resulting in falling stock prices and increasing interest rates.

The average citizen would find this to be a rather strange ritual. Isn't low unemployment good for the country? And why is low unemployment supposed to lead to higher inflation anyway? These are important and difficult questions. An influential economic theory, however, argues that the answers are easy and widely found in macroeconomics textbooks. Low

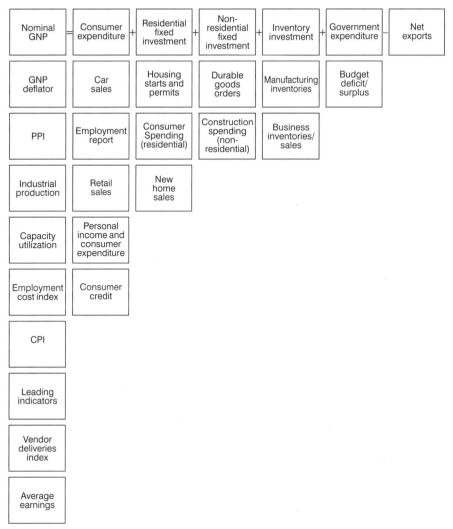

Figure 1.3 GNP broken down by its constituent market-sensitive economic indicators.

unemployment, this theory implies, is unambiguously 'good' only up to a point. If unemployment falls below this point, known as the non-accelerating inflation rate of unemployment (NAIRU), inflation tends to accelerate. Opinions about the current location of the NAIRU vary, but many published estimates in the US place it close to 5 per cent. Since recent unemployment figures have been consistently below that range, adherents to this theory predict that inflation will accelerate. We return to these ideas throughout the text and provide some flavour of the ideas below.

The Phillips curve, the natural rate and NAIRU

The idea that unemployment may be too low to be consistent with stable inflation is of relatively recent vintage. Its origins can be traced to the 1960s and 1970s discussion about how to interpret the then recently discovered 'Phillips curve', an empirical association between inflation and unemployment, named after the Australian economist based at the London School of Economics, A. W. Phillips, who popularized the idea. Some aspects of this debate are useful for the discussions that come later in the text.

Phillips's (1958) analysis of almost a century of UK data shocked the economics profession. Phillips focused on the relationship between wages and unemployment and discovered the striking fact that the rate of change in nominal wages had a negative correlation with unemployment. Soon afterward, Samuelson and Solow (1960) showed that a similar relation held using US data. Moreover, Samuelson and Solow argued that changes in nominal wages were positively related to overall inflation, thus recasting the wage unemployment relation discovered by Phillips into the inverse relation between price inflation and unemployment, which became more commonly known as the Phillips curve.

The discovery of the Phillips curve generated a heated debate about its implications for economic policy. In particular, research focused on whether a monetary authority, such as the Federal Reserve, could 'buy' less unemployment at the cost of faster inflation. Some argued that the existence of a Phillips curve implied that unemployment could be permanently lowered if inflation were kept at a permanently higher level. Others, in particular Friedman (1968) and Phelps (1968), argued that there was an inflation–unemployment trade-off in the short run but not in the long run. In justifying their thesis, Friedman and Phelps coined the term 'natural rate of unemployment'.

To understand Friedman and Phelps's argument consider first an economy without price surprises, so actual inflation is always equal to previously expected inflation. In such an economy, some workers would always be observed to be unemployed and looking for a job. This phenomenon may simply reflect the fact that, since workers and jobs are heterogeneous, unemployed workers and firms may take time to search for adequate matches. Hence, even if inflation were always perfectly foreseen, the economy would experience a positive rate of unemployment which is what Friedman and Phelps called 'natural'.

What if inflation was not perfectly foreseen? Friedman and Phelps argued that unexpectedly high inflation would make actual unemployment fall below its natural rate, but only in the short run. This decline would happen, in particular, if wage contracts had been negotiated on the basis of previously expected inflation, in which case an inflation surprise would reduce real (inflation-adjusted) wages and stimulate employ-ment. One implication of this idea is that a monetary author-ity could indeed 'buy' lower unemployment by inducing inflation to rise above previously expected inflation. But this effect would be only temporary, because economic agents would eventually learn to forecast inflation correctly, and the difference between expected inflation and actual inflation would tend to disappear.

Although unexpected accelerations in inflation, engendered by monetary policy, may 'cause' unemployment to fall below the natural rate, the converse need not hold. With a given monetary policy, the Friedman–Phelps theory had no implications for whether movements in the unemployment rate have an inde-pendent effect on inflation.

In subsequent research, a subtly but clearly different view on the relation between inflation and unemployment emerged. According to this view, inflation tends to accelerate whenever unemployment falls below a particular number, which has come to be known as the 'non-accelerating inflation rate of unemployment', or NAIRU. The NAIRU concept was first proposed by Modigliani and Papademos, who posited the existence of a rate of unemployment such that, 'as long as unemployment is above it, inflation can be expected to decline' (1975, p.142).

The intuition is that low unemployment is likely to intensify wage pressures and consequently to result in a generalized wage increase. Assuming that firms manage to pass this cost increase to consumers in the form of higher prices, a fall in unemployment is likely to be associated with an increase in inflation. Similarly, an increase in unemployment must result in a fall in inflation. There must, therefore, be a level of unemployment such that inflation can be expected to remain constant; this level is the NAIRU.

It is important to be aware that the Friedman–Phelps natural rate and the NAIRU are different concepts. Friedman and Phelps defined the natural rate as an equilibrium rate whose value was determined by the characteristics of the labour market. In contrast, the NAIRU is posited as an empirical value rather than an equilibrium value. More importantly, the theory of the NAIRU implies that low unemployment may cause inflation to increase independently of the causes of the low unemployment and, in particular, of monetary policy. This is not an implication of the Friedman–Phelps natural rate theory.

The NAIRU concept pervades current economic policy discussions. Since the publication of Modigliani and Papademos's article numerous studies have, not surprisingly, focused on the estimation of the NAIRU. If there were in fact a strong, stable relationship between unemployment, a known NAIRU, and inflation, then one could compare current unemployment with the NAIRU to predict future inflation accurately. However, there are serious limitations in the basic idea for policy makers applying the NAIRU concept and these are discussed further in Chapters 4 and 12.

2

The time value of money: the key to the valuation of financial markets

Time value of money is a critical consideration in under-standing the key areas in the economics of financial markets. Compound interest calculations are needed to determine future sums of money resulting from an investment. Discounting, or the calculation of present values, a concept inversely related to compounding, is a technique which is used to evaluate the cash flow associated with the valuation of financial markets.

Future values – compounding

A dollar in hand today is worth more than a dollar to be received tomorrow because of the interest it could earn from putting it in a savings account. This process of earning interest on money is known as compounding. Compounding interest means that interest earns interest. In order to appreciate the concepts of compounding and time value we need some definitions:

F_n = future value
   = the amount of money at the end of year n
P = principal
i = annual interest rate
n = number of years

Then,

F_1 = the amount of money at the end of year 1
   = principal and interest = $P + iP = P(1 + i)$

F_2 = the amount of money at the end of year 2
   = $F_1(1 + i) = P(1 + i)(1 + i) = P(1 + i)^2$

The future value of an investment compounded annually at rate i for n years is given by equation (2.1)

$$F_n = P(1 + i)^n = P \cdot FVIF_{i,n} \tag{2.1}$$

where $FVIF_{i,n}$ is the future value interest factor for $1. This can be found in Table 2.1.

Table 2.1 Compounded future value of $1 (FVIF)

Years Hence	1%	2%	3%	4%	5%	6%	7%	8%	9%
1	1.010	1.020	1.030	1.040	1.050	1.060	1.070	1.080	1.090
2	1.020	1.040	1.061	1.082	1.102	1.124	1.145	1.166	1.188
3	1.030	1.061	1.093	1.125	1.158	1.191	1.225	1.260	1.295
4	1.041	1.082	1.126	1.170	1.216	1.262	1.311	1.360	1.412
5	1.051	1.104	1.159	1.217	1.276	1.338	1.403	1.469	1.539
6	1.062	1.126	1.194	1.265	1.340	1.419	1.501	1.587	1.677
7	1.072	1.149	1.230	1.316	1.407	1.504	1.605	1.714	1.828
8	1.083	1.172	1.267	1.369	1.477	1.594	1.718	1.851	1.993
9	1.094	1.195	1.305	1.423	1.551	1.689	1.838	1.999	2.172
10	1.105	1.219	1.344	1.480	1.629	1.791	1.967	2.159	2.367

Example 2.1

Nadia placed $1000 in a savings account earning 8 per cent interest compounded annually. How much money will she have in the account at the end of 4 years?

$$F_n = P(1 + i)^n$$

$$F_4 = \$1000(1 + 0.08)^4 = \$1000 \cdot FVIF_{8,4}$$

From Table 2.1 the FVIF for 4 years at 8 per cent is 1.360. Therefore,

$$F_4 = \$1000(1.360) = \$1360.$$

Present values – discounting

Present value is the present worth of future sums of money. The process of calculating present values, or discounting, is actually the opposite of finding the compounded future value. In connection with present value calculations, the interest rate i is called the discount rate.

Recall that

$$F_n = P(1 + i)^n$$

Therefore

$$P = \frac{F_n}{(1 + i)^n} = F\left(\frac{1}{(1 + i)^n}\right) = F_n \cdot PVIF_{i,n} \qquad (2.2)$$

where $PVIF_{i,n}$ represents the present value interest factor for $1. This can be found in Table 2.2.

Table 2.2 Present value of $1 (PVIF)

Years Hence	1%	2%	4%	5%	6%	8%	10%	12%	15%
1	0.990	0.980	0.962	0.952	0.943	0.926	0.909	0.893	0.870
2	0.980	0.961	0.925	0.907	0.890	0.857	0.826	0.797	0.756
3	0.971	0.942	0.889	0.864	0.840	0.794	0.751	0.712	0.658
4	0.961	0.924	0.855	0.823	0.792	0.735	0.683	0.636	0.572
5	0.951	0.906	0.822	0.784	0.747	0.681	0.621	0.567	0.497
6	0.942	0.888	0.790	0.746	0.705	0.630	0.564	0.501	0.432
7	0.933	0.871	0.760	0.711	0.665	0.583	0.513	0.452	0.376
8	0.923	0.853	0.731	0.677	0.627	0.540	0.467	0.404	0.327
9	0.914	0.837	0.703	0.645	0.592	0.500	0.424	0.361	0.284
10	0.905	0.820	0.676	0.614	0.558	0.463	0.386	0.322	0.247

Example 2.2

Nadia has been given an opportunity to receive $20 000 six years from now. If she can earn 10 per cent on investing it, what is the most she should pay for this opportunity? To answer this question, one must compute the present value of $20 000 to be received six years from now at a 10 per cent rate of discount. F_6 is $20 000, i is 10 per cent, which equals 0.1, and n is six years. $PVIF_{10,6}$ from Table 2.2 is 0.564.

$$P = \$20\,000\left(\frac{1}{(1 + 0.1)^6}\right)$$

$$= \$20\,000(PVIF_{10,6}) = \$20\,000(0.564) = \$11\,280$$

This means that Nadia who can earn 10 per cent on her investment, should be indifferent to the choice between receiving $11 280 now or $20 000 six years from now since the amounts are time equivalent. In other words she could invest $11 280 today at 10 per cent and have $20 000 in six years.

Bond and stock valuation

The process of determining security valuation involves finding the present value of an asset's expected future cash flows using the investor's required rate of return. Thus the basic security valuation model can be defined mathematically as equation (2.3):

$$V = \sum_{t=1}^{n} \frac{C_t}{(1 + r)^t} \qquad (2.3)$$

where

V = intrinsic value or present value of an asset
C_t = expected future cash flows in period $t = 1, \ldots, n$
r = investors required rate of return.

Bond valuation

The valuation process for a bond requires a knowledge of three basic elements: (1) the amount of the cash flows to be received by the investor, which is equal to the periodic interest to be received and the par value to be paid at maturity; (2) the maturity date of the loan; and (3) the investor's required rate of return. The periodic interest can be received annually or semi-annually. The value of a bond is simply the present value of these cash flows.

If the interest payments are made annually then we derive equation (2.4)

$$V = \sum_{t=1}^{n} \frac{I}{(1 + r)^t} + \frac{M}{(1 + r)^n} = I(PVIFA_{r,n}) + M(PVIF_{r,n}) \quad (2.4)$$

where

I = interest payment each year = coupon interest rate (par value)
M = par value, or maturity value, typically $1000

r = investor's required rate of return

n = number of years to maturity

PVIFA = present value interest factor of an annuity of $1 (which can be found in Table 2.3)

PVIF = present value interest factor of $1 (which can be found in Table 2.2).

Table 2.3 Present Value of an Annuity of $1 (PVIFA)

Years	1%	2%	4%	5%	6%	8%	10%
1	0.990	0.980	0.962	0.952	0.943	0.926	0.909
2	1.970	1.942	1.886	1.859	1.833	1.783	1.736
3	2.941	2.884	2.775	2.723	2.673	2.577	2.487
4	3.902	3.808	3.630	3.546	3.465	3.312	3.170
5	4.853	4.713	4.452	4.329	4.212	3.993	3.791
6	5.795	5.601	5.242	5.076	4.917	4.623	4.355
7	6.728	6.472	6.002	5.786	5.582	5.206	4.868
8	7.652	7.325	6.733	6.463	6.210	5.747	5.335
9	8.566	8.162	7.435	7.108	6.802	6.247	5.759
10	9.471	8.983	8.111	7.722	7.360	6.710	6.145

Example 2.3

Consider a bond, maturing in 10 years and having a coupon rate of 8 per cent. The par value is $1000. Investors consider 10 per cent to be an appropriate required rate of return in view of the risk level associated with this bond. The annual interest payment is $80 (8% × $1000). The present value of this bond is given by equation (2.5):

$$V = \sum_{t=1}^{n} \frac{I}{(1+r)^t} + \frac{M}{(1+r)^n} = I(PVIFA_{r,n}) + M(PVIF_{r,n}) \quad (2.5)$$

$$= \sum_{t=1}^{10} \frac{80}{(1 = 0.1)^t} + \frac{1000}{(1+0.1)^{10}}$$

$$= \$80(PVIFA_{10\%,10}) + \$1000(PVIF_{10\%,10})$$

$$= \$80(6.145) + \$1000(0.386) = \$491.60 + \$386.00$$

$$= \$877.60$$

Common stock valuation

Like bonds, the value of a common stock is the present value of all future cash inflows expected to be received by the investor. The cash inflows expected to be received are dividends plus the future price at the time of the sale of the stock. For an investor holding a common stock for only one year, the value of the stock would be the present value of both the expected cash dividend to be received in one year (D_1) and the expected market price per share of the stock at year-end (P_1). If r represents an investor's required rate of return, the value of the common stock (P_0) would be given by equation (2.6).

$$P_0 = \frac{D_1}{(1 + r)^1} + \frac{P_1}{(1 + r)^1} \tag{2.6}$$

Example 2.4

Assume an investor is considering the purchase of stock A at the beginning of the year. The dividend at year-end is expected to be $1.50, and the market price by the end of the year is expected to be $40. If the investor's required rate of return is 15 per cent, then referring to Table 2.2 the value of the stock would be:

$$P_0 = \frac{D_1}{(1 + r)^1} + \frac{P_1}{(1 + r)^1} = \frac{\$1.50}{(1 + 0.15)} + \frac{\$40}{(1 + 0.15)^1}$$

$$= \$1.50(0.870) + \$40(0.870)$$

$$= \$1.31 + \$34.80 = \$36.11$$

Since common stock has no maturity date and is held for many years, a more general, multiperiod model is needed. The general common stock valuation model is defined as follows:

$$P_0 = \sum_{t = 1}^{\infty} \frac{D_t}{(1 + r)^t}$$

There are three cases of growth in dividends: zero growth, constant growth, and supernormal growth. In the case of *zero growth*, if

$$D_0 = D_1 = \ldots = D_\infty$$

then the valuation model becomes

$$P_0 = \sum_{t=1}^{\infty} \frac{D_t}{(1 + r)^t} \tag{2.7}$$

This reduces to

$$P_0 = \frac{D_1}{r} \tag{2.8}$$

Example 2.5

Assuming D equals $2.50 and r equals 10 per cent, then the value of the stock is:

$$P_0 = \frac{\$2.50}{0.1} = \$25$$

In the case of *constant growth*, if we assume that dividends grow at a constant rate of g every year, i.e., $D_t = D_0 (1 + g)^t$, then equation (2.7) is simplified to:

$$P_0 = \frac{D_1}{r - g} \tag{2.9}$$

This formula is known as the Gordon growth model.

Example 2.6

Consider a common stock that paid a $3 dividend per share at the end of last year and is expected to pay a cash dividend every future year with a growth rate of 10 per cent. Assume that the investor's required rate of return is 12 per cent. The value of the stock would be:

$$D_1 = D_0(1 + g) = \$3(1 + 0.10) = \$3.30$$

$$P_0 = \frac{D_1}{r - g} = \frac{\$3.30}{0.12 - 0.10} = \$165$$

Finally consider the case of *supernormal* growth. Firms typically go through life cycles, during part of which their growth is faster than that of the economy and then falls sharply. The value of stock during such supernormal growth can be found by taking the following steps:

1. compute the dividends during the period of supernormal growth and find their present value;
2. find the price of the stock at the end of the supernormal growth period and compute its present value; and
3. add these two present value figures to find the value (P_0) of the common stock.

Example 2.7

Consider a common stock whose dividends are expected to grow at a 25 per cent rate for two years, after which the growth rate is expected to fall to 5 per cent. The dividend paid last period was $2. The investor desires a 12 per cent return. To find the value of this stock, take the following steps:

1. Compute the dividends during the supernormal growth period and find their present value. Assuming D_0 is $2, g is 15 per cent and r is 12 per cent, then:

$$D_1 = D_0(1 + g) = \$2(1 + 0.25) = \$2.50$$

$$D_2 = D_0(1 + g)^2 = \$2(1.563) = \$3.125$$

or $$D_2 = D_1(1 + g)) = \$2.50(1.25) = \$3.125$$

$$PV \text{ of dividends} = \frac{D_1}{(1 + r)^1} + \frac{D_2}{(1 + r)^2}$$

$$= \frac{\$2.50}{(1 + 0.12)} + \frac{\$3.125}{(1 + 0.12)^2}$$

$$= \$2.50(PVIF_{12\%,1}) + \$3.125(PVIF_{12\%,2})$$

$$= \$2.50(0.893) + \$3.125(0.797)$$

$$= \$2.23 + \$2.49 = \$4.72$$

2. Find the price of stock at the end of the supernormal growth period. The dividend for the third year is:

$$D_2 = D_2(1 + g'), \text{ where } g' = 5\%$$

$$= \$3.125(1 + 0.05) = \$3.28$$

The price of the stock is therefore:

$$P_2 = \frac{D_3}{r - g'} = \frac{\$3.28}{0.12 - 0.05} = \$46.86$$

$$PV \text{ of stock price} = \$46.86(PVIF_{12\%,2}) = \$46.86(0.797)$$
$$= \$37.35$$

3. Add the two *PV* figures obtained in steps 1 and 2 to find the value of the stock.

$$P_0 = \$4.72 + \$37.35 = \$42.07$$

Simple interest and compound interest

Present values and future values for financial assets are very sensitive to the frequency with which interest is paid. In particular it is necessary to distinguish between simple interest and compound interest.

Simple interest

When money of value *P* on a given date increases in value to *S* at some later date, *P* is called the principal, *S* is called the amount or accumulated value of *P*, and *I* = *S* – *P* is called the interest.

When only the principal earns interest for the entire life of the transaction, the interest due at the end of the time is called simple interest. The simple interest on a principal *P* for *t* years at the rate *r* is given by

$$I = Prt \tag{2.10}$$

and the simple interest amount is given by

$$S = P + I = P + Prt = P(1 + rt) \tag{2.11}$$

Example 2.8

Find the simple interest on \$750 at 4 per cent for six months. What is the amount?

Here *P* = 750, *r* = 0.04, and *t* = $\frac{1}{2}$. Then

$$I = Prt = 750(0.04)\tfrac{1}{2} = \$15$$

and

$$S = P + I = 750 + 15 = \$765$$

Compound interest

If the interest due is added to the principal at the end of each interest period and thereafter earns interest, the interest is said to be compounded. The sum of the original principal and total interest is called the compound amount or accumulated value. The difference between the accumulated value and the original principal is called the compound interest. The interest period, the time between two successive interest computations, is also called the conversion period.

Interest may be converted into principal annually, semi-annually, quarterly, monthly, weekly, daily, or continuously. The number of times interest is converted in one year, or compounded per year, is called the frequency of conversion. The rate of interest is usually stated as an annual interest rate, referred to as the nominal rate of interest.

The following notation will be used :

$P \equiv$ original principal, or the present value of S, or the discounted value of S

$S \equiv$ compound amount of P, or the accumulated value of P

$n \equiv$ total number of interest (or conversion) periods involved

$m \equiv$ number of interest periods per year, or the frequency of compounding

$j_m \equiv$ nominal (yearly) interest rate which is compounded (payable, convertible) m times per year

$i \ \equiv$ interest rate per interest period.

The interest rate per period, i, equals j_m / m. For example $j_{12} = 12$ per cent means that a nominal (yearly) rate of 12 per cent is converted (compounded, payable) 12 times per year, $i = 1\% = 0.01$ being the interest rate per month.

Let P represent the principal at the beginning of the first interest period and i the interest rate per conversion period. It is necessary to calculate the accumulated values at the ends of successive interest periods for n periods. At the end of the first period, the interest due is Pi and the accumulated value is

$$P + Pi = P(1 + i)$$

At the end of the second period, the interest due is $[P(1 + i)]i$ and the accumulated value is

$$P(1 + i) + [P(1 + i)]i = P(1 + i)(1 + i) = P(1 + i)^2$$

At the end of the third period, the interest due is $[P(1 + i)^2]i$ and the accumulated value is

$$P(1 + i)^2 + [P(1 + i)^2]i = P(1 + i)^2(1 + i) = P(1 + i)^2$$

Continuing in this manner, we see that the successive accumulated values,

$$P(1 + i),\ P(1 + i)^2,\ P(1 + i)^3, \ldots$$

form a geometric progression whose nth term is

$$S = P(1 + i)^n \tag{2.12}$$

where S is the accumulated value of P at the end of the n interest periods.

The application of compound interest is most clearly seen by working through some real world applications.

Example 2.9

Assume you are asked to find (a) the simple interest on $1000 for two years at 12 per cent, and (b) the compound interest on $1000 for two years at 12 per cent compounded semi-annually (that is, $j_2 = 12$ per cent).

(a) $I = Prt - 1000(0.12)(2) = \$240$

(b) Since the conversion period is six months, interest is earned at the rate of 6 per cent per period, and there are four interest periods in two years, the answer can be seen from Table 2.4. The compound interest is $1262.48 - $1000 = $262.48.

Alternatively, from equation (2.12) with $P = 1000$, $i = 0.06$, and $n = 4$, then

$$S = P(1 + i)^n = 1000(1.06)^4 = \$1262.48$$

and the compound interest is $S - P = \$262.48$.

Table 2.4 Simple interest versus Compound Interest

At the End of Period	Interest	Accumulated Value
1	1000(0.06) = $60	$1060.00
2	1060(0.06) = $63.60	$123.60
3	1123.60(0.06) = $67.42	$1191.02
4	1191.02(0.06) = $71.46	$1262.48

Example 2.10

Assume you are asked to find the compound interest on $1000 at (a) j_{12} = 6 per cent for five years, and (b) j_{12} = 15 per cent for 30 years.

(a) We have P = 1000, i = 0.06/12 = 0.005, and n = 5 × 12 = 60. From equation (2.12),

$$S = P(1 + i)^n = 1000(1.005)^{60} = \$1348.85$$

The compound interest is $S - P$ = $348.85.

(b) We have P = 1000, i = 0.15/12 = 0.0125, and n = 30 × 12 = 360. From equation (2.12),

$$S = 1000(1.0125)^{360} = \$87,541.00$$

The compound interest is $S - P$ = $86,541.00, which is more than 86 times the original investment of $1000. If the investment had been at 15 per cent simple interest, the interest earned would have been only

$$I = 1000(0.15)(30) = \$4500$$

This illustrates the power of compound interest. A high rate of interest for a long period of time generates far more than receiving only simple interest.

Example 2.11

Assume you are asked to tabulate and graph the growth of $100 at compound interest rates j_{12} = 6%, 8%, 10%, 12% and for 5, 10, 15, 20, 25, 30, 35, 40, 45 and 50 years (see Table 2.5 and Figure 2.1).

Table 2.5 The power of compound interest

Years	n	j_{12} = 6%, i = 0.005	j_{12} = 8%, i = 0.08/12	j_{12} = 10%, i = 0.10/12	j_{12} = 12%, i = 0.01
5	60	134.89	148.98	164.53	181.67
10	120	181.94	221.96	270.70	330.04
15	180	245.41	330.69	445.39	599.58
20	240	331.02	492.68	732.81	1089.26
25	300	446.50	734.02	1205.69	1978.85
30	360	602.26	1093.57	1983.74	3594.96
35	420	812.36	1629.26	3263.87	6530.96
40	480	1095.75	2427.34	5370.07	11864.77
45	540	1478.00	3616.36	8835.42	21554.69
50	600	1993.60	5387.82	14536.99	39158.34

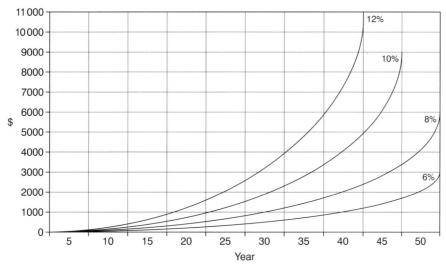

Figure 2.1 The power of compound interest.

Nominal and effective rates of interest

The annual rates of interest with different conversion periods are called equivalent if they yield the same compound amount at the end of one year. Again this is best understood using examples.

Example 2.12

At the end of one year the compound amount of $100 at:

(a) 4 per cent compounded quarterly is $100(1.01)^4 = \$104.06$
(b) 4.06 per cent compounded annually is $100(1.0406) = \$104.06$.

Thus 4 per cent compounded quarterly and 4.06 per cent compounded annually are equivalent rates.

When interest is compounded more often than once per year, the given annual rate is called the nominal annual rate or nominal rate. The rate of interest actually earned in one year is called the effective annual rate of the effective rate. In Example 2.12(a), 4 per cent is a nominal rate while in 2.12(b), 4.06 per cent is an effective rate. As noted above, 4.06 per cent is the effective rate equivalent to a nominal rate of 4 per cent compounded quarterly.

Example 2.13

What is the effective rate r equivalent to the nominal rate 5 per cent compounded monthly?

In one year 1 at r effective will amount to $1 + r$ and at 5 per cent compounded monthly will amount to $(1 + 0.05/12)^{12}$. Setting

$$1 + r = (1 + 0.05/12)^{12}$$

we find

$$r = (1 + 0.05/12)^{12} - 1$$

$$= 1.05116190 - 1 = 0.05116190$$

or   5.116%

Example 2.14

What is the nominal rate j compounded quarterly which is equivalent to 5 per cent effective?

In one year 1 at j compounded quarterly will amount to $(1 + j/4)^4$ and at 5 per cent effective will amount to 1.05. Setting

$$(1 + j/4)^4 = 1.05$$

we find

$$1 + j/4 = (1.05)^{1/4}$$

Then

$$j = 4[(1.05)^{1/4} - 1]$$

$$= 4(0.01227223) = 0.04908892$$

or   4.909%

3

The term structure of interest rates and financial markets

Decisions as to whether to spend or not to spend, whether to borrow (or lend) now or to postpone borrowing (or lending) for six or nine months, whether to buy securities today or hold cash for the present, whether borrowing or lending should be short-term or long-term, are all decisions influenced by current and expected interest rates. Interest rates are at the centre of the key issues in understanding the economics of financial markets. But what are the factors affecting interest rates and what exact role do interest rates play within the financial system?

Functions of interest rates

Interest rates serve a number of significant functions. First, they provide investors with a guide for allocating funds among investment opportunities. As funds are directed into projects that have higher expected rates of return (risk and other factors being taken into account), the funds are optimally allocated from the viewpoint of both consumer and investor, since the highest returns normally prevail where effective consumer demand is strongest. Unless an investment opportunity promises a return high enough to pay the market rate of interest, it does not justify the required capital outlay. The money market, by channelling funds into projects that have an expected return in excess of the interest rate, provides a valuable service to investors, borrowers, and society as a whole.

The interest rate also provides a measure of the relative advantage of current consumption compared to saving. By adjusting the available market rate for expected inflation and taxes, an individual can determine the real amount of additional future consumption that can be obtained by postponing current consumption.

Similarly, interest rates help businessmen decide among alternative production methods. Suppose a product can be made either solely with labour or with a combination of labour and machinery. By calculating the capital cost of the machine (the interest rate times the amount invested in the machine), the expected labour-plus-capital cost can be compared with the labour-alone cost to determine the least expensive means of production.

Determination of interest rates, demand and supply of funds

Interest rates are prices. Unlike other prices they are usually expressed as percentages of the amount borrowed or lent. But, like other prices, they are determined by supply and demand. Interest rates depend on the supply of and the demand for loanable funds. The sources of the supply of funds are savings, reductions in the demand for money and increases in the supply of money. The sources of the demand for funds are investment demands, consumption demands (for spending on consumer goods) and increases in the demand for money.

The supply of funds

Saving, which is the main source of supply of loanable funds, arises in all sectors of the economy and may take many forms. Personal saving, i.e., the excess of personal income over consumption spending, may consist, *inter alia*, of contributions to pension funds, the repayment of mortgage loans, deposits with mutual funds or banks, or the purchase of securities. Business saving comprises retained profits and, most important, depreciation charges. What is not reinvested in the business is usually held in a liquid form or used to reduce bank loans. The government may also contribute to saving in the economy by raising more in taxes than it needs for its own current expenditure; any surplus goes to offset part of the public sector's own investment.

It is important to distinguish between the potential and the actual supply of loanable funds. The reason for this is that households and businesses having savings may not be willing to make these funds available to borrowers. Money, remember, is a store of value. Households and businesses may not want to offer either their current savings or any of their accumulated savings to borrowers. On the contrary they may choose to add a portion of their current savings to their accumulated balances.

Having made choices as to how to divide their incomes and receipts between spending and saving, households and businesses must then decide on the specific form in which to hold their savings. The basic choice is between money in the form of either idle cash or bank accounts on the one hand, and securities of some sort on the other. Idle cash and bank accounts are highly liquid assets; securities acquired from borrowers are somewhat less liquid but generally yield a better rate of return. That part of savings (current or accumulated) which households and businesses want to hold as securities flows into the money market as the supply of loanable funds. That part of savings which households and businesses want to hold as cash obviously does not. This division depends upon the liquidity preferences of households and businesses (i.e., their preference to hold cash rather than spend it). More specifically, there are three main reasons why households and businesses prefer to hold cash rather than securities.

1. There is a transaction motive for holding money rather than securities. Households and businesses both need a stock of cash on hand to make ordinary day-to-day purchases. Households, for example, usually receive a sizeable chunk of income every week, or every month. Disbursements, on the other hand, occur more or less evenly over time. This means that households have an average money balance of some size bridging the gap between paydays. And it is simply more convenient to have one's assets in their most liquid form, that is, as idle cash balances or bank accounts, than in the form of securities. Furthermore, there are costs (brokerage fees) in transferring cash into securities and back again.
2. There is a precautionary motive for holding money. Households and businesses may hold cash balances to meet any rainy day contingencies that might arise. Particularly relevant are those risks which one cannot protect oneself against by purchasing insurance policies, e.g. prolonged illness, unemployment, and so forth.

3. There is a speculative motive for holding money. At any
time, there is a certain rate of interest that households and
businesses, as potential suppliers of loanable funds, consider to be about 'normal'. If the rate of interest is currently
low, i.e., 'below normal', households and businesses may
withhold a part of their savings that would otherwise flow
into the money market as a part of the supply of loanable
funds. They hold more money and fewer securities than
they normally would. Why? Because they expect that the
current below-normal interest rate will probably rise in the
future. Conversely, if the current interest rate is unusually
high, i.e., 'above normal', households and businesses will
choose to hold less money and more securities to take
advantage of high current interest rates as opposed to
the lower normal rate expected to prevail again in the
future.

The supply of loanable funds is critically influenced by the level
of interest rates, i.e., higher interest (real) rates will induce
households and businesses (but obviously not necessarily
governments) to be less liquid. At relatively high interest rates,
households and firms will prefer to hold their assets in the form
of interest-bearing securities rather than as non-interest bear-
ing current accounts and idle cash balances. The supply of
loanable funds depends on:

(i)   The rate of interest. A high rate of interest encourages
      savers to place their funds in financial institutions and the
      supply of loanable funds increases.
(ii) The amount of savings. Some countries, such as Japan, are
      very thrifty. This increases the amount of funds available
      for borrowers.
(iii) A Budget surplus. This occurs when the government spends
      less than its revenue. In these conditions the government
      has a surplus that it can lend to the private sector.
(iv) International factors. When foreigners buy assets in another
      country they are lending to those domestic residents. Low
      interest rates overseas encourage funds to flow from the low
      interest rate country into the countries with higher interest
      rates increasing the supply of funds available to borrowers
      in the high interest rate country (and vice versa).

The supply curve for loanable funds is upward sloping, i.e.,
higher interest rates increase the supply available, and vice
versa.

The demand for funds

Now let us turn to the demand for funds. Again this can be by private individuals, companies or governments. Private individuals borrow in order to increase their current level of consumption either for housing, automobiles, holidays or whatever. Companies borrow to pay for factories, plant and equipment. Finally, Governments borrow to pay for current and capital spending (e.g. on schools, roads etc. which they cannot finance from taxation).

The demand for borrowed funds depends on:

(i)   The rate of interest. When it becomes more expensive to borrow (i.e., when the interest rate rises) demand from the private sector falls (and vice versa).

(ii) The level of income. The higher the level of income, the more individuals and businesses will want to borrow. For example, if investment is to increase firms will in general require outside finance. Similarly, consumers borrow money to buy durable goods, washing machines, white goods, etc. More generally when incomes rise, individuals increase borrowing for all purposes (houses, automobiles, etc.) and firms need more working capital.

(iii) The government finances. In most countries governments are major borrowers of funds. This is known as the fiscal deficit or budget deficit (total government expenditure minus tax revenue).

(iv) International factors. When foreigners buy domestic assets they are lending to domestic residents of the country concerned. Low overseas interest rates encourage domestic borrowers to borrow these overseas funds, increasing the supply of funds available to domestic borrowers (and vice versa).

The demand curve for loanable funds is clearly downward sloping, i.e., lower interest rates raise the demand for funds. Businessmen will find it profitable to purchase larger amounts of capital goods when the price of loanable funds declines. Similarly, lower interest rates may encourage some increases in consumer and government borrowing. (In practice it is 'real' interest rates which are relevant.)

How are interest rates determined?

In equilibrium the interaction between the demand for loanable funds and the supply of loanable funds will determine the interest rate.

Elementary economic analysis tells us that if the demand rises (I) or the supply falls (II) then the interest rate rises. Similarly if the demand falls (III) or if the supply rises (IV) then interest rates will fall. This is illustrated in Figure 3.1.

The effect on the interest rate of any shift in demand or supply will depend on the elasticities of both supply and demand. Following a change in demand, the less elastic (more elastic) is the supply curve the greater (less) will be the change in interest rates. Following a change in supply, the less elastic (more elastic) is the demand curve the greater (less) will be the effect on interest rates.

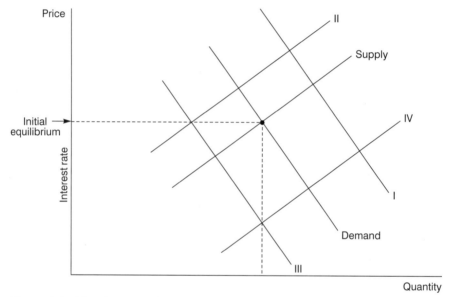

Figure 3.1   The determination of interest rates.

How can changes in the supply of funds and demand for funds change interest rates? If there is more saving (relative to demand) by businessmen and consumers, this will bring down interest rates. What happens if there is an increase in the supply of money? This adds to the savings in the capital market. To see how this can occur suppose that instead of raising new funds through the stock market companies borrow from their banks, and the banks increase the supply of money (remember bank loans create bank deposits which are in themselves the most important component of the money supply). Because companies are borrowing from the banks this will increase security prices (due to a lower demand) and the rate of interest on securities will fall correspondingly as companies can now raise funds more cheaply.

International factors affecting interest rates

Given the importance of international factors in affecting interest rates it is worth explaining, in some detail, the mechanics whereby overseas interest rates affect domestic interest rates. The speed of the impact of international factors depends on official exchange rate policy.

If a country has a fixed exchange rate (i.e., the government is committed to official intervention in order to keep the rate fixed) and the currency is weak (i.e., it is being heavily sold on the foreign exchange market), the government may be induced to raise official interest rates. The objective is to make it more attractive for overseas holders of the currency to hold it and to make it less attractive for domestic holders to transfer it overseas. If a country has a fixed and strong exchange rate there may be pressure for the authorities to lower the interest rate. As funds flow into the currency the authorities, being forced to increase the domestic money supply to keep the exchange rate fixed will, in an attempt to reduce the inflows, reduce domestic interest rates.

Under floating exchange rates the effects of capital flows on interest rates occur very quickly. With a weak currency investors will speedily reduce their holdings thereby driving up interest rates, e.g. by selling bonds. The link between bond prices and interest rates mentioned in Chapter 2 is outlined in more detail in the next section. Similarly investors will be keen to acquire liabilities in that currency since, if the exchange rate change occurs and is larger than the extra borrowing cost the investor can repay (say his bank loan) and make a profit. The combination of an increase in the supply of loanable funds and a decrease in the demand for loanable funds drives down interest rates.

The effect of international factors also depends on the size of the home economy and how developed the domestic financial system is. For a small economy a given foreign inflow of funds is likely to represent a relatively high proportion of the total capital market. The impact is likely to be bigger therefore in a country with limited facilities for foreign investors, for example, because the capital market is undeveloped or exchange controls are in operation.

Price and yield – a key relationship

The inverse relationship between price and yield is important in understanding how the financial system works. When interest rates rise, the market price of outstanding fixed-income securities, such as bonds and gilts (UK government securities), declines. When interest rates fall, the market price of fixed-income securities increases.

Holders of fixed-income securities then experience price depreciation on their portfolios during periods of rising interest rates. On the other hand those who defer the purchase of fixed-interest securities during a period of falling interest rates will later pay higher prices. The following example illustrates this inverse relationship.

Assume that a €1000 bond has a fixed coupon interest rate of 8 per cent and a maturity date of perpetuity (to make the arithmetic easy). The bond pays €80 in interest per year, and the face value, or principal amount, is of €1000. If, some time later, similar bonds of comparable maturity are paying €90 in interest a year, bond dealers will continue to buy and sell the 8 per cent issue, but they will lower its price until it also yields 9 per cent. The principle behind this is that no one would buy a bond with an 8 per cent yield when he could buy one of the same quality with a 9 per cent yield.

At what price will the 8 per cent coupon bond yield a 9 per cent current return? By using the formula for current yield:

$$\text{current yield} = \frac{\text{annual interest payment}}{\text{prevailing market price}}$$

and transposing it

$$\text{prevailing market price} = \frac{\text{annual interest payment}}{\text{current yield}}$$

the price can be determined

$$\frac{€80}{0.09} = €888.88$$

At a price of €888.88, the 8 per cent coupon bond will yield 9 per cent. Since the bond is selling for less than €1000, i.e., less than par value, it is said to be priced at a discount.

What if market interest rates fall and new bonds are being sold with 7 per cent coupons? Again, the 8 per cent coupon bond must be brought into line with similar securities. In this case, the 8 per cent bond will be 'bid up' to yield 7 per cent.

$$\frac{€80}{0.07} = €1,142.86$$

Since the bond is selling for more than par, i.e., €1142.86, it is said to be priced at a premium.

Instead of talking about the supply of and demand for credit or loanable funds determining the rate of interest, we could talk about the same thing in terms of the demand for and the supply of securities determining the price of securities (see Figure 3.2). To supply credit (lend) is equivalent to demanding financial assets (securities); financial institutions lend, for example, by purchasing financial assets. To demand credit (borrow) is the same as supplying securities; business firms borrow by selling their bonds or other IOUs. At a price of €833 (which corresponds, let us say, to a 6 per cent yield, assuming a 5 per cent coupon on a €1000 bond), relative eagerness to buy securities (or lend) would drive the price of securities up, and it would drive the rate of interest down. And at a price of €1250,

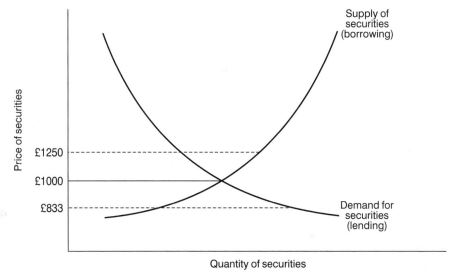

Figure 3.2 The determination of the price of securities.

corresponding to a 4 per cent yield, relative eagerness to sell securities (to borrow) would drive the price of securities down, and would drive the rate of interest up.

Now let us drop the assumption about a single rate of interest and consider why it is that rates of interest or yields on different financial instruments vary. Why do some borrowers pay more than others? Why are the yields on long-dated securities different from those on short-dated ones? Why do interest rates on different currency denominated assets vary? It is to these questions that we now turn.

The term structure of interest rates

The term structure of interest rates, or maturity structure as it is sometimes referred to, refers to the set of theories designed to explain why practically homogeneous bonds of different maturities have different interest rates. The starting point for understanding the term structure theories is the present value concept (discussed in detail in Chapter 2).

Because of the time value of money, one dollar received at a future date has a present value of less than one dollar. If we denote the present (that is, time 0) value of $1 received n periods from now by D_n, then the interest rate is the discount rate (denoted by R_n) that solves the following equation.

$$D_n = \frac{1}{(1 + R_n)^n} \qquad (3.1)$$

D_n represents both the present value of $1 received in n period and the spot price of a zero coupon bond with a par value of $1. The purchaser of this zero coupon bond pays the purchase price D_n at time zero and receives the par value of $1 at time n. The rate R_n is called the zero coupon discount rate or the spot interest rate. The spot market is the market for immediate delivery. Some observers call the spot market the 'cash' market.

The spot price D_n and the spot interest rate R_n are inversely related. When the spot interest rate goes up, the spot price goes down because the spot interest rate is the denominator. As the spot interest rate increases, the denominator increases, and the ratio (that is, the price) decreases. Figure 3.3 and Table 2.2

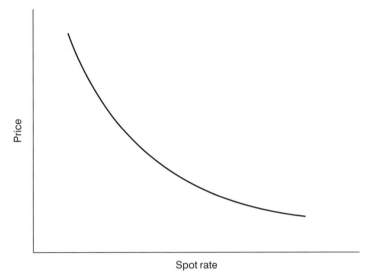

Figure 3.3   Spot price versus spot interest rate.

illustrate this point. Look across any row of Table 2.2. As you move to the right, the interest rate increases and the present value decreases. In Table 2.2 the present value decreases as maturity increases for a given interest rate. To see this point, look down any column of Table 2.2. The lowest present values are in the lower right corner of the table for long maturities and high interest rates.

Consider the examples in Figure 3.4. The spot interest rate is 8 per cent for one period, 10 per cent for two periods, and 12 per cent for three periods. D_1 equals 0.93, which means that the present value of $1 received one period from now is $0.93. D_2 is 0.83, which means that the present value of $1 received two periods from now is $0.83. The present value of $1 received three periods from now, D_3, is $0.71.

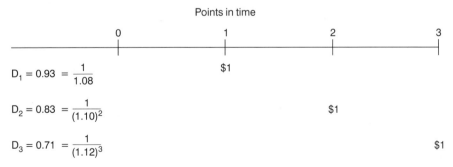

Figure 3.4   Present values.

The pattern of spot interest rates for different maturities is called the term structure of interest rates.

Determination of forward interest rates

Assume the one-year spot interest rate for a risk free security was determined to be 7 per cent. This means that the market has determined that the present value of $1 to be paid by the United States Treasury in one year is $1/1.07 or $0.9346. That means that the relevant discount rate for converting a cash flow one year from now to its present value is 7 per cent. If the two-year spot interest rate was 8 per cent, the present value of $1 to be paid by the US Treasury in two years is $1/1.08^2$, or $0.8573. (You are advised to check this with Table 2.2.)

An alternative view of $1 to be paid in two years is that it can be discounted in two steps. The first step determines its equivalent one-year value. That is, $1 to be received in two years is equivalent to $1/(1+f_{1,2})$ to be received in one year. The second step determines the present value of this equivalent one-year amount by discounting it at the one-year spot interest rate of 7 per cent. Thus its current value is given by:

$$\frac{\$1/(1 + f_{1,2})}{(1 + 0.07)} \tag{3.2}$$

However, this value must be equal to $0.8573 as, according to the two-year spot rate (as mentioned earlier), $0.8573 is the present value of $1 to be paid in two years. That is,

$$\frac{\$1/(1 + f_{1,2})}{(1 + 0.07)} = \$0.8573$$

which has solution for $f_{1,2}$ of 9.01 per cent.

This discount rate $f_{1,2}$ is known as the forward rate from year one to year two. That is, the discount rate for determining the equivalent value one year from now of a dollar that is to be received two years from now. In the example, $1 to be received two years from now is equivalent in value to $1/1.0901 = $0.9174 to be received one year from now (note that the present value of $0.9174 is $0.9174/1.07 = $0.8573).

The yield curve

Another important term it is important to be familiar with is the yield curve. A yield curve is a graph that shows the yields-to-maturity (on the vertical axis) for identical securities of various terms to maturity (on the horizontal axis) as of a particular date. In order to eliminate the risk of default the calculations are normally done for risk-free, government-issued securities.

The shape of the yield curve provides an estimate of the current term structure of interest rates and will change as yields to maturity change. Figure 3.5 illustrates the most commonly observed yield curves.

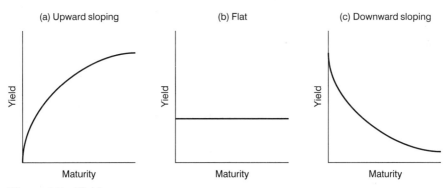

Figure 3.5   Yield curves.

Four primary theories are used to explain the term structure of interest rates: the unbiased expectations theory, the liquidity preference theory, the market segmentation theory, and the preferred habitat theory. In discussing them, the focus will be on the term structure of spot interest rates, because these rates are critically important in determining the price of any risk free security. Sharpe, Alexander and Bailey (1999) provide an excellent term structure survey and this has been drawn upon here.

Unbiased expectations theory

The unbiased expectations theory (or pure expectations theory, as it is sometimes called) holds that the forward rate represents the average opinion of what the expected future spot rate for the period in question will be. So a set of spot interest rates that is rising can be explained by arguing that the marketplace (that is, the general opinion of investors) believes that spot interest rates will be rising in the future. Conversely, a set of decreasing spot interest rates is explained by arguing that the marketplace expects spot interest rates to fall in the future.

Upward-sloping yield curves

In order to understand this theory more fully, consider an example in which the one-year spot rate was 7 per cent and the two-year spot rate was 8 per cent. The basic question is this: Why are these two spot interest rates different? Equivalently, why is the yield curve upward sloping?

Consider an investor with \$1 to invest for two years. This investor could follow a 'maturity strategy', investing the money now for the full two years at the two-year spot interest rate of 8 per cent. With this strategy, at the end of two years the dollar will have grown in value to \$1.1664 (= \$1 × 1.08 × 1.08). Alternatively, the investor could invest the dollar now for one year at the one-year spot interest rate of 7 per cent, so that the investor knows that one year from now the investor will have \$1.07 (= \$1 × 1.07) to reinvest for one more year. Although the investor does not know what the one-year spot rate will be one year from now, the investor has an expectation about what it will be. The expected future spot interest rate will hereafter be denoted as $es_{1,2}$. If the investor thinks that it will be 10 per cent, then the \$1 investment has an expected value two years from now of \$1.177 (= \$1 × 1.07 × 1.10). In this case, the investor could choose a 'rollover strategy', meaning that he or she would choose to invest in a one-year security at 7 per cent rather than in the two-year security, because one would expect to have more money at the end of two years by doing so, given that \$1.177 > \$1.1664.

However, an expected future spot interest rate of 10 per cent cannot represent the general view in the marketplace. If it did, investors would not be willing to invest money at the two-year spot interest rate, as a higher return would be expected from investing money at the one-year rate and using the rollover strategy. So the two-year spot interest rate would quickly rise as the supply of funds for two-year loans at 8 per cent would be less than the demand. Conversely, the supply of funds for one year at 7 per cent would be more than the demand, causing the one-year spot rate to fall quickly. Thus, a one-year spot interest rate of 7 per cent, a two-year spot interest rate of 8 per cent, and an expected future spot interest rate of 10 per cent cannot represent an equilibrium situation.

But now what if the expected future spot interest rate one year ahead is 6 per cent instead of 10 per cent? In this case, according to the rollover strategy the investor would expect $1 to be worth $1.1342 (= $1 × 1.07 × 1.06) at the end of two years. This is less than the value the $1 will have if the two year investment strategy is followed given that $1.1342 < $1.664, so the investor would choose the two-year investment period strategy. Again, however, an expected future spot interest rate of 6 per cent cannot represent the general view in the marketplace because if it did, investors would not be willing to invest money at the one-year spot interest rate.

We showed above (page 58) that the forward rate in this example was 9.01 per cent. What if the expected future spot interest rate was of this magnitude? At the end of two years the value of $1 with the rollover strategy would be $1.1664 (= $1 × 1.07 × 1.0901), the same as the value of $1 with the two-year investment period strategy. In this case, equilibrium would exist in the marketplace because the general view would be that the two strategies have the same expected return. Accordingly, investors with a two-year holding period would not have an incentive to choose one strategy over the other.

The unbiased expectations theory asserts that the expected future spot rate is equal in magnitude to the forward rate. In the example, the current one-year spot rate is 7 per cent, and, according to this theory, the general opinion is that it will rise to a rate of 9.01 per cent in one year. This expected rise in the one-year spot rate is the reason behind the upward-sloping term structure where the two-year spot rate (8 per cent) is greater than the one-year spot rate (7 per cent).

Equilibrium

In equation form, the unbiased expectations theory states that in equilibrium the expected future spot interest rate is equal to the forward rate:

$$es_{1,2} = f_{1,2} \qquad (3.3)$$

The previous example dealt with an upward-sloping term structure; the longer the term, the higher the spot interest rate. Whereas the explanation for an upward-sloping term structure was that investors expect spot rates to rise in the future, the reason for the downward-sloping curve is that investors expect spot interest rates to fall in the future.

Liquidity preference theory

The liquidity preference theory starts with the notion that investors are primarily interested in purchasing short-term securities. That is, even though some investors may have longer holding periods, there is a tendency for them to prefer short-term securities. These investors realize that they may need their funds earlier than anticipated and recognize that they face less 'interest rate risk' if they invest in shorter-term securities.

Interest rate risk

Investors with a two-year holding period would tend to prefer the rollover investment strategy because they would be certain of having a given amount of cash at the end of one year when it may be needed. An investor who followed a two-year investment strategy would have to sell the two-year security after one year if cash were needed. However, it is not known now what price that investor would get for the two-year security in one year. Thus there is an extra element of risk associated with the two-year investment strategy that is absent from the rollover strategy.

The upshot is that investors with a two-year holding period will not choose the two-year investment strategy if it has the same expected return as the rollover strategy because it is riskier. The only way investors will follow the two-year investment strategy and buy the two-year securities is if the expected return is higher. That is borrowers will have to pay the investors a risk premium in the form of a greater expected return in order to get them to purchase two-year securities.

Will borrowers be inclined to pay such a premium when issuing two-year securities? Yes, they will, according to the liquidity preference theory. First, frequent refinancing may be costly in terms of registration, advertising and paperwork. These costs can be lessened by issuing relatively long-term securities. Second, some borrowers will realize that relatively long-term bonds are a less risky source of funds than relatively short-term funds because borrowers who use them will not have to be as concerned about the possibility of refinancing in the future at higher interest rates. Thus borrowers may be willing to pay more (via higher expected interest costs) for relatively long-term funds.

In the earlier example, the one-year spot interest rate was 7 per cent and the two-year spot interest rate was 8 per cent. According to the liquidity preference theory, the only way investors will agree to follow a two-year investment strategy is if the expected return from doing so is higher than the expected return from following the rollover strategy. So the expected future spot rate must be less than the forward rate of 9.01 per cent. Assume it is 8.6 per cent. At 8.6 per cent the value of a $1 investment in two years is expected to be $1.1620 (= $1 × 1.07 × 1.086), if the roll-over investment strategy is followed. Because the value of a $1 investment with the two-year investment strategy is $1.1664 (= $1 × 1.08 × 1.08), it can be seen that the two-year investment strategy has a higher expected rate of return for the two-year period than can be attributed to its greater degree of risk.

Liquidity premium theory

The difference between the forward rate and the expected future spot interest rate is known as the liquidity premium. It is the 'extra' return given to investors in order to entice them to purchase the riskier longer-maturity two-year security. In the example given earlier, it is equal to 0.41 per cent (= 9.01 − 8.6 per cent). More generally it is given by:

$$f_{1,2} = es_{1,2} + L_{1,2} \tag{3.4}$$

where $L_{1,2}$ is the liquidity premium for the period starting one year from now and ending two years from now.

So how does the liquidity preference theory explain the slope of the term structure? In order to answer this question, note that with the rollover investment strategy the expected value of a dollar at the end of two years is $1 × (1 + s_1) × (1 + es_{1,2})$. Alternatively with the two year investment strategy, the expected value of a dollar at the end of two years is $1 \times (1 + s_2)^2$. According to the liquidity preference theory, there is more risk with the two-year investment strategy, which in turn means that it must have a higher expected return. That is, the following inequality, shown in the following equations, must hold:

$$\$1(1 + s_1) \times (1 + es_{1,2}) < \$1(1 + s_2)^2 \tag{3.5}$$

or:

$$(1 + s_1) \times (1 + es_{1,2}) < (1 + s_2)^2 \tag{3.6}$$

This inequality is the key to understanding how the liquidity preference theory explains the term structure.

Downward-sloping yield curves

Consider the downward-sloping case first, where $s_1 > s_2$. The above inequality will hold in this situation only if the expected future spot interest rate ($es_{1,2}$) is substantially lower than the current one-year spot interest rate (s_1). Thus a downward-sloping yield curve will be observed only when the market place believes that interest rates are going to decline substantially.

As an example, assume that the one-year spot interest rate (s_1) is 7 per cent and the two-year spot interest rate (s_2) is 6 per cent. Because 7 per cent is greater than 6 per cent, this is a situation in which the term structure is downward sloping. Now according to the liquidity preference theory, equation (3.6) indicates that,

$$(1 + 0.07)\,(1 + es_{1,2}) < (1.06)^2$$

which can be true only if the expected future spot rate ($es_{1,2}$) is substantially less than 7 per cent. Given the one-year and two-year spot interest rates, the forward rate ($f_{1,2}$) is equal to 5.01 per cent. Assuming the liquidity premium ($L_{1,2}$) is 0.41 per cent, then, according to equation (3.4) $es_{1,2}$ must be 4.6 per cent (= 5.01 – 0.41 per cent). Thus, the term structure is downward sloping because the one-year spot interest rate of 7 per cent is expected to decline to 4.6 per cent in the future.

The unbiased expectations theory would also explain the term structure by saying it was downward-sloping because the one-year spot rate was expected to decline in the future. However, the unbiased expectations theory would expect the spot rate to decline only to 5.01 per cent, not to 4.6 per cent.

Flat yield curve

Consider next the case of a flat yield curve, where $s_1 = s_2$. Equation (3.6) will be true in this situation only if $es_{1,2}$ is less than s_1. Thus a flat term structure will occur only when the marketplace expects spot interest rates to decline. Indeed, if $s_1 = s_2 = 7$ per cent and $L_{1,2} = 0.41$ per cent, then $f_{1,2} = 7$ per cent, and, according to equation (3.4), the expected future spot rate is 6.59 per cent (= 7.00 – 0.41 per cent), a decline from the current one-year spot rate of 7 per cent. This outcome is in contrast to the unbiased expectations theory, which would interpret a flat rate structure to mean that the marketplace expected interest rates to remain at the same level.

Upward-sloping yield curves

The last case is an upward-sloping yield curve where $s_1 < s_2$. A slightly upward-sloping curve can be consistent with an expectation that interest rates are going to decline in the future. For example, if $s_1 = 7$ per cent and $s_2 = 7.2$ per cent, then the forward rate is 7.2 per cent. In turn, if the liquidity premium is 0.41 per cent, then the expected future spot rate is 6.79 per cent (= 7.20 – 0.41 per cent), a decline from the current one-year spot rate of 7 per cent. Thus the reason for the slight upward slope in the term structure is that the marketplace expects a small decline in the spot rate. In contrast, the unbiased expectations theory would argue that the reason for the slight upward slope was the expectation of a small increase in the spot rate.

If the term structure is more steeply sloped, then it is more likely that the marketplace expects interest rates to rise in the future. For example, if $s_1 = 7$ per cent and $s_2 = 7.3$ per cent, then the forward rate is 7.6 per cent. Continuing to assume a liquidity premium of 0.41 per cent, equation (3.4) indicates that the marketplace expects the one-year spot interest rate to rise from 7 per cent to 7.19 per cent (= 7.6 – 0.41 per cent.) The unbiased expectations theory also would explain this steep slope by saying that the spot rate was expected to rise in the future, but by a larger amount. In particular, the unbiased expectations theory would state that the spot interest rate was expected to rise to 7.6 per cent, not to 7.19 per cent.

In summary, with the liquidity preference theory, down-ward-sloping term structures are indicative of an expected decline in the spot interest rate, whereas upward-sloping term structures may indicate either an expected rise or decline, depending on how steep the slope is. In general, the steeper the slope, the more likely it is that the marketplace expects spot interest rates to rise. If roughly half the time investors expect that spot rates will rise and half the time investors expect that spot interest rates will decline, then the liquidity preference theory suggests that there will be more occurrences of upward-sloping term structures than down-ward-sloping ones.

The market segmentation theory

A third explanation for the determination of the term structure rests on the assumption that there is market segmentation. Various investors and borrowers are thought to be restricted by law, preference, or custom to certain maturities. Some investors may prefer short-term securities, others intermediate-term securities, whilst others prefer long-term securities. According to the market segmentation theory, spot interest rates are determined by supply and demand conditions in each market. Furthermore, it is assumed investors and borrowers will not leave their market and enter a different one even when the current rates suggest to them that there is a substantially higher expected return available by making such a move.

With this theory, an upward-sloping term structure exists when the intersection of the supply and demand curves for shorter-term funds is at a lower interest rate than the intersection for longer-term funds. This situation could be due to either a relatively greater demand for longer-term funds by borrowers or a relatively greater supply of shorter-term funds by investors, or some combination of the two. Conversely, a downward-sloping term structure would exist when the intersection for shorter-term funds was at a higher interest rate than the intersection for longer-term funds.

The preferred habitat theory

According to this theory, investors and borrowers have segments of the market in which they prefer to operate, similar to the market segmentation theory. However, they are willing to leave their desired maturity segments if there are significant differences in yields between the various segments. These yield differences are determined by the supply and demand for funds within the segments.

As a result the term structure under the preferred habitat theory, as under the liquidity preference theory, reflects both expectations of future spot interest rates and a risk premium. Unlike the risk premium associated with the liquidity preference theory, under the preferred habitat theory the risk premium does not necessarily rise directly with maturity. Instead, it is a function of the extra yield required to induce borrowers and investors to shift out of their preferred habitats. The risk premium may, therefore, be positive or negative in the various segments.

The decomposition of the yield curve

Consider the term structure as of 22 January 2001 from Table 3.1. The simple interest yield is 5.69 per cent for a 176-day maturity Treasury security and 5.13 per cent for an 85-day maturity. If the expectations hypothesis holds, over the 176-day holding period, the 5.69 per cent yield must be equalized with the yield on two consecutive transactions: the purchase of the 85-day Treasury today followed by, on the date of the maturity of the 85-day Treasury security, the purchase of a 91-day Treasury security for a total holding period of 85 plus 91 which equals 176 days. We know the yield on the first leg of this transaction: the spot interest rate on the 85-day Treasury security, or 5.13 per cent (in simple interest format). If all 176-day holding period yields are equal, then we can solve for the 91-day implied forward rate, i.e., the rate on the 91-day Treasury security that will be delivered in 85 days, denoted by $_{85}i_{91}$.

Table 3.1 The Term Structure of Interest Rates, January 22, 2001

Time to Maturity, t (days)	Rate of Discount, d (%)	Simple Interest Yield, i (%)
85	5.00	5.13
176	5.46	5.69
274	5.67	6.01
358	5.85	6.30

Figure 3.6 shows the decomposition of the yield curve for the 176-day and 85-day spot yields. In the top transaction, the investor buys the 176-day security, with a face value set at $1 (for simplicity) as shown in equation (3.7) for a price of:

$$P = \frac{F}{1 + {}_0i_{176}(176)/365} = \frac{1}{1 + 0.569(176)/365}$$

$$= \$0.973295959 \tag{3.7}$$

If the unbiased expectations hypothesis holds, then this investment must be the equivalent to the bottom transaction in Figure 3.6: the purchase of a spot 85-day security followed by the purchase of a 91-day security in 85 days. Setting the price of the 85-day security equal to $0.973295959, we find that the face value, upon maturity, is

$$F = P\left(1 + \frac{it}{365}\right) = 0.973295959\left(1 + \frac{0.0513(85)}{365}\right)$$

$$= \$0.984923512$$

thereby yielding the 85-day spot yield of 5.13 per cent.

This is immediately reinvested in a 91-day forward security to mature 176 days from today at a face value of $1. The yield on that security is given in equation (3.8)

$$\frac{F - P}{P}\left(\frac{365}{t}\right) = \frac{1 - 0.984923512}{0.984923512}\left(\frac{365}{91}\right) = 6.14\% \qquad (3.8)$$

This yield is the implied forward rate on the 91-day bill to be delivered in 85 days, denoted by $_{85}i_{91}$.

Restating this in a simplified formula, we obtain

Price of 176-day spot = Price of 85-day spot × Price of 91-day implied forward

$$\frac{1}{1 + \frac{_0i_{176}(176)}{365}} = \left(\frac{1}{1 + \frac{_0i_{85}(85)}{365}}\right) \times \left(\frac{1}{1 + \frac{_{85}i_{91}(91)}{365}}\right)$$

$$\frac{1}{1 + \frac{0.0569(176)}{365}} = \left(\frac{1}{1 + \frac{0.0513(85)}{365}}\right) \times \left(\frac{1}{1 + \frac{_{85}i_{91}(91)}{365}}\right)$$

where $_{85}i_{91}$ denotes the implied forward rate.

The implied forward rate of 6.14 per cent can be interpreted as the market's consensus that the expected spot interest rate on 91-day securities will be 6.14 per cent in 85 days from today. Thus, the upward slope of the yield curve suggests that the market expects interest rates to rise in the future. The implied forward rate can be used as an estimate of how high interest rates are expected to rise.

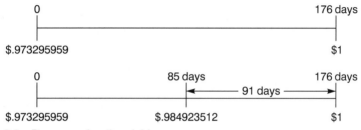

Figure 3.6 Decomposing the yield curve.

This process can be repeated for other maturity pairs of spot interest rates. For instance, we can use the 85-day and the 274-day spot rates of 22 January 2001 to solve for the implied forward rate, $_{85}i_{189}$ = 6.33 per cent, on a 189-day maturity security to be delivered in 85 days. Similarly, using the 85-day and 358-day securities, we can show that the implied forward rate, $_{85}i_{273}$, on a 273-day maturity security to be delivered in 85 days is 6.59 per cent. Plotting the implied forward rates (see 6.14 per cent, 6.33 per cent and 6.59 per cent in Figure 3.7) expected to prevail in 85 days, we obtain a forward yield curve, which graphically depicts the implied forward rates for different maturities on a specific date in the future. This can be used as a consensus estimate of expected future spot interest rates.

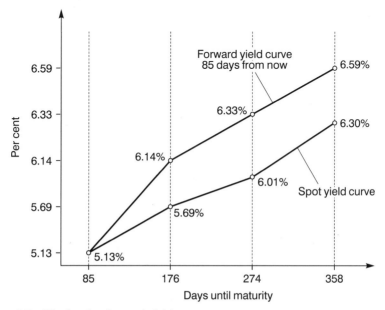

Figure 3.7 Plotting the forward yield curve.

The implied forward rate is a forecast of expected future spot rates. If the expectations hypothesis holds, then the implied forward rate tells us the rate that investors expect to prevail on deferred delivery securities. This implied forward rate should be equal to the spot interest rate that is expected to prevail on the deferred delivery date.

4

How can investors forecast the behaviour of financial markets?

The role of business cycles

The business cycle refers to the phenomena whereby there are ups and downs in the level of economic activity over time and that these ups and downs invariably recur. The fact that these peaks and troughs of economic activity do recur means that an understanding of the business cycle gives one a forecasting framework. This framework can be used confidently to analyse the way financial markets can be expected to behave in the future, given that we know at which stage of the business cycle the economy is currently operating at. Without some form of economic model it is impossible to forecast the impact of new information. The business cycle model enables us to predict the effect of the behaviour of stocks, bonds and currencies as new information arrives in the market place.

The exact response of financial markets to different stages of the business cycle will be analysed later in this chapter but at this stage it is useful to summarize some of the conclusions for the bond, stock and foreign exchange markets.

- Bonds. Too much economic activity is bad news, as it may force up interest rates. Too little economic activity is good news, as it could result in falling interest rates.
- Stocks. Economic activity is good news as long as there is no rise in interest rates. Economic activity increases the likelihood of higher earnings and subsequently dividends. An economic slowdown would have the opposite effect.

● Currency Market. If interest rates rise this is normally good news for the domestic currency, increasing, as it does, the returns from holding the currency. However, if there are domestic reasons to prevent rising interest rates, such as high unemployment, and there is simultaneously bad news on the inflation side then this is bad for the domestic currency. Falling interest rates normally cause the currency to weaken.

Business activity historically goes through waves of expansion followed by waves of contraction. At one stage of the cycle production, employment and profits rise, which is then followed by another phase when profits, prices and output fall, resulting in rising unemployment. Then the entire cycle repeats itself again. During the expansion phase, demand, production, income and wealth all grow. Houses and factories are constructed, and investment in machinery and equipment take place. House prices, stock prices and other assets grow in value. But then comes the inevitable contraction and the forces that caused wealth to rise go into reverse. Demand, production and incomes fall. The amount of housebuilding and investment in factories are drastically reduced. Assets fall in value as house prices and stock prices fall.

Although no two business cycles are identical, all (or most) cycles have features in common. This point has been made strongly by a leading business cycle theorist and recent Nobel prize winner, Robert E. Lucas, Jr., (1977) of the University of Chicago:

> 'Though there is absolutely no theoretical reason to anticipate it, one is led by the facts to conclude that, with respect to the qualitative behaviour of comovement among economic variables, *business cycles are all alike*. To theoretically inclined economists, this conclusion should be attractive and challenging, for it suggests the possibility of a unified explanation of business cycles, grounded in the *general* laws governing market economies rather than in political or institutional characteristics specific to particular countries or periods.'

Lucas's statement that business cycles are all alike (or more accurately that they have many features in common) is based on examinations of co-movement among economic variables over the business cycle.

That business cycles occur and repeat themselves is not in dispute. The causes of regularity and the length and duration of the phases of the cycle have not been completely satisfactorily explained, although Table 4.1 shows what seems to be the most

Table 4.1   Key Features of the Business Cycle

Forces of supply and demand condition every cycle. Supply creates its own demand. By producing goods incomes are increased which enables employees to buy more goods and services.

Neither businesses nor consumers are constrained in their spending pattern to rely solely upon the income they have generated in the process of production. Credit is available.

Every expansion carries with it the inevitability of over-expansion and subsequent contraction. Over-borrowing takes place. This need to repay as interest rates rise stretches the ability of individuals to keep spending, forcing a reducing in spending.

During contractions production and income recede to a sustainable level (i.e. a level not reliant upon a continuous growth in credit).

Every contraction sows the seed of the subsequent recovery. As interest rates fall borrowing becomes cheaper, investment and spending rise, and the cycle starts over again.

Source: Lehmann (1990)

plausible explanation. The only certain factor is that the business cycle is created by internal forces from within the economic system. Certain key features of the cycle do recur and it is to these that we now turn. Table 4.1 provides a summary of many of these characteristics.

It must be stressed here that the analysis below does not take account of the whole 'New Economy' version of macroeconomics, which is discussed further in Chapter 12. The sustainability of the New Economy version of macroeconomics is as yet untested. It may well indeed change the rules of the business cycle but until the evidence has been collected through a recession, as well as a boom, then our version of where financial market volatility comes from will remain in place.

It is useful to examine these features in more detail, following the Lehman (1990) analysis.

1. *The forces of supply and demand condition every cycle.*
   Our ability to enjoy increasing income depends on our ability to supply or create increased production or output; we must produce more to earn more. But the level of demand, and the expenditures made in purchasing this output, must justify the level of production. That is, we must sell what we produce in order to earn. With sufficient demand, the level of production will be sustained and will grow, and incomes will

increase; if demand is insufficient, the reverse will occur. During the expansionary phase of the cycle, demand and supply forces are in a relationship that permits the growth of production and incomes; during the contractionary phase, their relationship compels a decrease in production and incomes.

2. *Neither consumers nor businesses are constrained to rely solely on the income they have generated in the process of production.*

They have recourse to the credit market; they can borrow money and spend more than they earn. Spending borrowed funds permits demand to take on a life of it's own and bid-up a constantly and rapidly growing level of production. This gives rise to the expansionary phase of the cycle. Eventually, the growth in production becomes dependent on the continued availability of credit, which sustains the growth in demand. But once buyers can no longer rely on borrowed funds (because of market saturation, the exhaustion of profitable investment opportunities, or tight credit), demand falls and, with it, the bloated level of production and income. The contractionary phase has begun.

3. *Every expansion carries with it the inevitability of 'over-expansion' and the subsequent contraction.*

Over-expansion may be propelled by businesses that invest too heavily in new plant and equipment in order to take advantage of a seemingly profitable opportunity, or by consumers who borrow too heavily in order to buy homes, autos, or other goods. But when businesses realize that the expected level of sales will not support additional plant and equipment, and when consumers realize that they will have difficulty paying for that new home or car, then businesses and consumers will curtail their borrowing and expenditure. Since production and income have spurted ahead to meet the growth in demand, they fall when the inevitable contraction in demand takes place.

4. *During contractions, production and incomes recede to a sustainable level, i.e., to a level not reliant on a continuous growth in credit.*

The contraction returns the economy to a more efficient level of operation.

5. *Every contraction sows the seeds of the subsequent recovery.*

Income earned in the productive process, rather than bloated levels of borrowing, maintains the level of demand. Consumers and businesses repay their debts. Eventually, lower debt burdens and interest rates encourage consumer and business borrowing and demand. The economy begins expanding once more and *the cycle begins to repeat itself.*

The cyclical behaviour of economic variables: direction and timing

Two characteristics of the cyclical behaviour of macroeconomic variables are important to the discussion of the business cycle facts. The first is the direction in which a macroeconomic variable moves, relative to the direction of aggregate economic activity. An economic variable that moves in the same direction as aggregate economic activity (up in expansions, down in contractions) is said to be procyclical. A variable that moves in an opposite direction to aggregate economic activity (up in contractions, down in expansions) is said to be countercyclical. Variables that do not display a clear pattern over the business cycle are said to be acyclical.

The second characteristic of this macroeconomic behaviour is the timing of the variable's turning points (peaks and troughs) relative to the turning points of the business cycle. An economic variable is a leading variable if it tends to move in advance of aggregate economic activity. In other words, the peaks and troughs in a leading variable occur before the corresponding peaks and troughs in the business cycle. A coincident variable is one whose peaks and troughs occur at about the same time as the corresponding business cycle peaks and troughs. Finally, a lagging variable is one whose peaks and troughs tend to occur later than the corresponding peaks and troughs in the business cycle.

The fact that some economic variables consistently lead the business cycle suggests that they might be used to forecast the future course of the economy. This idea is behind the index of leading indicators, discussed later. In some cases the cyclical timing of a variable is obvious from a graph of its behaviour over the course of several business cycles; in other cases elaborate statistical techniques are needed to determine timing. Conveniently, the Statistical Indicators Branch of the Bureau of Economic Analysis (BEA) has analysed the timing of dozens of

Table 4.2   The Cyclical Behaviour of Key Macroeconomic Variables

Variable	Direction	Timing
Production		
Industrial production	Procyclical	Coincident
Durable goods industries are more volatile than nondurable goods and services		
Expenditure		
Consumption	Procyclical	Coincident
Business fixed investment	Procyclical	Coincident
Residential investment	Procyclical	Leading
Inventory investment	Procyclical	Leading
Government purchases	Procyclical	
Investment is more volatile than consumption		
Labour Market Variables		
Employment	Procyclical	Coincident
Unemployment	Countercyclical	Unclassified
Average labour productivity	Procyclical	Leading
Real wage	Procyclical	
Money Growth and Inflation		
Money growth	Procyclical	Leading
Inflation	Procyclical	Lagging
Financial Variables		
Stock prices	Procyclical	Leading
Nominal interest rates	Procyclical	Lagging
Real interest rates	Acyclical	

Source: *Survey of Current Business*, May 1993.

economic variables. This information is published monthly in the *Survey of Current Business*, along with the most recent data for these variables (see Table 4.2).

The stages of the business cycle

From the point of view of analysing financial market behaviour during the business cycle, again following Lehman (1996), it is useful to break down the cycle into four phases: trough to

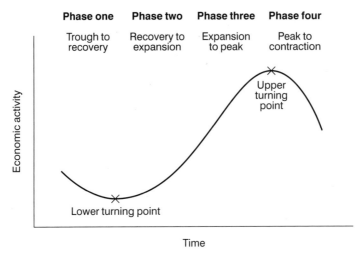

Figure 4.1   Phases of the business cycle.

recovery; recovery to expansion; expansion to peak; and peak to contraction. The phases are summarized in Figure 4.1.

Phase one: from trough to recovery

During this phase GDP and industrial production are falling and capacity utilization is declining. This leads to an increase in labour productivity and a fall in unit labour costs, driving down the rate of inflation, as measured by producer prices. Pressures for a fall in interest rates build up, changing the shape of the yield curve (see Figure 4.2).

The Federal Reserve, seeing rising unemployment, will be actively stimulating the economy with an easing of monetary policy.

Phase two: from recovery to expansion

At this stage economic activity starts to pick up, reinforced by cheap credit and low inflation. Fluctuations in consumer prices are a key determinant of consumer real income, so a fall in inflation is a boost to real income. This leads to improved consumer sentiment and demand, which in turn drives economic expansion. This is evidenced by increased demand in the economy fuelled by a rise in consumer credit and increased spending on automobiles, a rise in retail sales and a rise in the

Gross domestic product	↓
Industrial production	↓
Capacity utilization	↓
Labour productivity	↑
Unit labour costs	↓
Producer prices	↓

Phase one: trough to recovery

Recession progresses

– Yield curve becomes positively sloped

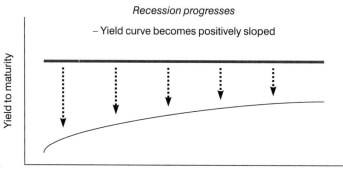

Figure 4.2 The yield curve in phase 1.

demand for housing. The trend in interest rates is one in which pressures are starting to build for rising rates. The yield curve moves, as can be seen from Figure 4.3.

Phase three: from expansion to peak

From phase two of the business cycle we are aware that all the indicators of economic expansion, e.g. car sales, consumer credit, retail sales, and housing starts, are showing improvements. This will initiate broad-based growth as incomes increase in the construction, car and other durable goods industries spill over boosting demand for other consumer goods. Boom conditions will intensify as business invests in additional factories and machinery to meet the extra orders.

As the expansion unfolds, capacity utilization increases with the growth in demand and production. Soon factories move from, say, 70 per cent to 80 per cent of their maximum capacity. Productive facilities strain to meet demand and to retain the loyalty of customers.

Consumer price index	↓
Consumer real income	↑
Consumer sentiment	↑
Consumer demand Car sales Consumer credit Retail sales Housing starts	↑ ↑ ↑ ↑ ↑

Phase two: recovery to expansion

Adequate physical and financial resources promote balanced growth

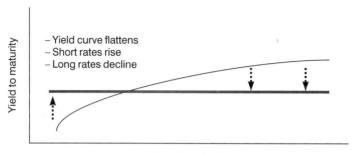

– Yield curve flattens
– Short rates rise
– Long rates decline

Yield to maturity

Time to maturity

Figure 4.3 The yield curve in phase 2.

Next, high levels of capacity utilization drive labour productivity down, at least until the recent 'new economy' behaviour, and unit labour costs move up as efficiency is sacrificed in the name of increased output. Machinery that is always in use cannot be adequately maintained and will tend to break down. Inexperienced workers cannot make the same contribution as old hands. The amount of labour employed increases more rapidly than output, and as output per worker falls, the labour cost per unit of output rises. This generates a surge in production costs. These rapidly increasing costs are translated into rapidly increasing prices, and a renewed round of inflation begins.

At this stage there will be pressures for the Federal Reserve to raise interest rates in an attempt to restrain the inflation. The yield curve moves again, as can be seen from Figure 4.4.

This third phase of the business cycle (from expansion to peak) is the inverse of the first. All the forces that led to a reduction in inflationary pressures are now reversed.

Gross domestic product	↑
Industrial production	↑
Capacity utilization	↑
Labour productivity	↓
Unit labour costs	↑
Producer prices	↑

Phase three: expansion to peak

Pressure on capacity causes economy to overheat

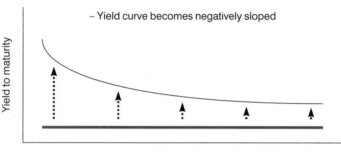

− Yield curve becomes negatively sloped

Time to maturity

Figure 4.4   The yield curve in phase 3.

Phase four: from peak to contraction

From phase three we know that economic expansion generates reduced efficiency and heightened inflation. As production grows, and with it capacity utilization, labour productivity falls, again the trend prior to the 'new economy' behaviour. Labour costs increase, driving prices upward. The economy has reached a level of activity that cannot be sustained.

The fourth phase of the business cycle is the inverse of the second. In that phase of the cycle, from recovery to expansion, a declining rate of inflation pushed consumer real income upward, prompting consumers to borrow and spend, thus fuelling the economic expansion. Now, in the last phase of the cycle, a rising rate of inflation has the opposite impact on the consumer. Real income falls, and consumer sentiment erodes. Consumers become pessimistic when their salaries don't keep up with inflation, giving them less and less real buying power. They respond by restricting their purchase of postponable items, especially those that require heavy borrowing. The downturn in consumer activity will lead to a general contraction in demand, which will continue until the trough of the cycle is reached and the whole cycle starts again. As the Federal Reserve moves to stimulate the economy by cutting interest rates the yield curve moves to the one shown in Figure 4.5.

Phase four: peak to contraction

Recession progresses

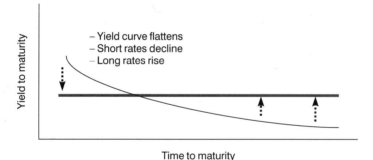

Time to maturity

Figure 4.5 The yield curve in phase 4.

The role of inventories in recessions

Historically, most post-war recessions have been characterized by a significant reduction in aggregate inventory investment relative to the reduction from peak to trough of GNP. In trying to predict the duration of a recession, one should watch the behaviour of business inventories. Indeed economic recessions can be triggered by an oversupply of business inventories. The effect of an oversupply of inventories, which results in inventory reductions, accounted for more than 40 per cent of the real GNP decline in each of the nine recessions since 1947. In the recessions of 1948 and 1960, all of the decline in real GNP can be attributed to a drop in inventory investment to negative levels.

Inventory investment, or changes in business inventories, is pro-cyclical and a leading indicator but it is also extremely volatile. For example, between 1982 and 1990 inventory investment fluctuated sharply despite the fact that the economy was continuously in expansion.

Inventory behaviour cannot be ignored, despite its volatility. Consequently it must be monitored if the future stage of the business cycle is to be anticipated.

The business cycle and monetary policy

As already indicated the outlook for the economy and expectation of households and businesses plays a central role in the magnitude and timing of monetary policy effects on the economy. Households' own experience with the cyclical rise and fall in interest rates may affect their actions. A sustained sharp rise in interest rates, for example, may suggest more uncertain prospects for employment and incomes, resulting in greater household caution towards spending on consumer goods and house purchases. Conversely, a significant fall in interest rates during a period of weak economic activity may encourage greater consumer spending by increasing the value of household assets. Lower mortgage rates, together with greater availability of mortgage credit, may also stimulate the demand for housing.

Businesses plan their inventories and additions to productive capacity (i.e., capital spending) to meet future customer demands and their own sales expectations. Since internal resources, i.e., retained earnings and depreciation allowances, do not provide all of their cash requirements, businesses are often obliged to use the credit markets to finance capital spending and inventories.

During a business cycle expansion, the business sector's need for external financing rises rapidly, as firms accumulate inventories to ensure that sales rise rapidly. Firms accumulate inventories to ensure that sales will not be lost because of shortages. At the same time, businesses attempt to finance additions to capacity. Greater business demand for funds tends to bid-up interest rates. In making investment decisions, such investors take into account recent experience with inflation and inflation expectations, as well as numerous other factors, such as long-term interest rates and the credibility of monetary policy. These same considerations are also important in the transmission of monetary policy to the foreign exchange market.

How does monetary policy affect the economy?

By causing changes in interest rates, financial markets and the dollar exchange rate, monetary policy actions have important effects on output, employment and prices. These effects work through many different channels, affecting demand. Figure 4.6 shows the main contours of the transmission of monetary policy to the economy. Monetary policy actions influence

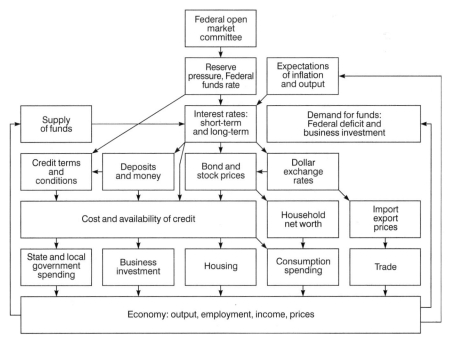

Figure 4.6   The transmission of monetary policy.

output, employment and prices through a number of complex channels. These channels involve a variety of forces in financial markets that cause changes in: (1) the cost and availability of funds to businesses and households, (2) the value of household assets or net worth, and (3) the foreign exchange value of the dollar with direct consequences for import/export prices. All changes, in due course, affect economic activity and prices in various sectors of the economy.

When the Federal Reserve tightens monetary policy (for example, by draining bank reserves through open market sales of Government securities) the Fed funds rate and other short-term interest rates rise more or less immediately, reflecting the reduced supply of bank reserves in the market. Sustained increases in short-term interest rates lead to lower growth of deposits and money as well as higher long-term interest rates. Higher interest rates raise the cost of funds, and, over time, have adverse consequences for business investment demand, home buying and consumer spending on durable goods, other things remaining the same. This is the conventional money or interest rate channel of monetary policy influence on the economy.

A firming of monetary policy may also reduce the supply of bank loans through higher funding costs for banks or through increases in the perceived riskiness of bank loans. Similarly, non-bank sources of credit to the private sector may become more scarce because of higher lending risks (actual or perceived) associated with tighter monetary conditions. The reduced availability, as distinct from costs, of loans may have negative effects on aggregate demand and output. This is the so-called 'credit channel' that may operate alongside the interest rate channel.

Higher interest rates and lower monetary growth may also influence economic activity through the 'wealth channel' by lowering actual or expected asset values. For example, rising interest rates generally tend to lower bond and stock prices, reducing household net worth and weakening business balance sheets. As a consequence, business and household spending may suffer.

Finally, a tightening of monetary policy affects economic activity by raising the foreign exchange value of the dollar – the exchange rate channel. By making US imports cheaper and by increasing the cost of US exports to foreigners, the appreciation of the dollar reduces the demand for US goods, and, therefore, has adverse consequences for the trade balance and output. On the positive side, lower import prices help in improving the US inflation performance.

Needless to say, all these effects work in the opposite direction when the Federal Reserve eases monetary policy.

Fundamental analysis, the business cycle and financial markets

Fundamental analysis, as it is known in financial markets, is closely tied to the supply of and demand for money. The money supply, in turn, affects the level of interest rates, bond prices and the currency markets. Because so many factors, discussed in earlier chapters, influence the supply of and demand for money, the reaction of financial markets is somewhat complex.

In general, however, traders watch three major sources of information:

1. the key economic reports issued by various government agencies and private organizations;
2. the Federal Reserve; and
3. the US Treasury Department.

The major financial markets key in on different types of economic indicators. Table 4.3 and Chapters 5, 6 and 7 provide a survey of some of the more important economic indicators. Fixed-income markets are primarily concerned with reports that address the pace of economic growth and inflation. The foreign exchange markets also look at these figures, as well as at foreign trade imbalances. The stock market is affected by economic growth to the extent that this affects general earnings, but stocks are also dependent on specific company and industry fundamentals. In addition, changes in interest rates will affect the stock market to the extent that rate shifts may cause investors to be more or less attracted to stocks relative to bonds.

Prior to the release of an economic report, many of the news services survey the major dealers and publish forecasts. These surveys are an excellent barometer of the financial markets' expectations and are built into market prices prior to the report's release date.

Table 4.3 Major Economic Reports

Report	Description	Degree of Impact	Typical Release Date	Released by	Period Covered
CPI	The Consumer Price Index measures the average change in prices for a fixed basket of goods and services	High	10th Business Day	Labour Dept. Bureau of Statistics	Prior month
Durable Goods	One of a series of manufacturing and trade reports. Focuses on new orders	Moderate	18th Business Day	Commerce Dept. Census Bureau	Prior month
Employment	A survey of households providing very timely information on the rate of unemployment	Very high	First Friday of the month	Labour Dept. Bureau of Economic Analysis	Prior month
GDP	Gross Domestic Product measures the value of items produced within the US	Very high (for initial est.)	20th Business Day	Commerce Dept. Bureau of Economic Analysis	Prior quarter
Housing Starts	Measures new residential units started. Most significant for the financial markets during turning points in the business cycle	Moderate	15th Business Day	Commerce Dept. Census Bureau	Prior month
Industrial Production	Industrial Production measures output in manufacturing, mining and utility industries	Moderate	15th Business Day	Federal Reserve	Prior month
Merchandise Trade	Details the monthly exports and imports of US goods	Moderate to high	Third week of the month	Commerce Dept. Census Bureau	Two months prior
NAPM	The (National Association of) Purchasing Managers Index is a composite index of new orders, production, supplier deliveries, inventories and employment	High	First business day of the month	National Association of Purchasing Managers	Prior month
PPI	The Producer Price Index measures the average domestic change in prices, less discounts received, by wholesale producers of commodities	High	10th business day of statistics	Labour Dept. Bureau	Prior month
Retail Sales	A measure of consumer spending, reporting on sales of both nondurable and durable consumer goods	High	Mid-month	Commerce Dept. Census Bureau	Prior month
Unemployment Insurance Claims	Reflects actual initial claims for unemployment insurance filed with state unemployment agencies	Moderate	Every Thursday	Labour Dept. Employment and Training Administration	Prior week

Table 4.4 The impact of economic news on financial markets

Market	If Business Conditions are Stronger than expected	If Inflation is Higher than expected	If Business Conditions are Weaker than expected	If Inflation is Lower than expected
Fixed-Income Prices	▼	▼	▲	▲
Stock Market Prices	▲	▼	▼	▲
Foreign Exchange (value of the dollar)	▲	▲	▼	▼

Source: Niemira and Zukowski (1994)

But the forecasts are not always accurate. Once the number is released, prices quickly adjust to reflect the new information. Table 4.4 summarizes how the major financial markets typically react to news that varies from initial expectations.

Consider the fixed-income markets for example. Assume that the so-called employment report, discussed in detail in Chapter 6, showed a lower unemployment rate than expected. This would signal stronger business conditions, more consumer income, and increased spending – all signs that the economy is heating up. This news would tend to drive interest rates up and, because prices and yields move inversely in the fixed-income markets, this increase in interest rates would mean a decrease in bond prices.

Over time, the markets tend to favour and follow certain reports over others. For example, if the current concern is centred on inflation, then the CPI and PPI reports, discussed in detail in Chapter 5, will take on more significance. If the value of the dollar and its impact on international trade becomes a major issue, then the merchandise trade report becomes more important.

The NBER and business cycles

In the United States the National Bureau of Economic Research (NBER), a private non-profit organization of economists founded in 1920, pioneered business cycle research. The NBER developed and continues to update business cycle chronology, providing a detailed history of business cycles in the United States and other countries. The NBER has also sponsored many studies of business cycles. One landmark study was the 1946 book *Measuring Business Cycles* by Arthur Burns (who also served as Federal Reserve chairman) and Wesley Mitchell (a principal founder of the NBER). This work was among the first to document and analyse the empirical facts about business cycles. It begins with the following definition:

> 'Business cycles are a type of fluctuation found in the aggregate economic activity of nations that organise their work mainly in business enterprises. A cycle consists of expansions occurring at about the same time as many economic activities, followed by similarly general recessions, contractions, and revivals which merge into the expansion phase of the business cycle; this sequence of changes is recurrent but not periodic; in duration business cycles vary from more than one year to ten or twelve years.'

Five points in this definition should be clarified and emphasized.

Aggregate economic activity

Business cycles are defined broadly as fluctuations of 'aggregate economic activity' rather than fluctuations in any single specific economic variable such as real GDP. Although real GDP may be the single variable that most closely measures aggregate economic activity, Burns and Mitchell also thought it important to look at other indicators of activity, such as employment and financial market variables.

Expansion and contractions

Figure 4.7, a diagram of a typical business cycle, helps to explain what Burns and Mitchell meant by expansions and contractions. The dashed line shows the average, or normal, growth path of aggregate economic activity, and the solid curve shows the rises and falls of actual business activity. The period of time during which aggregate economic activity is falling is a contraction or recession. If the recession is particularly severe, it becomes a depression. After reaching the low point of the contraction, the trough (*T*), economic activity begins to increase. The period of time during which aggregate economic activity grows is an expansion or a boom. After reaching the high point of the expansion, the peak (*P*), aggregate economic activity begins to decline again. The entire sequence of decline followed by recovery, measured from peak to peak or trough to trough, is a business cycle.

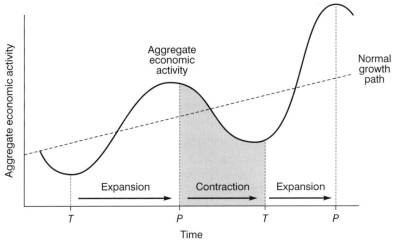

Figure 4.7 A typical business cycle.

Peaks and troughs in the business cycle are known collectively as turning points. One goal of business cycle research is to identify when turning points occur. Aggregate economic activity is not measured directly by any single variable, so there is no simple formula that tells economists when a peak or trough has been reached. In practice, a small group of economists who form the NBER's Business Cycle Dating Committee determine that date. The committee meets only when its members believe that a turning point may have occurred. By examining a variety of economic data, the committee determines whether a peak or trough has been reached and, if so, the month it happened. However, the committee's announcements usually come well after a peak or trough occurs, so their judgements are more useful for historical analysis of business cycles than as a guide to current policymaking.

A specific cycle is a set of turning points observable in a particular series. These turns may or may not correspond to the overall business cycle turning point dates. The selection of a turn must meet the following criteria.

1 The cycle duration must be at least 15 months, as measured from either peak to peak or trough to trough.
2 If the peak or trough zone is flat, then the latest value is selected as the turn.
3 Strike activity or other special factors are generally ignored, if their effect is brief and fully reversible.

Co-movement

Business cycles do not occur in just a few sectors or in just a few economic variables. Instead, expansions or contractions occur at about the same time in many economic activities. Thus, although some industries are more sensitive to the business cycle than others, output and employment in most industries tend to fall in recessions and rise in expansions. Many other economic variables, such as prices, productivity, investment, and government purchases, also have regular and predictable patterns of behaviour over the course of the business cycle. This tendency is called co-movement.

Recurrent but not periodic

The business cycle is not periodic, in that it does not occur at regular, predictable intervals and does not last for a fixed or predetermined length of time. Although the business cycle is not periodic, it is recurrent; that is, the standard pattern of contraction–trough–expansion peak recurs again and again in industrial economies.

Persistence

The duration of a complete business cycle can vary greatly, from about a year to more than a decade, and predicting it is extremely difficult. However, once a recession begins, the economy tends to keep contracting for a period of time, perhaps for a year or more. Similarly, an expansion once begun usually lasts a while. The empirical evidence on this is discussed below. This tendency for declines in economic activity to be followed by more growth, is called persistence. Because movements in economic activity have some persistence, economic forecasters are always on the lookout for turning points, which are likely to indicate a change in the direction of economic activity.

How do you identify a recession?

A conventional definition used by the financial media, i.e., that a recession has occurred when there are two consecutive quarters of negative real GDP growth, is not widely accepted by economists. The reason that economists tend not to like this definition is that real GDP is only one of many possible indicators of economic activity.

A more complete statement, used by the NBER for spotting a recession, would include the following.

1. Real GDP should decline at least one-quarter and industrial production contract for at least four to six months.
2. There should be a contraction, for at least four to six months, in one or more of the following series:
    *   industrial production
    *   real disposable personal income
    *   employment and/or
    *   aggregate hours worked.
3. The employment diffusion index, described in detail in Appendix A, should decline below 40 per cent of all industries expanding their workforce, on a one-month change basis, and remain below that point for at least four to six months.

The unemployment rate criteria seems less useful since it can be affected by demographic influences. For example, during the 1990 recession, the unemployment rate was held down by a demographic bonus – a shrinking or very slowly growing labour force.

So the NBER definition, which is 'a recurring period of decline in total output, employment and trade, usually lasting from 6 months to a year, and marked by widespread contractions in many sectors of the economy', is the one officially applied. In simpler terms the NBER refer to a recession as the three Ds: depth, duration, and dispersion. That means that it cannot be just one part of the economy, such as the manufacturing sector, for example. In addition it cannot be too short or too mild.

The American business cycle: the historical record

An overview of American business cycle history is provided by the NBER's monthly business cycle chronology, as summarized in Table 4.5. It gives the dates of the troughs and peaks of the 31 complete business cycles that the US economy has experienced since 1854. Also shown are the number of months that each contraction and expansion lasted.

Table 4.5 NBER Business Cycle Turning Points and Duration's of Post-1854
Business Cycles

Troughs	Expansion (months from trough to peak)	Peak	Contraction (months from peak to next trough
Dec. 1854	30	June 1857	18
Dec. 1858	22	Oct. 1860	8
June 1861	46	Apr. 1865	32
Dec. 1867	18	June 1869	18
Dec. 1870	34	Oct. 1873	65
Mar. 1879	36	Mar. 1882	38
May 1885	22	Mar. 1887	13
Apr. 1888	27	July 1890	10
May 1891	20	Jan 1893	17
June 1894	18	Dec. 1895	18
June 1897	24	June 1899	18
Dec. 1900	21	Sep. 1902	23
Aug. 1904	33	May 1907	13
June 1908	19	Jan. 1910	24
Jan. 1912	12	Jan. 1913	23
Dec. 1914	44 WWI	Aug. 1918	7
Mar. 1919	10	Jan. 1920	18
July 1921	22	May 1923	14
July 1924	27	Oct. 1926	13
Nov 1927	21	Aug. 1929	43 (Depression)
Mar 1933	50	May 1937	13 (Depression)
June 1938	80 WWII	Feb. 1945	8
Oct. 1945	37	Nov. 1948	11
Oct. 1949	45 (Korean War)	July 1953	10
May 1954	39	Aug. 1957	8
Apr. 1958	24	Apr. 1960	10
Feb. 1961	106 (Vietnam War)	Dec. 1969	11
Nov. 1970	36	Nov 1973	16
Mar. 1975	58	Jan. 1980	6
July 1980	12	July 1981	16
Nov. 1982	92	July 1990	8
Mar 1991			

Source: US Department of Commerce, Survey of Current Business, October 1994, Table
C-51: Business Cycle Expansions and Contractions

Post-world war II US business cycles

As World War II was ending in 1945, economists and policy-
makers were concerned that the economy would relapse into
depression. As an expression of this concern, Congress passed
the Employment Act of 1946, which required the government to

fight recessions and depressions with any measures at its disposal. But instead of falling into a new depression, as feared, the US economy began to grow strongly.

Only a few relatively brief and mild recessions interrupted the economic expansion of the early post-war period. None of the five contractions that occurred between 1945 and 1970 lasted more than a year, whereas 18 of the 22 previous cyclical contractions in the NBER's monthly chronology had lasted a year or more. The largest drop in real GDP between 1945 and 1970 was 3.3 per cent during the 1957–1958 recession, and throughout this period unemployment never exceeded 8.1 per cent of the work force. Historically, there has been a strong correlation between economic expansion and war. The 1949–1953 expansion corresponded closely to the Korean War, and the latter part of the strong 1961–1969 expansion occurred during the military build-up to fight the Vietnam War. More recently economic expansion has occurred in the absence of wartime conditions.

Because no serious recession occurred between 1945 and 1970, some economists suggested that the business cycle had been 'tamed', or even that it was 'dead'. This view, which continues today, was especially popular during the record 106-month expansion of 1961–1969, which was widely attributed not only to high rates of military spending during the Vietnam War but also to the macroeconomic policies of Presidents Kennedy and Johnson. Some argued that policy-makers should stop worrying about recessions and focus their attention on inflation, which had been gradually increasing over the 1960s.

Unfortunately, reports of the business cycle's death proved premature. Shortly after the Organization of Petroleum Exporting Countries (OPEC) succeeded in quadrupling oil prices in the fall of 1973, the US economy and the economies of many other nations fell into a severe recession. In the 1973–1975 recession American real GDP fell by 4.1 per cent and the unemployment rate reached 9 per cent – not a depression but a serious downturn, nonetheless. Also disturbing was the fact that inflation, which had fallen during most previous recessions, shot up to unprecedented double-digit levels. Inflation continued to be a problem for the rest of the 1970s, even as the economy recovered from the 1973–1975 recession.

More evidence that the business cycle was not dead came with the sharp 1981–1982 recession. This contraction lasted 16 months, the same length as the 1973–1975 decline, and the unemployment rate reached 11 per cent, a post-war high. Inflation did drop dramatically, from about 11 per cent to less than 4 per cent per year. The recovery from this recession was strong, however, and the ensuing expansion continued until the summer of 1990.

In July 1990 the expansion of almost eight years ended, and the economy entered a recession. This recession was relatively short (the trough came in March 1991, only eight months after the peak) and shallow (the unemployment rate peaked in mid 1992 at 7.7 per cent, not particularly high for a recession).

The business cycle expansion period that commenced in March 1991 continues to this day.

The Goldilocks economy

Figure 4.8 illustrates recent behaviour of real gross domestic product since 1972. The shaded areas indicate recessions. It is the length of the non-shaded areas that have suggested to many economists that the business cycle is dead. This recent enviable combination of steady growth and low inflation is widely referred to as a 'Goldilocks economy' after the fairy tale story, The Three Bears, in which the character Goldilocks eats the bear's food which is 'neither too hot nor too cold'.

Are long expansions followed by short contractions?

Simple graphical analysis seems to indicate that, in the post-war period, long expansions are followed by short contractions (see Figure 4.9).

The long expansion (106 months) of the 1960s was followed by a short contraction of only 11 months. The shorter expansion (36 months) in the early 1970s was followed by a somewhat longer contraction of 16 months. The next expansion in the late

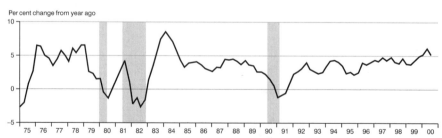

Figure 4.8 Real gross domestic product. Source: National Economics Trends. Shaded area signifies a recession.

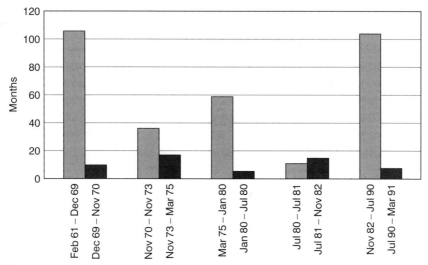

Figure 4.9 Lengths of the last five expansions and contractions.

1970s (58 months) was longer, and the following contraction was shorter (six months). Then there was a very short expansion from July 1980 to July 1981 (12 months) followed by a long contraction (16 months). Finally, the great expansion of November 1982 to July 1990 was followed by a brief contraction that ended in March 1991. The expansion from that time continues until today.

The Non-Accelerating Inflation Rate of Unemployment (NAIRU) – a new target for the Federal Reserve

NAIRU is sometimes referred to as the natural rate of unemployment, namely that rate which can be sustained without a change in the inflation rate. The NAIRU concept, discussed further in Chapter 12, is related to the Phillips curve, which was discussed in Chapter 1. The Phillips curve is the relationship which shows that high rates of unemployment are associated with low rates of change of money wages, whilst low rates of unemployment are associated with high rates of change of money wages.

The importance of the Phillips curve was that policy makers (and particularly governments) applying this concept, changed their views about how the economy might be managed. Many became convinced that there was a trade-off between unemployment and inflation. Zero inflation (i.e., price stability) could be achieved but only by keeping unemployment at what, for the time, seemed a relatively high level. On the other hand, lower unemployment could be achieved by accepting higher levels of inflation. The key point about the Phillips curve was that it demonstrated that it was impossible to fix both the rate of unemployment and the rate of inflation at desirable levels.

The concept of the NAIRU has acquired significance since it seems to be embraced by both Laurence Meyer, a Governor of the Federal Reserve, and Alan Greenspan, Chairman of the Federal Reserve. The application of NAIRU to predicting Federal Reserve actions would suggest that if the Federal Reserve foresees low unemployment it will tighten monetary policy and slow the economy. If the current unemployment rate is below the non-accelerating rate there will be wage and price pressures with inflation rising. Periods when the actual unemployment rate is below the national rate suggests a booming economy and pressure for the Federal Reserve to raise interest rates. Periods when the actual unemployment rate is above the natural rate are said to be periods of recessionary pressures when the Federal Reserve could be expected to lower interest rates.

The fact that unemployment can remain in an economy that is booming reflects imperfections in labour markets, imperfections that exist regardless of the overall state of the economy. Unemployment may exist as people may have the wrong skills, live in the wrong areas, or have little incentive to accept the jobs they are offered. Consequently this unemployment remains irrespective of the cyclical nature of the economy.

Recent estimates of the actual unemployment rate and the natural unemployment rate are given in Figure 4.10. The relationship between unemployment and inflation are given in Figure 4.11. The unemployment gap is calculated from Figure 4.11 by subtracting the natural rate of unemployment from the actual unemployment rate.

Historically, the gap between the actual unemployment rate and the natural unemployment rate has been a reliable indicator of future increases in inflation. Until very recently it was very unusual for the actual unemployment rate to fall

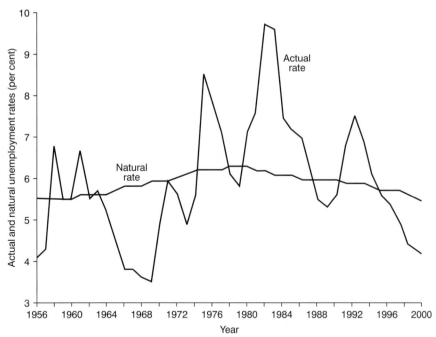

Figure 4.10 Actual unemployment rate and estimates of the natural unemployment rate (1956–2000). (Sources: Unemployment rate; all civilian workers, Economic Report of the President, 2000. Natural unemployment rate; Congressional Budget Office, The Economic and Budget Outlook, Fiscal Years 2001–2010.)

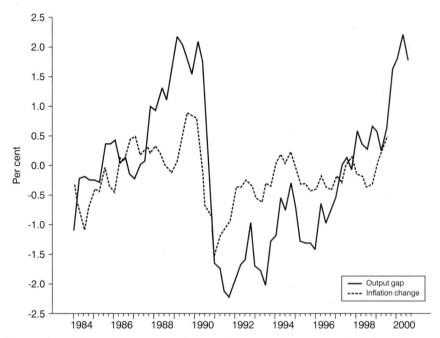

Figure 4.11 The output gap and the subsequent four quarter inflation change. (Sources: Federal Reserve Bank of New York.)

below the natural rate without the economy ultimately experiencing a rise in inflation.

The output gap, defined as the percentage difference in percentage terms between real GDP and 'potential output' also illustrates that when this goes below the zero line in Figure 4.11 inflation pressures build up.

Why might NAIRU be useful to central banks?

One of the problems with monetary policy is that there are time lags between when a policy action is taken and when it takes effect. Therefore in controlling inflation it is dangerous to look only at current rates of inflation. By the time inflation actually begins to rise, inflationary pressures may have been brewing for a year or two and it may take a substantial tightening of policy (possibly leading to a recession) to slow them down.

According to standard thinking of the way the economy works, using the NAIRU concept, if there is an increase in overall spending in the economy it will be followed by inflation. So increases in demand raises real GDP relative to its potential level, which increases the demand for labour to produce the additional goods and services, and therefore lowers the unemployment rate relative to the NAIRU. Excess demand in goods and labour markets leads to higher inflation in goods, prices and wages with a lag. Because of this, the unemployment rate can help in generating the inflation forecasts that are crucial in formulating monetary policy.

What are the limitations of the use of NAIRU?

There are both empirical and theoretical problems with NAIRU. On the empirical side the estimated NAIRU for the US has varied in the post-war period. In the 1960s, the NAIRU commonly was estimated at around 5 per cent. By the mid-1970s, it had climbed to around 7 per cent. And by the mid to late 1990s, it had fallen back to 5.5–6 per cent. A number of factors can affect the NAIRU, including changes in labour force demographics, governmental unemployment programmes, regional economic disturbances, and the recent improvements in technology enabling unemployed workers to search more efficiently for available jobs.

A related empirical criticism is that the NAIRU cannot be estimated with much precision. Based upon comprehensive empirical analysis of Phillips curves, the evidence seems to suggest that by the early twenty-first century, the NAIRU falls within a range of 4.8–6.6 per cent. Given this kind of uncertainty, the NAIRU can provide misleading signals for monetary policy at various times.

A theoretical objection to the use of the NAIRU for monetary policy is that the short-run trade-off between unemployment and inflation may be unstable over time. This trade-off is sensitive to the way in which expectations about inflation are formed, which in turn will depend upon the nature of the monetary policy regime itself.

A further theoretical objection is that the NAIRU makes sense as an indicator of future inflation only when the economy is subjected to a large increase in the demand for goods and services. However, the economy could also be affected by supply shocks or unexpected changes in the aggregate supply of goods and services. An example of a supply shock would be a sudden increase in productivity, as recently provided by the so-called 'new economy' phenomena. Initially, this kind of shock raises the quantity of goods and services produced relative to the quantity demanded, and thus put downward pressure on prices. At the same time, the increase in real GDP raises the demand for labour and reduces the unemployment rate. Thus, a falling unemployment rate would be associated with reduced pressure on prices. If a central bank were using the NAIRU to guide policy, it might mistakenly see the lower unemployment rate as a reason to fear higher inflation in the future, and therefore might tighten policy.

Some observers argue that a supply shock in recent years is having an effect on the economy. One explanation for this recent development is a surge in productivity due to the introduction of new computer related technologies. So a rising real GDP can occur at the same time as falling inflation. Therefore standard Phillips curve analysis would over-forecast inflation.

Federal Reserve Chairman, Alan Greenspan, speaking at his July 1997 Humphrey–Hawkins Testimony, expressed the view that technological change has added to workers insecurity in recent years and made them less willing to push for higher wages, and this may be thought of as one version of the effect of new technology. Greater insecurity might reduce the upward pressure on wage rates at any unemployment rate and so lower the threshold rate at which wages (and prices) would begin to move upwards.

What is the future of the business cycle?

There is considerable empirical evidence that business cycles have manifested themselves in all market-orientated industrialized economies since detailed statistics have been in existence. Their existence is here to stay, albeit not necessarily in the same shape, form, diffusion and duration. Chapter 12 returns to this idea in discussing what has become known as the New Economic Paradigm. At least four underlying forces are likely to shape the business cycle of the future. These are:

- the maturity of the economy
- the degree of globalization of the economy and related technological developments
- demographic change
- the rapidity at which the former soviet bloc countries integrate into the post cold-war environment.

The ability of an economy to thrive is bound up with the ability of other economies to thrive. In contemplating growth and stability for any open economy the problems posed by the diverse stages of maturity reached by other economies are crucial. The relationship between the structural requirements imposed by the labour force, by advancing technology, by demographic change, and of growth in mature economies has implications for domestic consumption, investment and government spending, with spillover effects on the demand for goods from the rest of the world.

What evidence is there that the business cycle is dead and buried?

There have been several structural changes to the US economy that have increased the longevity of US economic expansions.

- The increased adoption of just-in-time inventories, which has led to the ratio of inventories to sales in the manufacturing sector hitting historic lows. Because US companies now respond more quickly to a fall in demand, this reduces the risk of a large inventory overhang, which, historically, has accounted for a significant share of the GDP decline during recessions.

- 'Just-in-time' capital. This refers to shorter delivery lags for capital equipment. Capital equipment is now shipped less than three months after the order is booked, twice as fast as it was in the early 1980s.
- International diversification. Because the share of foreign goods and services in final sales to US agents has doubled since 1980, a demand slump in the US has less impact on US production than it previously did.
- Increased globalization has led to greater price/wage flexibility.

What evidence is there that the business cycle may still be alive and kicking?

There are at least two reasons to be sceptical of commentators claiming that the business cycle is no more. First, one should recall that previous, long-lived economic expansions also led to the misplaced belief that the business cycle was a thing of the past. Writing in the late 1920s, it would have been almost equally easy to come up with statistics suggesting that recessions were much less likely than previous decades.

Secondly, and perhaps most importantly, Greenspan (1998a) asserts that

> '. . . there is one important caveat to the notion that we live in a new economy, and that is human psychology . . . The way we evaluate assets, and the way changes in those values affect our economy, do not appear to be coming out of a set of rules that is different from the one that governed the actions of our forebears . . .'

If for some reason the US stock market level does mean-revert to some estimates of 'fair value', the notion that the US does not experience recessions will quickly be seen as rather misguided.

In discussing the future of the business cycle it is instructive to bear in mind the comments made by Alan Greenspan in his February 1997 Humphrey–Hawkins Testimony.

> 'We have had 15 years of economic expansion interrupted by only one recession – and that was six years ago. There is no evidence, however, that the business cycle has been repealed. Another recession will

doubtless occur some day owing to circumstances that could not be, or at least were not, perceived by policy makers and financial market participants alike.

History demonstrates that participants in financial markets are susceptible to waves of optimism, which can in turn foster a general process of asset-price inflation that can feed through into markets for goods and services.

Excessive optimism sows the seeds of its own reversal in the form of imbalances that tend to grow over time. When unwarranted expectations ultimately are not realized, the unwinding of these financial excesses can act to amplify a downturn in economic activity, much as they amplify the upswing.'

It would be a fool who ignored the lessons of history!

5

Which US economic indicators really move the financial markets?†

As already discussed in Chapter 1 it is essential in analysing what moves financial markets to be able to breakdown the components of Nominal GNP. Table 1.1 in Chapter 1 provides the framework for analysing the effect of economic indicators on financial markets which are developed further in Chapters 5, 6 and 7. Appendix B gives the announcement time, title and reporting entities for 18 monthly economic indicators and one weekly economic indicator.

We will analyse economic data using the following classification system, in order that a consistent analytical approach can be applied. For each indicator we will discuss

- definition
- who publishes it and when?
- how should you interpret it?
- what is its impact on financial markets?

The key indicators affecting nominal GNP/GDP are listed in Figure 5.1 and are discussed in detail in this chapter.

Gross national product and gross domestic product

Definition

Gross domestic product (GDP) measures the total value of US output. It is the total of all economic activity in the US,

---

† The contents of this chapter are discussed in more detail in Kettell, B. (1999) *What Drives Financial Markets?* Financial Times-Prentice Hall.

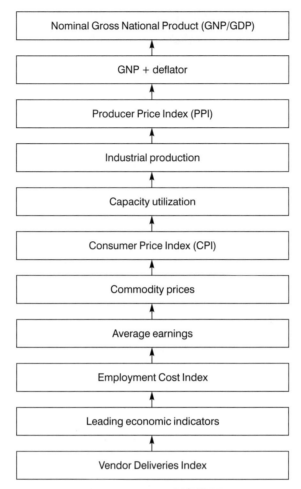

Figure 5.1 Key indicators affecting nominal GNP/GDP.

regardless of whether the owners of the means of production reside in the US. It is 'gross' because the depreciation of capital goods is not deducted.

GDP is measured in both current prices, which represent actual market prices, and constant prices, which measure changes in volume. Constant price, or real, GDP is current-price GDP adjusted for inflation.

The financial markets focus on the seasonally-adjusted annualized percentage change in real expenditure-based GDP in the current quarter compared to the previous quarter.

The difference between GDP and gross national product (GNP) is that GNP includes net factor income, or net earnings, from abroad. This is made up of the returns on US investment abroad (profits, investment income, workers' remittances) minus the return on foreign investments in the US. It is national, because it belongs to US residents, but not domestic, since it is not derived solely from production in the US.

Given that US investment abroad is broadly similar to foreign investment in the US then GDP is approximately equal to GNP and the terms are often used interchangeably.

Who publishes it and when?

Three reports on quarterly GDP are published by the Department of Commerce. Advance, Preliminary and Final GDP growth rates are released during the first, second and third months of the following quarter.

How should you interpret it?

Look at the annualized growth in seasonally-adjusted real expenditure-based GDP for the latest quarter compared to the previous quarters. Breaking the figure down to final sales and inventories can suggest the future behaviour of the economy.

What is its impact on financial markets?

Financial market reaction to this economic indicator is often restrained since it is usually expected news, with many of its key components having already been published. When there is a reaction in the financial markets it will always be to an unexpected Advance report rather than to the other two measures.

GDP deflator

Definition

The GDP deflators are comprehensive measures of inflation since they encompass changes in prices in all sectors of the economy: consumer products, capital goods, the foreign sector, and the government. In general it is calculated as:

$$\text{GDP price deflator} = \frac{\text{Nominal GDP}}{\text{Real GDP}} \times 100$$

There are actually three GDP deflators: the implicit price deflator, the fixed weight deflator, and the chain-price index. Until the late 1980s, the implicit price deflator was the primary focus of attention. Since 1989, the Commerce Department has promoted the fixed weight index instead. The implicit price deflator measures changes in prices as well as changes in the composition of output. Some goods are less expensive than other goods, so depending on the combination of goods and services produced in any given quarter, regardless of the price changes, the implicit price deflator can rise or fall. It is rare to see an outright decline in the implicit GDP deflator, but its rate of increase varies significantly from one quarter to the next.

The fixed weight deflator works on the same principle as the consumer and producer price indexes since it measures prices for a composition of GDP chosen in a certain time-period; 1987 weights are currently used. Consequently, the fixed weight deflator only reflects changes in prices.

The chain-price index combines the variable and fixed weight baskets. For any given quarter, it shows the basket of goods of the previous quarter. Over time, however, the basket of goods is changing. Admittedly, this has questionable relevance to the inflation picture and gets little attention, if any.

Who publishes it and when?

The Bureau of Economic Analysis releases the GDP deflators together with the gross domestic product and national income statistic about four weeks after the end of the quarter. The figures are seasonally adjusted and annualized.

How should you interpret it?

The fixed weight GDP deflator is more meaningful than the implicit price deflator. The implicit price deflator reflects changes in the composition of GDP as well as changes in prices. Although less frequent, reports such as these quarterly deflators might have less volatility than more frequent reports (such as the monthly indicators). Both the implicit and fixed weight GDP deflators can have quirks from time to time, as do the PPI and the CPI. For example, government pay rises typically occur in the first quarter, boosting the GDP deflator overall. Seasonal adjustment factors can not be used to account for the annual pay rise because the magnitude of increase is not stable from year to year.

See Appendix B for details of how price indices can be measured.

What is its impact on financial markets?

Financial market participants eagerly await the GDP deflators. In the past few years, more attention has focused on the fixed weight deflator than on the implicit price deflator. An acceleration in the deflator is unfavourable news to all markets. Stock prices will decline, bond prices will fall (yields will rise), and the value of the dollar will also decrease. A moderation in the inflation measure will lead to the opposite effect. Stock prices, bond prices, and the foreign exchange value of the dollar will increase.

Producer price index (PPI)

Definition

The PPI measures prices that manufacturers and farmers charge to the shops. The US producer price indices (PPIs) are calculated in three different ways: type of commodity produced; net output of particular industries; and stage of the production cycle. Of these variations the latter is by far the most relevant for financial markets.

Under the 'stage of processing' methodology, there are three indices:

- crude materials for further processing, covering things like oil and livestock that cannot be sold to consumers before being used in manufacturing;
- intermediate materials, supplies and components, including items that have been manufactured but require work before they are saleable;
- finished goods, which can be used by consumers.

By separating the stages of production in this way it is possible to gauge inflation as it works its way through the production process. A fourth index combines the three subdivisions into the 'all commodities index'. Financial market attention is focused on the percentage change in the monthly finished goods PPI. However, because food prices tend to be seasonal, and energy prices are frequently volatile, analysts prefer to watch the 'core' rate of producer price inflation, which strips out food and energy prices.

Who publishes them and when

The PPIs are published in a Department of Labour press release towards the middle of the month following that to which they refer.

How should you interpret it?

Concentrate on the seasonally-adjusted finished goods PPI and look at how this has behaved on a month-to-month, quarter-on-quarter, six-monthly and year-on-year basis. This should give a good guide as to whether the trend is changing.

To establish whether the change is merely due to volatile items, repeat the above for 'core' PPI, i.e., headline PPI minus food and energy. However, core PPI includes the sometimes volatile auto component. This makes up about 5 per cent of the finished goods index and may be subject to huge volatility as the result of incentive programmes and discounts. Care should be taken to ensure that what appears to be an underlying change in trend is not just due to this 'noisy' component. Particularly vulnerable months are September and October; September is when prices usually fall by as much as 3 per cent ahead of the new model year.

What is its impact on financial markets?

Financial market participants pounce on the PPI figures when they are reported. The fixed-income market will obviously prefer to see low inflation over high inflation. Thus, the larger the monthly rise in the PPI, the more negative the impact on the bond and the money markets. High inflation leads to high interest rates; low inflation points to declining interest rates.

The stock and foreign exchange markets will also view accelerating inflation negatively. Stock prices may decline and the value of the dollar will probably drop when producer price increases are large and accelerating, unless the markets expect the Federal Reserve to respond by raising interest rates, which in turn would make the dollar more attractive.

As mentioned above, financial market participants will often look at the Producer Price Index for Finished Goods, excluding food and energy prices. Large spurts in these components are less likely to cause negative market reactions than increases in the core rate.

The index of industrial production

Definition

The industrial production figures are a set of index numbers that measure the monthly physical output of US factories, mines, and gas and electric utilities. The index is broken down by type of industry (manufacturing, mining or utilities) and by type of market (consumer, equipment, intermediate or materials). The financial markets tend to focus on the seasonally-adjusted monthly change in the aggregate figure.

Who publishes it and when?

The Federal Reserve publishes the preliminary estimate of the previous month's industrial production in a press release around the 15th of each month. The first revision of the index comes with the next month's preliminary data about 45 days after the reference month, and there are second, third and fourth estimates in the following months. After the fourth estimate the index is regarded as final (although it may be further revised with the annual benchmarking exercise in the autumn).

How should you interpret it?

The US Index of Industrial Production is a derivative statistic, based in a large part on the BLS employment report which comes out two to three weeks earlier, and consequently is usually expected news. The employment report is discussed further in Chapter 6.

Industrial production is pro-cyclical, i.e., it rises during economic expansions and falls during contraction. It is included as one of the four coincident indicators, discussed in Chapter 4. It is typically used as a proxy for GDP even though it only covers 20 per cent of total production in the country.

What is its impact on financial markets?

A rise in industrial production signals economic growth, whereas a decline in production indicates contraction. Thus fixed income participants view a rise in industrial production as a warning of inflationary pressures. This means that there are pressures for interest rates to rise, which is bad news for fixed income markets. Similarly a drop in industrial production provides a warning signal that economic contraction is on the way with an expectation that interest rates will fall; good news for fixed income markets.

Participants in the stock and foreign exchange markets favour gains in industrial production together with the capacity utilization rate, discussed below, since they portend economic strength. Stock market professionals will look towards increases in corporate earnings, whereas foreign exchange professionals will look towards higher interest rates. High interest rates in the United States relative to other countries increase the demand for US securities and therefore US dollars.

Capacity utilization rate

Definition

Capacity utilization measures the extent to which the capital stock of the nation is being employed in the production of goods. Technically defined, the utilization rate for an industry is equal to the Output Index divided by the Capacity Index.

Output is measured by the Index of Industrial Production. Capacity attempts to capture 'sustainable practical capacity', as indicated by work schedules and the availability of inputs to operate the machinery and equipment already in place.

Who publishes it and when?

The Federal Reserve Board publishes it at the same time as industrial production, about two weeks after the end of the month.

How should you interpret it?

Once capacity reaches a certain point it is expected that excess demand pressures will result in inflation. The actual point at which these pressures have occurred has risen over time, largely due to technological progress. At certain times the market has used this indicator as a good leading indicator of inflation, although its value has become limited as it has risen.

One problem with this index is that it covers many industries that do not uniformly suffer inflationary pressures at the same level. The paper industry, for example, normally operates at around 95 per cent capacity, whereas non-electrical machinery normally operates at 78 per cent capacity.

The capacity utilization rate rises during expansions and falls during recessions.

What is its impact on financial markets?

A rise in capacity utilization has the same effect on financial markets as a rise in industrial production since the two indicators are inextricably linked. It is not necessary to view them as two separate indicators. They always move in the same direction, and they will always tell a similar story. However, they serve a different purpose.

Industrial production will signal economic growth. The capacity utilization rate reflects the extent of resources utilization and the point at which inflationary pressures set in. For example, a 1 per cent rise in industrial production should not cause fears of inflationary pressures when the operating rate is 78 per cent. However, it could indicate that inflation will accelerate when the utilization rate is around 85 per cent.

Commodity prices

Inflationary pressures can often come from increases in commodity prices. A list of the key commodity prices which financial markets focus on is given below in Table 5.1.

Oil and food prices are closely scrutinized key commodities. Oil, as a source of energy or a natural resource in the production of goods, is a key component of economic activity used in manufacturing, and it is an important product used by consumers as well. Food is an indispensable item in every person's budget.

Crude oil prices

Definition

Crude oil is traded at the New York Mercantile Exchange (NYMEX). Both spot and futures prices of crude oil are determined in the market. The spot price reflects the current

Table 5.1 Key commodity prices for financial markets

Commodity Prices	Unit
Agricultural raw material	yoy %
Cotton (Liverpool index)	cts/lb
Wool (Aus-NZ; UK)	cts/kg
Rubber (New York)	cts/lb
Food	yoy %
Cocoa (LCE)	USD/t
Coffee (CSCE)	cts/lb
Sugar (CSCE)	cts/lb
Wheat (CBT)	USD/bu
Base metals	you %
Aluminium (LME)	USD/t
Copper (LME)	USD/t
Nickel (LME)	USD/t
Crude oil	yoy %
Brent	USD/bl
WTI	USD/bl
Gold	USD/ounce

value of the commodity, whereas the futures price reflects the price at some point in the future, such as three or six months hence.

Who publishes it and when?

The price is quoted continuously and is available on screen-based information systems.

How should you interpret it?

This is not straightforward. Financial market participants in the fixed income, stock and foreign exchange markets often look at the future price of crude oil as an indicator of inflation. Oil is an important commodity in the US economy. However, oil prices change hourly and it is not always clear as to what the inflationary implications are. Oil prices are particularly prone to movements based on rumour, which may or may not prove to be fact.

What is its impact on financial markets?

Financial markets are well aware that the oil price rises of the 1970s did cause major US recessions. Largely speaking the announcement that oil prices are rising in a sustainable manner will cause a negative reaction in the bond and stock markets, but it could well strengthen the prospects for the dollar. All price falls will provoke the opposite reaction.

Food prices

Definition

Food prices are also monitored closely by financial market participants. The most monitored indicator of food prices is the Index of Prices Received by Farmers, more commonly known as the 'Ag Price Index'.

The Index of Prices Received by Farmers comprises crops (44.2 per cent) and livestock and products (55.8 per cent). For the most part, the price changes are based on average prices for all grades and qualities at the point of sale (such as the local market) about the middle of the month.

Who publishes it and when?

The Department of Agriculture releases the Index of Prices Received by Farmers at the end of the month for the current month, but it only reflects price changes through the middle of that month. The index is not adjusted for seasonal variation.

How should you interpret it?

The 'Ag Price Index' needs to be compared to other inflation indicators. Although it is related to food price changes in the Producer Price Index and the Consumer Price Index, it can vary significantly over time. First, the Ag Price Index is not adjusted for seasonal variations. The food components in both the Consumer Price Index and the Producer Price Index are seasonally adjusted. Second, the Ag Price Index measures prices at the first point of sale and is based on an average price for all grades. The Producer Price Indexes and the Consumer Price Index typically adjust for quality and grades. Generally speaking, the index should decline or post small increases during periods of harvest, and larger increases during off seasons.

What is its impact on financial markets?

The Ag Price Index is reported late in the afternoon and gets little attention from financial market participants. However, an unexpectedly large rise in the index can spur a drop in bond prices if market psychology is already negative. Conversely, an unexpectedly large drop in the index may lead to a rise in bond prices if market psychology is positive. The foreign exchange and stock markets ignore this index altogether.

Commodity price indicators: a checklist

The most popular commodity price indicators for financial markets have been the Commodity Research Bureau (CRB) futures index, the Journal of Commerce (JOC) index, the crude PPI, the change in the Sensitive Materials Prices Index (SMPs), the National Association of Purchasing Managers Prices index, and the Philly Index.

The CRB index

The Commodity Research Bureau's future index (CRB), compiled since 1957, measures prices of non-financial contracts traded on public futures exchanges. The CRB contains nearby and deferred (up to, but not including, one year away) futures prices for 21 separate commodities contracts (see Table 5.2). Since 13 of the 21 commodities are foodstuffs and the remaining eight are atypical industries, the CRB is not the best indicator of general inflation.

Table 5.2   CRB Component Groups

Imports	Cocoa, coffee, sugar
Precious metals	Gold, platinum, silver
Industrials	Cotton, copper, crude oil, lumber, silver.
Livestock and meats	Cattle, hogs, pork bellies
Grains	Corn, oats, soybean meal, wheat
Energy	Crude oil, heating oil, unleaded gasoline

The journal of commerce industrial index (JOC)

The Journal of Commerce tracks an index of prices of 17 industrial materials and supplies used in the first stage of manufacturing, energy production, or building construction. The components have been chosen on the basis that they have been sensitive to price pressures that show up six to nine months later in the Producer Price index (PPI) or Consumer Price Index (CPI). The JOC index is more sensitive to actual economic developments than the CRB.

Each commodity in the JOC index is weighted by its importance to overall economic output and how well it predicts inflation. The base year is 1980. The JOC index is subdivided into three major categories: textiles, metals, and other (see Table 5.3).

Table 5.3 JOC Index Composition

Category	Material
Textiles	Cotton (5.9%), Burlap (5.5%), Polyester (2.7%), Print cloth (3.3%)
Metals:	Scrap steel (6.3%), Copper scrap (6.7%), Aluminium (6.1%), Zinc (5.1%), Tin (5%)
Miscellaneous	Hides (5.5%), Rubber (6.3%), Tallow (5.2%), Plywood (7.9%), Boxes (5%), Red Oak (6.3%), Benzene (4.7%), Crude oil (7.1%)

The change in sensitive materials prices (SMPs)

This index is calculated on spot prices of 12 crude and intermediate materials and 13 raw industrial materials. It is calculated as a moving average and is compiled by the US Department of Commerce, US Department of Labour, and Commodity Research Bureau Institute. Table 5.4 compares the CRB, JOC and the SMP.

The crude PPI

The crude PPI is divided into three parts: food, energy, and other. It is weighted according to the actual value of commodity shipments.

Table 5.4 Composition of Commodity Price Indexes

	CRB	JOC	SMPS
Prices	Futures	Spot	Spot
Components	21	17	25
Weights	Equal	Individual	Equal
Weights by Category:			
Metals	19%	38%	38%
Energy	14%	12%	0%
Livestock	14%	0%	0%
Grains, food and fibre	43%	17%	29%
Other	10%*	36%†	33%‡

* *Orange juice and lumber*
† *Rubber, red oak, hides, tallow, boxes and plywood*
‡ *Rubber, hides, resin, tallow, wastepaper, sand and timber*

The NAPM prices index

The NAPM Prices Index measures the percentage of manufacturing firms reporting higher material prices, plus half the percentage of those firms reporting no change in prices. It therefore has a value of roughly 50 per cent when aggregate prices are unchanged. The NAPM index is discussed further in Chapter 7.

The Philadelphia index (Philly)

The Philly Index, calculated a bit differently from the NAPM index, is the percentage of firms in the Philadelphia region reporting higher prices, minus the percentage reporting lower prices; hence, it should have a value of roughly zero when aggregate prices are unchanged. The Philly index is discussed further in Chapter 7.

Consumer price index (CPI)

Definition

The consumer price index (CPI) is a measure of the prices of a fixed basket of consumer goods. There are two versions, the

CPI-U and the CPI-W. The CPI-U is more widely used because it measures inflation as it affects all urban households (including the unemployed and the retired). The CPI-W covers only urban wage earners and clerical workers in blue-collar occupations, but is used by many unions in wage negotiations.

Who publishes it and when?

The CPI is published monthly in a press release from the Bureau of Labor Statistics, a division of the US Department of Labor. Publication of the data is usually in the second week of the following month. The CPI is seasonally adjusted.

How should you interpret it?

Financial markets generally disregard the CPI-W, which covers only urban wage earners and clerical workers in blue-collar occupations. The seasonally-adjusted CPI-U is the main starting point for analysis. However, there are times when seasonal factors diverge from the trends embodied in the official seasonal adjustment. The most notable case of this is when a drought occurs.

The month-on-month CPI change is regarded as being too 'noisy', or volatile, to give any clues on a change in the trend of inflation. The year-on-year comparison is the most widely used.

Reluctantly, many economists exclude pieces of the index for analytical purposes: 'reluctantly', because those excluded prices affect inflation. Food and energy prices are the usual candidates for exclusion owing to their extreme volatility. The CPI-U minus food and energy is commonly referred to as the 'core' rate of inflation. Some analysts watch the CPI minus housing and medical costs.

What is its impact on financial markets?

Financial market participants anxiously await the Consumer Price Index because it drives much activity in the market place. The fixed income, stock and foreign exchange markets all react adversely to sharp increases in inflation. Interest rates will rise; stock prices will fall; and the value of the dollar will decline in the foreign exchange market because the rise in interest rates is due to price increases, not economic expansion. Market participants, in a similar fashion to their approach with the Producer

Price Indexes, discount increases in food and energy prices to some degree. A sharp increase in the CPI excluding food and energy prices will bring about a more negative reaction than an increase in the total CPI.

Markets do consider the total CPI as well as the index excluding food and energy prices. They will ignore an increase in food and energy prices when they are certain prices will reverse in coming months. Food and energy prices constitute about 25 per cent of consumer expenditure.

Average hourly earnings

Definition

Average hourly and weekly earnings measure the level of wages and salaries for workers on private non-farm payrolls. These monthly payroll figures are derived from the Establishment Survey, which is discussed in Chapter 6.

Who publishes it and when?

Average hourly and weekly earnings data are published with the monthly employment report from the BLS. This is normally released on the third Friday after the week containing the 12th, with data for the month earlier.

Real average weekly earnings are published in a press release from the Labor Department on the day of release of the CPI. This is usually published in the second week of each month with data for the month earlier.

How should you interpret them?

Average hourly earnings for workers in private industry are derived by dividing total non-farm payrolls by total hours reported for each industry except government employees. The hourly earnings figures reflect changes in basic hourly rates as well as increases in premium pay because of overtime hours worked. The markets focus on the monthly and year-on-year percentage changes in seasonally-adjusted average hourly and weekly earnings.

Because of the inconsistency in the series from changes in employment or overtime, you should not place a lot of weight on average hourly earnings; they do not represent labour costs to the employer. But just as other measures of inflation tend to move in tandem, so do the measures of wage inflation. This is the only monthly indicator of wage inflation, so it is a good proxy for other measures that are calculated quarterly but are adjusted for occupation or industry shifts, and overtime pay.

What is their impact on financial markets?

Average hourly earnings is the earliest available indicator of underlying trends in industry's wage and salary costs and it is an indicator closely monitored by the Federal Reserve. Their main disadvantage from the point of view of financial markets is that they exclude non-wage costs, such as insurance, retirement, savings and other benefits. The Employment Cost Index (ECI), described below, includes these items and is a better measure of total labour costs.

Despite its volatility and limitations, financial market participants pounce on the average hourly earnings data. It is the first inflation news for the month. A rapid rise in hourly wages is negative for all the markets – stock, fixed-income, and foreign exchange – because it signals inflationary pressures.

The employment cost index (ECI)

Definition

Wage pressures can be measured in two ways: average wages, and the employment cost index. Average earnings measure the level of wages and salaries for employees on non-farm payrolls. The Employment Cost Index tracks all civilian employee compensation. Apart from wages and salaries it also includes many of the other benefits that employees receive. These include:

- paid leave (vacations, holidays, sick leave)
- supplemental pay (for overtime and shift differentials, and non-production bonuses)
- insurance benefits (life, health, sickness, and accident)
- retirement and savings benefits (pension, savings, and thrift plans)

- legally required benefits (social security, railroad retirement and supplemental retirement, federal and state unemployment insurance, workers' compensation, and other legally required benefits)
- other benefits, such as severance pay and supplemental unemployment plans.

Who publishes it and when?

The ECI is published quarterly by the Bureau of Labor Statistics. The survey is conducted quarterly for the pay period including the 12th day of the four months, March, June, September and December. Data is released on the fourth Tuesday in the month following the survey.

How should you interpret it?

The Labor Department, which designed and conducts the survey, cautions users to the limitations of this index. The Employment Cost Index is not a measure of change in the total cost of employing labour. For example, it does not include training costs. Also, it does not report retroactive pay. The index does not cover all employers and employees in the United States, although it does cover nearly all workers in the civilian non-farm economy. The main group not covered is the self-employed.

What is its impact on financial markets?

Financial market participants react to the Employment Cost Index as they would to any other inflation measure. Because it is a quarterly release, and a more stable series than most, the market impact can be muted. Financial markets focus on the quarterly percentage change in the seasonally-adjusted ECI compared with the previous quarter and the same quarter of the year before. The advantage of the ECI over average earnings is that it includes non-wage costs, which can add 30 per cent to total labour costs.

It is known to be watched closely by Alan Greenspan, the Chairman of the Federal Reserve, giving it extra impetus should the outcome be significantly different from market expectations.

Index of leading indicators (LEI)

Definition

The Index of Leading Indicators is a weighted average of the economic variables that lead the business cycle. It is part of the family of indicators designed to provide information on the current stage of the business cycle.

As discussed in Chapter 4, the direction of a variable relative to the business cycle can be procyclical, countercyclical, or acyclical. A procyclical variable moves in the same direction as aggregate economic activity, rising in booms and falling in recessions. A countercyclical variable moves oppositely to aggregate economic activity, falling in booms and rising in recessions. An acyclical variable has no clear cyclical pattern.

The timing of a variable relative to the business cycle may be coincident, leading, or lagging. A coincident variable's peaks and troughs occur at about the same time as peaks and troughs in aggregate economic activity. Peaks and troughs in a leading variable come before, and peaks and troughs in a lagging variable come after the corresponding peaks and troughs in aggregate economic activity.

The 10 variables that make up the index are listed in Table 5.5. They were chosen because each has a tendency to predict

Table 5.5 Indicators included in Leading Economic Indicators (LEI)

---

1 Average work week in manufacturing measured by hours worked.
2 Average weekly initial jobless, measured by claims for unemployment insurance.
3 Manufacturers new orders for consumer goods and materials – $1982.
4 Vendor delivery performance – percentage experiencing slower deliveries to their factories. (Derived from the NAPM.)
5 Plant and equipment contracts and orders – $1982.
6 New private sector building permits 1967=100.
7 Money supply, M2 – $1982.
8 S&P 500 index of stock prices.
9 Michigan Index of Consumer Sentiment. This consists of two parts:
  (i) Consumers' assessment of current economic conditions – **not included** in the LEI
  (ii) Expected economic changes – **included** in LEI
10 Yield spread – 10 year Treasury bond yield minus the fed funds rate.

(lead) economic activity and because data on them are frequently and promptly reported. This second characteristic is essential because a variable cannot be of much help in forecasting if accurate data on the variable arrive only after a long delay.

Who publishes it and when?

The indices are published in a monthly press release by the Bureau of Economic Analysis in the Commerce Department. The data are released about one month after the end of the reference month. The BEA lists the components from the largest negative/positive contributor to the smallest. The preliminary data are subject to revision in each of the following five months, as new source data become available.

How should you interpret them?

The interpretation of the index of leading indicators was discussed in detail in Chapter 4. Although the components of the index are varied, there are good economic reasons why each component helps to predict economic activity. For example, new orders for plant and equipment, and new building permits are all direct measures of the amount of future production being planned in the economy. The index of stock prices reflects the optimism or pessimism of stock market participants about the economy's future. However, the index is not without problems, including the following.

- Despite the emphasis on the use of data that are promptly available, the data on the 10 components of the index, and thus the index of leading indicators itself, are usually revised during the first two months after their initial releases. As a result, an early signal of recession or recovery may be reversed when the revised data become available.
- On several occasions the index has given false warnings, predicting a recession when in fact no recession occurred in the several months following the drop in the index. A recent example of this was when the index fell in five successive months early in 1995 but the economy kept moving briskly forward.
- Although it may forecast that a recession is coming, the index does not provide much information about how far in the future the recession will occur nor how severe it will be when it arrives.

- Changes in the structure of the economy over time may cause some variables to become better predictors of the economy and others to become worse. For this reason, the index of leading indicators must be revised periodically, either to change the list of component indicators or to change the weights of the components.

It is essential to determine whether increases or decreases in the index are broadly based. If six indicators rise and four indicators fall it is difficult to generalize about the trend. The LEI is, however, particularly useful around business cycle turning points.

What is their impact on financial markets?

The percentage change in the index of leading indicators is reported monthly, with two or three consecutive monthly declines being regarded as the warning sign that a recession is on the way (but see Chapter 4 for serious caveats regarding this general rule). The index tends to turn down in advance of cyclical peaks. On the whole, the index is a valuable and much watched forecasting device, correctly predicting a large majority of economic turning points during the post-World War II period.

Consequently the financial markets will certainly react violently to large shifts in the index. Large rises in the LEI will boost stocks and the dollar, with adverse effects on bonds. The markets will react in the opposite direction to large falls in the LEI. Even small changes in the LEI will be seized upon by market participants in order to prove their point when market sentiment is particularly negative or positive. This is particularly true around business cycle turning points.

Vendor deliveries index

Definition

This index is a diffusion index, a concept discussed in detail in Chapter 4 and in Appendix A. The National Association of Purchasing Managers (discussed in detail in Chapter 7) are asked how the overall delivery performance from vendors compared with the month before is changing. The index is calculated by dividing the percentage of vendors who said 'the same' by two. The answer is then added to the per cent of vendors who said deliveries were slower. The outcome is then multiplied by a seasonal adjustment factor.

Who publishes it and when?

This index is one of the indices published in the index of the National Association of Purchasing Managers, and is published monthly.

How should you interpret it?

The index is benchmarked at 50. An index greater than 50 indicates that more manufacturers are reporting slower deliveries rather than faster deliveries. So if the index was 65 then this can be interpreted that 65 per cent are reporting slower deliveries and 35 per cent are reporting faster deliveries. This would be seen as evidence of an acceleration of economic activity with the possibility of price increases.

An index of less than 50 indicates that more manufacturers reported faster deliveries than slower deliveries. So an index of 35 would be interpreted as 35 per cent reporting slower delivery and 65 per cent reporting faster delivery. This would be interpreted as evidence of an economic slowdown with less pressure for price increases.

What is its impact on financial markets?

If manufacturers are reporting prompter deliveries then this is seen as evidence of slackness in the economy, taking pressures off price increases. Slower deliveries provide evidence that capacity constraints are being hit, provoking fears of inflationary pressure. Again this is an index that Alan Greenspan has, at times, drawn attention to, making it at those times very market sensitive.

A major limitation of the index is that it is centred on the manufacturing sector, which represents only 20 per cent of the economy, and gives us no information about pressures to raise wages in the service sector.

6

Consumer expenditure, investment, government spending and foreign trade: the big picture†

Consumer expenditure accounts for two-thirds of US GDP. Consequently it is a major component of nominal GDP and its behaviour is of great interest to the financial markets. A strong consumer sector signals a healthy economy which can lead to inflation and higher interest rates.

Consumer indicators that point to robust spending are bearish for the fixed-income market, bullish for the stock market, and favour a strong dollar. Consumer indicators that point to sluggish spending are bullish for the fixed income market, bearish for the stock market, and unfavourable for the foreign exchange value of the dollar.

The majority of the consumer sector indicators are reported monthly although a couple of them are available more often. The more frequently the indicator is reported, the more it is beloved by financial market participants, but the more careful they must be in interpreting it. The stock, fixed income, and foreign exchange markets are constantly moving, as traders revise their expectations of economic activity based on economists' forecasts, market rumours, or actual economic reports. As a result, the more frequent the economic data, the more readily the market can incorporate new economic information.

As with the indicators discussed in Chapter 5 we will then analyse economic data using the following classification system,

† The contents of this chapter are discussed in more detail in Kettell, B. (1999) *What Drives Financial Markets*. Financial Times-Prentice Hall.

in order that a consistent analytical approach can be applied. For each indicator we will discuss:

1. definition
2. who publishes it and when?
3. how should you interpret it?
4. what is its impact on financial markets?

The key indicators affecting consumer expenditure are listed in Figure 6.1.

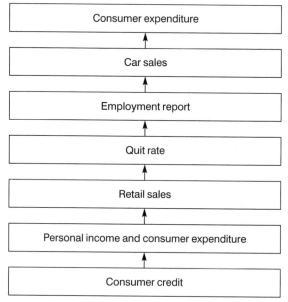

Figure 6.1   The economic indicators which influence consumer expenditure.

Car sales

Definition

The most frequently reported indicator of consumer spending is the 10-day unit auto sales. Unit car sales report the number of cars that were sold during that particular 10-day period.

Who publishes it and when?

The major auto manufacturers of domestically produced cars report their sales for the first 10 days, the middle 10 days, and the last 10 days of each month. These sales figures are available on the third business day following each 10-day period. Sales for the first 10 days of any month are usually reported on the 13th of the month; sales for the middle 10 days, on about the 23rd; and for the last 10 days, on the third business day of the subsequent month.

How should you interpret them?

Most importantly, car sales provide the very first piece of information concerning the strength or weakness of the economy. No other indicator is as timely because none is released during the course of that same month.

Car sales have a second great strength. They can provide us with an important clue concerning the retail sales and personal consumption expenditures (PCE) data to be released later in the month, both of which can be big market movers. Automobile sales represent about 25 per cent of retail sales and about 8 per cent of consumption.

Car sales have a third important feature. They can give the markets an early warning signal of an impending recession, and tell the markets when they can begin to expect a recovery. The underlying reason for this is that car sales are very sensitive to changes in interest rates and consumer psychology. If consumers get nervous about the economic outlook, or are bothered by rising interest rates, one of the first things they do is cancel plans to buy a new car. This makes sense because automobiles and housing are obviously the largest expenditures in the family budget. If you are going to cut costs, this is the place to start! Historically, the automobile and housing sectors of the economy are the first to dip into recession when times are bad. They are also the first to experience a recovery. Thus, car sales tend to be a leading indicator of economic activity, and can provide some clues concerning when the economy is about to change direction. This is why financial markets consider car sales data to be so valuable.

What is their impact on financial markets?

Participants in the fixed income or bond market prefer to see weak auto sales in turn signalling an economic slowdown. Players in the stock and foreign exchange markets would prefer to see a rise in auto sales. In the case of the stock market, strong auto sales signal a healthy economy and good earnings in auto and related industries, as well as companies in general. The foreign exchange market favours strength, so that rising interest rates increase the demand for the dollar. However, if the market share of foreign-produced cars increases at the expense of domestically produced cars, the demand for foreign currencies will go up and the exchange value of the dollar will decline. Strong auto sales can provoke bond market participants to push up interest rates and thereby push down bond prices.

The employment report

Definition

The Employment Report consists of employment related data which in turn comes from two separate surveys, the Establishment Survey and the Household Survey. The Establishment Survey provides information on non-farm payroll employment, the average hourly workweek and the average hours index. The Household Survey provides information on the labour force, household employment and the unemployment rate (see Figure 6.2). The Establishment Survey, used to compile non-farm payrolls is based on a much larger sample than the Household Survey used to compile unemployment figures.

Non-farm payroll employment measures the number of people in gainful employment in all non-farm industries, such as manufacturing and services. The financial markets focus on the seasonally-adjusted monthly change in the number of payroll jobs. Average weekly hours represent the length of the working week in private non-agricultural industries. They are

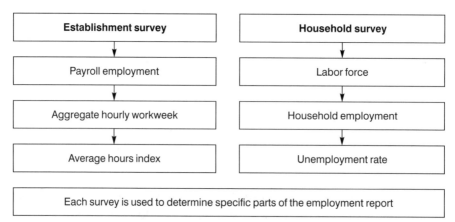

Figure 6.2 The Establishment Survey and the Household Survey.

based on reports of paid hours for production, construction and non-supervisory workers.

Average weekly hours are derived by dividing the total hours paid for by the number of employees during the pay period. Pay periods longer than a week are adjusted to represent a week. The average weekly hours derived from the total hours reflect the effect of factors such as absenteeism, labour turnover, part-time work and strikes. The effect of strikes can be significant as was seen from the effects of the General Motors strike in 1998.

The headline civilian unemployment rate, based on the household survey, is the number of unemployed persons as a percentage of the total civilian labour force (which includes unemployed and employed persons in the US). The unemployed include both people collecting unemployment benefits or public assistance, and those who are not eligible, for example, because they have exhausted their unemployment insurance or are former students who have not accumulated unemployment benefits. Students (including those aged 16 years old and above who are still at school) are counted as unemployed if they have looked for a job and are available for at least a part-time position.

People without a job and not actively looking for work are not in the labour force and, therefore, are not counted as unemployed.

Once we know the number of people who are employed along with the number of people who are unemployed, we can calculate the unemployment rate. The labour force is the sum of employed plus unemployed individuals. The unemployment rate is equal to the number of unemployed persons divided by the total number of persons in the labour force:

$$\frac{\text{Unemployed}}{\text{Employed} + \text{Unemployed}} = \text{Unemployment rate}$$

Either the numerator (number of employed) or denominator (number in the labour force) can cause changes in the unemployment rate. The unemployment rate will increase whenever the labour force increases (barring an equal increase in the number of employed persons) and whenever the number of unemployed persons increases (barring any change in the labour force). Conversely, either a drop in the labour force, or a decline in the number of unemployed persons, will cause the jobless rate to decrease.

Employment figures based on the establishment survey are restricted to wage and salary employees in the non-farm sector and government civilian workers.

Who publishes it and when?

As already mentioned the employment information comes from two separate surveys, the establishment survey and the household survey. Both surveys are conducted by the Bureau of Labor Statistics (BLS) for the calendar week that includes the 12th of the month. The data are generally released the first Friday of the following month, which makes this date very market sensitive.

The household survey is carried out for the BLS by the Census Bureau. It is based on a sample of about 60 000 households, out of a total of more than 95 million. Information is obtained each month for only about 144 000 people, 75 000 of whom are actually in the labour force.

The data for a given month actually relate to a particular week. A special group of 1600 Census Bureau interviewers visit or telephone households in the calendar week including the 19th of the month and ask about their employment status during the week including the 12th of the month, which is called the survey week. The number of weeks from survey to survey can be easily calculated: about every third month, it is five weeks instead of four, which can sometimes provide the markets with misleading numbers if they are not aware of the sample period.

The non-farm payroll data are compiled from the monthly establishment survey of employer payroll records. The data are obtained from a postal survey of employers. The survey sample covers about 360 000 employers who employ more than 40 million people, or about 40 per cent of non-farm employment.

How should you interpret it?

It is essential to concentrate on the seasonally adjusted monthly unemployment rate and the change in non-farm payrolls. Since monthly payroll changes can be volatile, financial markets concentrate on the 3- and 6-month average changes in non-farm payrolls to gauge the underlying trend.

The unemployment rate and non-farm payrolls can move in opposite directions rendering labour market activity unclear. The establishment survey, which generates the non-farm payroll data, generally has much smaller movements on a monthly basis and offers a smoother short-term trend than the household survey used in calculating the unemployment rate. This is because the establishment survey has a much larger sample, adjusts for new companies (which reduces the like-lihood of a fall in the payroll) and aims to maintain its sample base while trying to ensure that the companies in the sample respond to the survey.

Average weekly hours worked reflect the demand for labour since employers typically increase or reduce hours worked before hiring or laying off workers in response to changes in demand. Aggregate weekly hours, published as an index, are the product of employment and the average working week. A rise in the average working week can offset a fall in employment, and vice versa. The average working week falls relatively less quickly in the early stages of an economic slowdown because employees with shorter working hours (particularly in indus-tries with many part-time workers, such as the retail trade) tend to be dismissed first.

Weekly reports of jobless figures contain two useful pieces of information for forecasters: initial claims for unemployment benefits, and the number of insured unemployed. When workers are laid off they can apply for unemployment insur-ance. These applications, called initial claims for state unem-ployment benefits, are one of the most closely watched pointers to employment trends and a good indicator of the pace of layoffs. Initial claims are available $2\frac{1}{2}$ weeks after applications are recorded.

What is its impact on financial markets?

The Employment Report has frequently been referred to as the 'Jewel in the Crown' of all the economic indicators to which financial markets will react. Financial market participants can extract a wealth of market sensitive information from the fine details of this report (see Figure 6.3).

Players in the fixed income market favour small increases or outright declines in non-farm payrolls because they signal economic weakness. Economic weakness usually signals lower interest rates through decreased market demand for loans or Federal Reserve easing.

Conversely, large increases in non-farm payrolls could indi-cate a healthy economy and suggest higher interest rates as credit demands pick up or the Federal Reserve tightens to

Figure 6.3 Why the employment report is so market sensitive.

prevent inflationary pressures. The potential for higher interest
rates makes foreign exchange market participants eager for
robust gains in non-farm payrolls, as they will push up the value
of the dollar. Participants in the stock market will also favour
healthy employment gains because a strong economy means
healthy corporate profits, which is a boon for stock prices.

Stock prices and the foreign exchange value of the dollar rise
when the unemployment rate falls. A rising unemployment rate
is associated with a weak or contracting economy and declining
interest rates. Conversely, a decreasing unemployment rate is
associated with an expanding economy and potentially rising
interest rates. This is bad news for the bond market.

The quit rate

Definition

The quit rate, published monthly in the BLS Employment
Report, is officially defined as: job leavers as a per cent of the
total unemployed. It is essentially the share of unemployed
people who have chosen to leave their jobs. Job leavers are not
workers who have been fired or laid off, they are those who
leave voluntarily.

Who publishes it and when?

It is published in the BLS Employment Report.

How should you interpret it?

Presumably most people who quit their jobs do so because they
have better, higher-paying jobs lined up. This view is certainly

supported by the empirical evidence. A higher quit rate is not a leading indicator of wage pressure; it is the result of it.

What is its impact on financial markets?

The quit rate acquired the status in 1997 and 1998 of being one of the indicators that Alan Greenspan, the Federal Reserve Chairman, follows when setting the course of monetary policy.

Retail sales

Definition

Retail sales include all merchandise sold for cash or credit by establishments primarily engaged in retail trade.

Who publishes them and when?

Sales of non-durable and durable consumer goods are reported between the 11th and 15th of each month for the previous month. This series is published by the Commerce Department's Bureau of the Census and is derived from a sample of establishments of all sizes and types across the country. Because the sales figures come from a sample, and not all businesses report their sales in a timely fashion, they are subject to substantial revision for several months after the initial report.

How should you interpret them?

Retail sales are reported in current, or nominal, dollars, i.e., they are not adjusted for inflation. Auto sales constitute the largest single component of retail sales, about 25 per cent of the total. Although monthly auto sales are not as volatile as 10-day auto sales, they still jump around from month to month, and the wild fluctuations can obscure the underlying trend. For this reason financial market participants talk about retail sales excluding autos. By removing the volatile component of the series, financial markets assess the underlying spending behaviour of consumers.

Financial market analysts believe that when the Federal Reserve look at the retail sales data it is not so much concerned with the trend in the total but in that of discretionary spending which is taken to be retail sales minus energy, food and drug store sales. This represents a better picture of consumer confidence.

What is their impact on financial markets?

Participants in the fixed income market favour a drop in retail sales or at least weakness in the figures because that points to a weakening economy. There is then pressure for the Federal Reserve to cut interest rates, which is good for bond prices. If retail sales rise sharply bond market participants will push up interest rates and push down bond prices.

Stock market professionals favour rising retail sales. Strong consumer spending figures indicate a healthy economy and that augurs well for corporate profits. Stock prices, especially those directly related to the retail sector, are likely to rise on this news. If retail sales decline, or show only a small rise, stock prices will fall or at best not show any upward momentum.

Foreign exchange participants also favour a healthy rise in retail sales because it points to a strong US economy and suggests that the Federal Reserve may force up interest rates. Rising interest rates relative to the rest of the world lead to a rise in demand for the dollar. If retail sales decline, however, interest rates are likely to drop, and the softer demand will then cause the dollar to fall.

The Johnson Redbook

The Johnson Redbook series is compiled by a unit of Lynch, Jones and Ryan, a New York brokerage firm. Johnson conducts a weekly survey of 25 retailers across the country including chain stores, discounters and department stores. This weekly indicator of retail sales is reported every Tuesday afternoon and describes sales for the previous week. Johnson Redbook figures are faxed to customers, but as is the case with all economic indicators, the data are picked up by the media.

Bond traders do react to the Johnson Redbook data, so it is worth keeping an eye on the series. The market reaction will be similar to auto sales: if retailers post higher sales, suggesting healthy or improving economic growth, bond prices will fall and cause yields to rise; a weak report signals economic sluggishness and allows interest rates to fall. The market reaction to the Johnson Redbook series only affects the bond market.

Personal income and consumer expenditure

Definition

Personal income represents the compensation that individuals receive from all sources. That includes wages and salaries, proprietor's income, income from rents, dividends and transfer payments, such as social security, unemployment and welfare benefits. Personal income is important for financial markets as it clearly holds the key to future spending and hence economic activity.

Consumer expenditure data also involves data collection from many different sources. Personal consumption expenditures include durable goods, non-durable goods and services. Motor vehicles, furniture, appliances, boats and pleasure craft, jewellery, watches and books would be durable goods. Food, clothing, shoes, gasoline and fuel oil would be non-durable goods.

The services sector represents roughly half of consumer spending. This would include electricity, gas, telephone, domestic services, motor vehicle repairs, insurance, medical care, investment services, beauty parlours, etc.

Who publishes it and when?

The income and consumption data are prepared monthly by the Commerce Department's Bureau of Economic Analysis. Given the many different types of income, there is a wide variety of source data. The income and expenditure figures are compiled, edited and eventually released one day after the GNP report, which generally appears in the third week of the month.

How should you interpret it?

Personal consumer expenditures (PCE) are the 'C' portion of the GDP equation $C + I + G + (X - IM)$.

Since consumer spending is two-thirds of GDP, the financial markets have thus two-thirds of their forecast. The data tend to be relatively stable, given that the service sector spending has traditionally been less volatile than spending on durable and non-durable goods.

Personal income has to be adjusted for inflation, giving a figure for real income, a more accurate barometer of spending power. The personal income figures also provide information on savings behaviour. A sharp drop in the savings rate indicates that the consumer is dipping into savings to finance purchases. This is not a sustainable situation, and one should expect to see slower consumption and GDP growth in the months ahead.

What is its impact on financial markets?

Financial market participants are likely to respond mildly to personal income data. Increases in personal income generally point to increases in consumer spending and gains in economic activity overall. That is bad news for the fixed-income market because bond traders fear that economic expansions are inflationary. Consequently, bonds are likely to fall in price and rise in yield. Decelerating or falling personal income growth, being signs of economic weakness in consumer spending, is favourable news to bond traders because it suggests recession and a deceleration of inflationary pressures or potential Federal easing. This would cause bond prices to rise and yields to decline.

Stock market participants view personal income as well as personal consumption expenditure growth favourably. Strong consumer spending points to healthy corporate profits. Thus, stock prices are likely to rise when personal income growth increases and fall when personal income growth declines.

The foreign exchange markets will take the same perspective as the equity trader. Rising personal income growth bodes well for the economy pointing to higher interest rates and therefore an increase in the demand for dollars. This will raise the exchange value of the dollar. Sluggish gains in personal income or outright declines (which are unusual) clearly indicate economic weakness. Consequently, interest rates would fall and lead to a drop in the demand for the dollar (pushing down its value in the foreign exchange market).

Financial market participants (either in the fixed income, stock, or foreign exchange markets) do not tend to react forcibly to monthly data on personal consumption expenditures due to the fact that it is highly predictable and consequently is 'expected' news.

Consumer instalment credit

Definition

Consumer instalment credit covers loans to households, which are scheduled to be repaid in two or more monthly payments, for purchases of goods and services and the refinancing of consumer debt. Secured and unsecured loans, (except those secured with real estate, which are defined as mortgage loans) are included. Securitized consumer loans, which are those made by finance companies, banks and retailers and sold as securities, are also included.

Who publishes it and when?

The net change in consumer instalment credit is reported by the Federal Reserve Board between five and six weeks after the end of the month.

How should you interpret it?

For the most part, when consumer credit increases, it suggests gains in consumer spending and a sense of optimism about the economy. This will happen during economic expansions. When consumer credit decreases, it suggests decreased consumer spending, possibly coupled with a sense of pessimism about future economic activity. This often happens during recessions.

Consumer credit outstanding usually rises, but the rate of increase is quicker during expansions than recessions. The rare monthly falls in consumer credit show up during recessions. Consumer credit therefore magnifies cyclical changes in consumer spending, particularly for durable goods.

What is its impact on financial markets?

Consumer credit data is difficult to interpret on its own. Financial markets will include this along with other indicators in order to gain a clearer picture of the economy. For example, increases in consumer credit coupled with increases in auto sales and retail sales clearly point to consumer optimism and healthy economic activity. Conversely, if retail sales and auto sales decline, but consumer credit increases, consumers may not be repaying their debt as rapidly. It could signal lack-lustre economic activity along with some cautious consumer behaviour. Finally, declines in consumer credit coupled with increases in retail sales or auto sales, suggest that consumers are repaying their loans more rapidly than they are under-taking new loans. This would also indicate squeamishness about the economy.

In practice financial market participants do not usually react to consumer credit data. It is old news by the time it is reported, having followed all the other consumer indicators.

Investment spending, government spending and foreign trade

Investment spending refers to the creation of capital: the purchase or putting in place of buildings, equipment, roads, houses and the like. Sound investment in capital results in future benefits that are more valuable than the present cost. Capital is also able to generate future benefits in excess of cost by increasing the productivity of labour. A person who has to dig a hole can dig a bigger hole with an excavator than with a shovel. A computer can do in several seconds what it took bookkeepers hours to do only a few years ago. This increase in productivity makes it less costly to produce products.

While many factors influence business, people's desire to invest, the state of business confidence, which in turn depends on expectations about the future, are very important. While difficult to measure it does seem obvious that busi-nesses will build more factories and purchase more machines when their expectations are optimistic. Conversely, their investment plans will be very cautious if the economic outlook appears bleak.

There are fewer indicators of investment spending than there are of consumer spending because investment spending accounts for only about one-fifth of gross domestic product. Despite its smaller contribution to GDP, investment spending is significant because the volatility inherent in investment spend-ing exacerbates the business cycle. Growth in investment expenditure outpaces GDP growth during a cyclical upswing but also declines more sharply during recessions. In general, most of these investment indicators are not followed as intimately as the consumer indicators.

It is useful to break down investment spending into the major components, these being Residential Fixed Investment, Non-residential Fixed Investment, and Inventory Investment, and then to examine the individual subcomponents. The format we will follow is outlined in Figure 6.4.

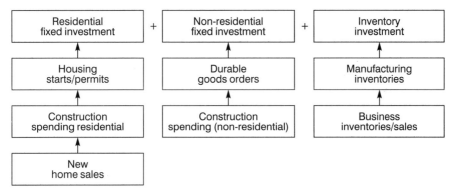

Figure 6.4 Investment spending.

In theoretical discussions it is common to lump all the components of investment together, which is very misleading because the investment components of GDP consist of several distinct categories that vary considerably over the business cycle. Whereas all three investment categories – residential fixed investment, non-residential fixed investment, often called business fixed investment, and changes in business inventories – are substantially more volatile than the remaining GDP components, their individual behaviour can vary widely. They differ with respect to both the magnitude of changes and the timing of changes over a business cycle.

In recent recessions the dollar decline in real investment expenditure was larger than the total decline in real GDP. Furthermore a large portion of the total decline in investment was owing to the swing in inventory accumulation from positive values at the start of the recession to large negative values. It is clear that investment is the most volatile part of GDP, and even though it represents less than one-fifth of total GDP, it is responsible for much of the cyclical change that takes place.

Residential fixed investment

Housing starts and permits

Definition

The level of activity in the US housing market is measured monthly at each stage of construction; the number of permits issued authorizing a new house to be built; the number of houses actually started; the number of houses completed; and the number of houses sold. The Bureau of the Census equates the granting of a building permit with authorizations to build. A housing unit is considered started when excavation begins for the footings or foundations.

Who publishes them and when?

The Bureau of the Census, within the Department of Commerce, reports housing starts and permits about two to three weeks after the end of the month.

How should you interpret them?

Housing construction plays a critical role in the economy. Increases in housing starts raise construction employment, and recent homebuyers often purchase other consumer durables leading, through a multiplier effect, to increased employment. Construction is especially important for the business cycle, because changes in residential construction tend to lead recessions and recoveries. In addition, the supply of new housing is a determinant of movements in house prices, which affect both housing affordability and the wealth position of homeowners.

Building permits is a pointer to housing starts, which is a pointer to completions and, ultimately, sales. There is no pointer to building permits, which are regarded as a forward indicator for the US economy. Building permits are included in the leading, coincident and lagging indicators of US economic activity.

What is their impact on financial markets?

Participants in the fixed-income market view a rise in housing starts unfavourably because it signifies economic growth. They will sell bonds which will push down bond prices, causing yields to rise. When housing starts decline, bond and money market traders will view this favourably, pushing up prices, and causing bond yields to fall.

In contrast, an increase in housing starts will encourage stock market professionals. A healthy economy provides potentially robust corporate earnings. Similarly, foreign exchange market participants will favour the rise in housing starts that brings about the bond market reaction of higher interest rates. Although rising interest rates are unfavourable for bond market professionals, they are a positive factor for the foreign exchange markets because they push up the value of the dollar. A drop in housing starts bodes poorly for stock prices and for the dollar because it signals weak domestic growth.

Financial market reaction to housing starts data is not as strong as the reaction to some other figures, but it can move the markets when the changes are significant and compatible with market psychology. As already mentioned housing starts typically lead the economy out of recession, so they are closely monitored at turning points of the business cycle. They are particularly watched at the early stages of recovery, when market participants assess the magnitude of strength of the recovery; and at expansion peaks, when market participants anticipate declines in housing activity.

Residential construction spending

Definition

The definition includes residential buildings and new housing. New housing is broken down into single units and new units.

Who publishes it and when?

This is included in all construction expenditures and is published by the Bureau of Census about five weeks after the end of the month.

How should you interpret it?

Residential construction provides information about the residential component of investment. Together with non-residential construction and state and local government spending on construction they account for 20 per cent of GNP, a number too

large to be ignored. Residential spending accounts for around 5
per cent of GNP.

Construction industries, together with automobiles, are typically the first two sectors to go into recession when the bad
times arrive and the first two sectors to recover when conditions
improve. Analysts track home and automobile sales for hints
about when these changes are beginning to occur, and they
revise their forecasts accordingly.

What is its impact on financial markets?

Unfortunately, there are two problems with the monthly report
on construction spending which includes residential construction spending as well as other construction spending. First, it is
not very timely. It is released on the first business day of the
month for two months prior. That makes it one of the last pieces
of information the financial markets receive about the state of
the economy for any given month. Second, the report tends to
be quite volatile and revisions can be sizeable.

New home sales

Definition

Sales of new and existing single-family houses are another
indicator of housing demand. Figures are issued on the
number of houses sold, homes for sale, and the month's
supply of unsold homes.

Who publishes them and when?

The statistics on sales of new and existing single family homes
are reported about four to five weeks after the end of the month.
New single-family home sales are published by the Bureau of
the Census. Existing single-family home sales are compiled by
the National Association of Realtors.

How should you interpret them?

New home sales are an important indicator of the degree of
strength of the housing market. As discussed earlier large
changes in consumer spending first appear in housing and
automobiles.

The problem with the house sales data is that they tend to be quite volatile. This obviously limits the data's usefulness. For the most part, sales of new and existing homes move in tandem. If sales of existing homes are rising more rapidly than sales of new homes, the relative price differential between new and used homes may have shrunk.

Home sales tend to follow the same seasonal pattern as housing starts. As a result, unusually warm weather during winter months can cause a temporary spurt in home sales, especially in the American Midwest or Northeast. Similarly, unusually rainy seasons in the spring or summer months can hold down home sales temporarily.

What is their impact on financial markets?

Since they are so volatile, new home sales are difficult to predict. If home sales rise unexpectedly and market partici-pants conclude that this is the beginning of a new trend, the participants react adversely and push interest rates higher. An unanticipated decline prompts the opposite response.

The stock market and the foreign exchange market do not appear to attach a great deal of importance to this report and, as a result, it is rare to find a reaction in either market.

Non-residential fixed investment

Advance durable goods orders: manufacturers shipments, inventories and orders release

Definition

Durable goods are goods designed to last for three years or more. The report when published is referred to as 'advance' because it is an early release of the manufacturers' shipments, inventories and new orders. New orders are leading indicators of production three to six months hence. Shipments, which are the same as sales, are indicators of current production and sales of manufactured goods. Inventories, often referred to as unfilled orders, are also part of this report.

The durable goods report is divided into broad categories, such as defence and non-defence capital goods.

Who publishes it and when?

The Bureau of Census, within the Department of Commerce, produces an advance report of manufacturers' shipments, new orders, and unfilled orders of durable goods about three weeks after the end of the month.

About one week after the advance report on durable goods, the Census Bureau releases the entire report on manufacturers' goods. The monthly survey of manufacturers has a response rate of roughly 55 per cent. This complete report includes figures on non-durable goods as well as durable goods. Non-durable goods, which make up roughly half the total, do not tend to be as unstable as durable goods.

The reported data are supposed to represent firm orders for immediate or future delivery. These orders must be legally binding and supported by a signed contract, a letter of intent, or some similar document.

The shipments data represent the sum total of sales for that month whether for domestic use or export.

How should you interpret them?

Durable goods orders have the potential to provide market participants with hard information. Orders are generally believed to be a front runner for activity in the manufacturing sector because a manufacturer must have an order before contemplating an increase in production. Conversely, a drop-off in orders eventually causes production to be scaled back; otherwise the manufacturer accumulates inventories which must be financed.

Unfortunately the orders report has two major drawbacks. The first problem with the orders data is that they are extremely volatile. This is because they include civilian aircraft and defence orders. If an aircraft carrier or two is included in one month's figures then they will dwarf the other components.

The second problem with the orders data is that they are notable for sizeable revisions once more data becomes available one week later. The revised data, as discussed above, are contained in the report on manufacturing orders, shipments and inventories.

What is their impact on financial markets?

Strictly speaking, fixed-income market participants will consider a rise in orders and shipments indicative of economic strength; a decline in durable orders and shipments signals weakness. As a result, strong orders and shipments lead to rising interest rates, whereas weak orders and shipments signal lower interest rates. However, shipments are much less relevant to the markets than orders, since shipments represent present conditions and orders represent future conditions. Financial market professionals are future oriented.

Stock market players, along with foreign exchange market professionals, prefer economic strength to weakness and would favour strong durable orders to declines in the series. Those in the stock market are looking for growth in corporate profits, whereas those in the foreign exchange market are looking to push up the value of the dollar on rising interest rates. A decline in orders could lower the value of the dollar if interest rates fall.

Economic growth is unfavourable to fixed-income market professionals because it either signals inflationary pressures (during economic expansions) or the end of Federal Reserve easing (during recoveries). Neither foreign exchange or stock market professionals want to see economic growth accompanied by inflation. But, foreign exchange professionals tend to prefer high interest rates, so they would be relieved to see the end of a period of Federal Reserve easing.

Non-residential construction spending

Definition

Non-residential construction spending includes spending on buildings, industrial, offices, hotels/motels, religious, educational buildings and hospitals.

Who publishes it and when?

It is published at the same time as residential construction spending.

How should you interpret it?

The statistics are incorporated directly into GDP by the Bureau of Economic Analysis. If you follow the pattern you can develop a feel for GDP revisions.

What is its impact on financial markets?

As with residential construction spending these statistics contain little new information on the state of the economy and are largely ignored.

Inventory investment

Manufacturing inventories/business inventories/sales

Definition

Total business inventories can be broken down into:

- manufacturing inventories
- wholesale inventories
- retail inventories

In addition to a more complete and detailed report of ship-ments, new orders, and unfilled orders, the manufacturers' release on factory orders also includes data on manufacturing inventories.

Who publishes them and when?

Data on manufacturing inventories is published as part of the factory orders report, by the Bureau of the Census of the Department of Commerce. It is published in the first week of the month and refers to the two months prior.

How should you interpret it?

Inventories are stocks of goods on hand, which may be raw materials, goods in process or finished products. They are generally thought of as being a necessary evil, providing a cushion against unexpected orders. Businesses are anxious to keep inventories at low levels in order to minimize the funds tied up as working capital. Their role tends to aggravate both the upswing and the downswing of the business cycle. It is essential to follow both the business upswing and the downswing.

Business upswing

If demand rises businesses must increase production. If this is not done speedily enough sales grow quicker than production and this results in an unplanned draw down of inventories. This is known as involuntary inventory depletion. If a business has too few inventories sales could be jeopardized. Consequently an expected rise in demand means businesses will increase output, increase capacity utilization, face productivity de-creases and rises in unit labour costs, which all force up the rate of inflation. Consequently inventory accumulation adds to the inflationary cycle, and this aggravates the upswing.

Business downswing

As sales weaken, inventories build up and businesses will cut back production. This will then provoke attempts to liquidate inventories by price cutting in an attempt to reduce working capital. As goods are sold from inventories, production and employment are reduced by more than sales since orders can be filled from inventories rather than current production. Consequently inventory liquidation aggravates the downswing.

Desired versus undesired inventories

As mentioned earlier, inventories are a necessary evil. Should these be produced in order to face an expected increase in demand then this is a signal that prices are rising with the possibility that interest rates may be rising. Similarly an expected drop in sales and a consequent reduction in inventories will be a natural forerunner to falling prices and a reduction in interest rates. Consequently falls in desired inventories suggest interest rate falls. Rises in desired inventories indicate pressures for interest rate rises.

In order to know whether inventories are desired or not it is essential to compare them with sales. If the ratio of inventories to sales rises then there are pressures for interest rates to fall, and vice versa (see Figure 6.5).

Manufacturing inventories represent about one half of total business inventories. To this manufacturing inventory figure one must add inventories at the wholesale and retail levels to obtain overall business inventories available about two weeks later.

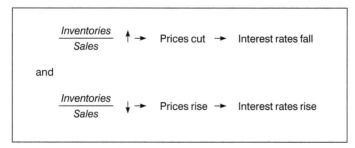

Figure 6.5 Effect of inventories on interest rates.

What is their impact on financial markets?

The report on business inventories and sales comes on the back of several previously published reports. The durable goods data (which contains information on the sales of durable goods by manufacturers), the report on factory orders, shipments and inventories, the retail sales report, and the wholesale inventories and sales data have all been published.

Given that so much of this inventory and sales information is published throughout the month, by the time business inventories/sales information is published most of the information is already known. Consequently it has a very limited effect on the financial markets. However, at business cycle turning points, the markets will react to business inventories.

Inventory accumulation during a sluggish economic period suggests producers will have to unload unwanted inventories and production will suffer. Declines in production are favourable news for the bond market participants because they indicate possible recession and lower interest rates (see Figure 6.5). Production declines are not favourable news to stock market participants nor to foreign exchange players looking for a strong dollar. A weak economy means lacklustre earnings. Low interest rates indicate capital flows to the United States will be reduced and a drop in demand for the dollar will ensue.

Inventory liquidation portends future rebuilding of inventories and increases in production. Bond market participants will not be happy as interest rates climb and bond prices sag. In contrast, stock market players will view the potential rise in production favourably as corporate earnings move upward. Similarly, foreign exchange participants favour the potential for upward momentum in the economy and in the dollar.

Government spending and taxation

In January of each year, the President of the United States sends his budget message to Congress. For over a decade now the event has set off an annual debate over how best to reduce the budget deficit, the amount by which the government expenditures exceed its receipts during a specified period of time, usually one year. These debates have been acrimonious, time consuming, and highly political. But they also have an important economic aspect, for the two sides are arguing over the government's fiscal policy, that is the overall balance of government spending and taxation.

Government purchases of goods and services (G) are a direct component of total spending. As we discussed in Chapter 1, they are to be added to Investment (I), Consumption (C) and Net Exports (X – IM) if we are to foresee the likely trend in GDP.

The interpretation of budget deficits and surpluses can be ambiguous. Since a falling GDP means higher expenditures and lower tax receipts, the deficit rises in a recession and falls in a boom, even with no change in fiscal policy.

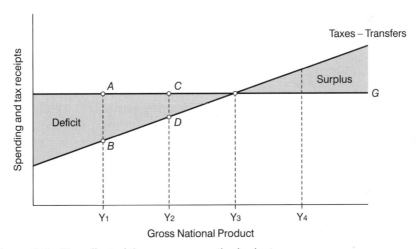

Figure 6.6   The effect of the economy on the budget.

Figure 6.6 depicts the relationship between GNP and the budget deficit. The government's fiscal programme is summarized by the two black lines. The horizontal line labelled G indicates that federal purchases of goods and services are approximately unaffected by GNP. The rising line labelled 'Taxes minus Transfers' indicates that taxes rise and transfer payments fall as GNP rises. Notice that the same fiscal policy (that is the same two black lines) can lead to: a large deficit if GNP is Y_1, to a small deficit if GNP is Y_2, and to a balanced budget if GNP is Y_3, or even to a surplus if GNP is as high as Y_4. The deficit itself cannot be a good measure of the government's fiscal policy as it clearly depends on what is happening to GNP.

For this reason, many economists pay less attention to the actual deficit or surplus and more attention to what is called the structural deficit or surplus. This is a hypothetical construct that replaces both the spending and taxes in the actual budget by estimates of how much the government would be spending and receiving, given current tax rates and expenditure rates, if the economy were operating at some fixed high-employment level. For example, if the high-employment benchmark in Figure 6.6 was Y_2, while actual GNP was only Y_1, the actual deficit would be AB while the structural deficit would be only CD.

Because the structural deficit is based on the spending and taxing the government would be doing at some fixed level of GNP, rather than on actual expenditures and receipts, it is insensitive to the state of the economy. It changes only when policy changes. That is why most economists view it as a better measure of the thrust of fiscal policy than the actual deficit.

Interpreting a budget deficit

In interpreting a budget deficit it is essential to distinguish between the structural deficit or surplus and the actual deficit and surplus. The structural deficit is sometimes known as the full employment deficit and the actual deficit as the cyclical deficit.

As discussed earlier the same fiscal programme can lead to a large or small deficit, depending on the state of the economy. Failure to appreciate this point has led many people to assume that a larger deficit always signifies a more expansionary fiscal policy. But that is not always true.

Think, for example, about what happens to the budget when the economy experiences a recession and GNP falls. The government's most important sources of tax revenue, i.e., income taxes, corporate taxes and payroll taxes, all shrink because firms and people pay lower taxes when they earn less. Similarly, some types of government spending, notably transfer payments like unemployment benefits, rise when GNP falls because more people are out of work.

Remember that the deficit is the difference between government expenditures and tax receipts:

Deficit = G + Transfers − Taxes

Supply side economics

Active macroeconomic stabilization policy can be carried out either by means that tend to expand the size of government (by raising either G or taxes when appropriate) or by means that hold back the size of government (by reducing either G or taxes when appropriate). Expansionary fiscal policy can cure recessions, but it normally exacts a cost in terms of higher inflation. This dilemma led to a great deal of interest in 'supply-side' tax cuts designed to stimulate the output of the economy, known as aggregate supply.

The co-existence of high unemployment and inflation in the US during the 1970s questioned the contribution made by orthodox economics in controlling the business cycle. A new group calling themselves supply-side economists came to the policy forefront.

The essential argument of the supply-siders was quite simple. Basically, they said that all the attention to demand orthodox macroeconomic theory distracted attention from the real problem with the US economy. The real problem, according to the supply-siders, was that high rates of taxation and heavy regulation had reduced the incentive to work, to save, and to invest. What was needed was not a demand stimulus but rather better incentives to stimulate supply.

Supply-siders would argue that if taxes were cut so that people took home more of their paycheques, they would work harder and save more. Similarly if business got to keep more of their profits they would invest more. This added labour supply and investment, or capital supply, would lead to an expansion of the supply of goods and services, which in turn would reduce inflation and unemployment at the same time. Thus the solution was to be found on the supply side of the economy.

At their most extreme, supply-siders argued that the incentive effects were likely to be so great that a major cut in tax rates would actually increase tax revenues. That is, even though tax rates would be lower, more people would be working and earning income and firms would earn more profits, so that the increases in the tax bases (profits, sale, and income) would outweigh the decreases in rates, resulting in increased government revenues.

Figure 6.7 presents one of the key diagrams of supply-side economics. The tax rate is on the vertical axis, and tax revenue is on the horizontal axis. The assumption behind the way that the curve is drawn is that there is some tax rate beyond which the supply response is large enough to lead to a fall in tax revenue for further increases in the tax rate. There is obviously some tax rate between zero and 100 per cent at

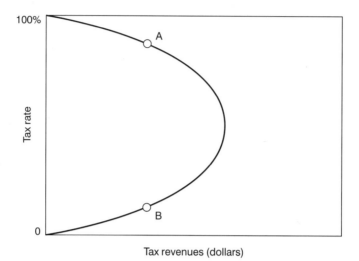

Figure 6.7 The Laffer curve.

which tax revenue is at a maximum. At a tax rate of zero, work effort is high but there is no tax revenue. At a tax rate of 100 per cent the labour supply is presumably zero, since no-one would be allowed to keep any of the income he or she makes. Somewhere in between zero and 100 is the maximum-revenue rate.

The diagram in Figure 6.7 is called the Laffer curve, after Arthur Laffer, who first proposed it. The Laffer curve had some influence on the passage of the Economic Recovery Tax Act of 1981, the tax package put forward by the Reagan administration that brought with it substantial cuts in both personal and business taxes. The individual income tax was to be cut by 25 per cent over 3 years. Corporate taxes were cut sharply in a way designed to stimulate investment. The new law allowed firms to depreciate their capital at a very rapid rate for tax purposes, and the bigger deductions led to taxes that were significantly lower than before.

The effect of these tax cuts was felt just as the US economy was in the middle of the deepest recession since the Great Depression. The unemployment rate hit 10.7 per cent in the fourth quarter of 1982.

Controversy has resolved around the impact of supply-side effects. While conceptually simple, the Laffer curve came under increasing scrutiny after tax cuts based on supply-side arguments apparently failed to 'deliver the goods'. Tax rates fell but tax revenues did not rise accordingly, and the United States resorted to deficit spending.

The Laffer Curve shows that the amount of revenue that the government collects is a function of the tax rate. It also shows that when tax rates are very high, an increase in the tax rate could actually cause tax revenues to fall. Similarly, under the same circumstances, a tax rate cut could actually generate enough additional economic activity to cause revenues to rise. Certainly, when rates are zero, revenues are zero. Likewise, it must be agreed that if rates are 100 per cent, no-one would work or invest, and revenues would also be zero. The supply side school claimed in 1980 that the US was at a point like A on the curve and that taxes should be cut. In fact, experience and evidence have shown that the US was rather at a point like B. The 1981 tax cuts reduced revenues substantially below what they would have been without the cuts.

Supply-side tax cuts aim to push the economy's aggregate supply curve higher. If successful, they can expand the economy and reduce inflation at the same time – a highly desirable outcome. But critics point out five problems of supply-side tax cuts:

- they also stimulate aggregate demand
- the beneficial effects on aggregate supply may be small
- the demand-side effects occur before the supply-side effects
- they make income distribution more unequal
- large tax cuts lead to large budget deficits.

Budget deficits and financial markets

Financial markets distrust budget deficits under most circumstances, as they fear that they are inflationary. The reasoning behind this is that when government policy pushes up aggregate demand, firms may find themselves unwilling or unable to produce the higher quantities that are being demanded at the going prices. Prices will therefore have to rise. Deficit spending will not cause much inflation if the economy has lots of slack. But deficit spending is likely to be highly inflationary in a fully employed economy. Remember that budget deficits involve the government issuing bonds to finance the difference between revenues and taxation.

The monetization issue

Deficit spending normally drives up real GNP and the price level. The increased transactions demand for money associated with rising GNP tends to force up interest rates. Suppose now that the Federal Reserve does not want interest rates to rise. What can it do? To prevent the rise in interest rates it must engage in expansionary monetary policies. Expansionary monetary policies normally take the form of open market purchases of government bonds. So deficit spending might induce the Federal Reserve to increase its purchases of government bonds, that is, to buy up some of the newly issued government debt.

But why is this called monetizing the debt? Open market purchases of bonds by the Federal Reserve gives banks more reserves, which leads, eventually, to an increase in the money supply. So a monetized deficit results in an increase in the money supply which increases inflationary pressures and forces up real interest rates. Financial markets, particularly bond markets and currency markets are very wary of inflation.

Financial markets worry about structural deficits, which appear permanent, but are happy with cyclical deficits, which are likely to be temporary.

Budget deficits: a historical curiosity?

In November 1995 the US Congress passed the Balanced Budget Act. The Bill provided a fiscal package that would, according to Congressional Budget Office projections, balance the federal budget by fiscal year 2002. On 20 November 1995, President Clinton signed into law a Continuing Resolution for Fiscal year 1996 that provided short-term financing for most federal government operations. It also heralded an agreement between the President and Congress on the goal of producing a long-term budget plan that would eliminate the federal deficit on the seven-year schedule proposed in the Balanced Budget Act.

In 1992, the year of his election as President, the deficit in the $1.3 trillion budget was $290 billion. Figure 6.8 gives the US budgetary position for 1975–1999, a period where budget deficits were the usual fiscal outcome. However, as can be seen from Figure 6.9, the projections for the foreseeable future are for large budget surpluses. The Congressional Budget Office report for the year 2001 gives projections for a cumulative budget surplus of $5.61 trillion for the years

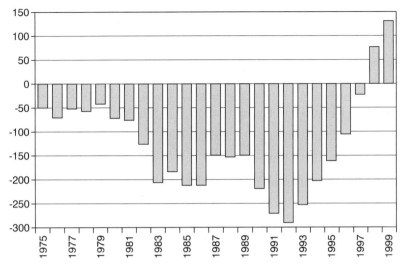

Figure 6.8 US budget 1975–1999. (Source: United States Treasury Department.)

2002–2011. These projections have largely taken the US budget deficit out of the picture as a factor influencing financial markets, for the first time for 40 years. Future economic policy making issues will focus on whether these surpluses should be used to finance tax cuts or whether they should be used to redeem government debt.

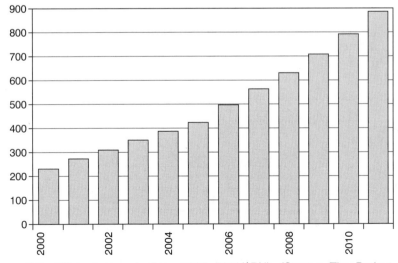

Figure 6.9 US budget projections 2000–2011($BN). (Source: The Budget and Economic Outlook. Fiscal Years 2002–2011. Congressional Budget Office.)

Foreign trade

Net exports, trade and current accounts

Definition

The balance of payments is the collective term for the accounts of US transactions with the rest of the world. It has several components.

- Merchandise Trade. This is the raw balance on trade in visible goods, published monthly. The financial markets focus on the seasonally adjusted monthly trade data.
- Current Account. This is the balance of trade plus services (passenger and freight transportation, insurance, telecommunications, construction, engineering and income from royalties, patents, etc.) plus defence transactions (transfers under foreign military sales programmes, defence purchases) plus remittances and government grants.
- Statistical Discrepancy. This is the difference between total credits (exports of goods and services, unilateral transfers to the US, and capital inflows) and total debits (imports of goods and services, unilateral transfers overseas, and capital outflows) in the balance of payments.

Who publishes them and when?

There are two sources for US trade data. The Bureau of the Census in the Department of Commerce provides monthly trade figures about 45 days after the month to which they refer. The Bureau of Economic Analysis (BEA) provides monthly figures about 55 days after the relevant month.

How should you interpret them?

Focus on the seasonally-adjusted trade numbers. A single month's trade figures are not regarded as a reliable guide to the underlying trend, so take a three-month moving average at the very least. If the three-monthly comparison suggests a change of trend, check to see whether the six- and nine-monthly averages fit in with that picture.

Once evidence of a change in trend has been established, find out whether it is import- or export-driven by looking at the way total imports and total exports have moved. Look for corroborative evidence from other economic releases. If imports are depressed, does this tally with readings of domestic demand from retail sales? If exports are booming, how does that fit in with the data on factory orders, industrial production?

When the price of oil has been moving sharply, look at the trade balance minus oil for an underlying picture of trade trends, since this is regarded as a better guide to competitiveness.

Occasionally, other categories are excluded (aeroplanes when there is a bunching of export deliveries, non-monetary gold when the Japanese were importing a large volume in 1988 for a medal struck in honour of Emperor Hirohito), the reason being to identify lasting trends and to refrain from extrapolating on non-recurring events. However, the full deficit does have to be financed and most economists say such exclusions should be used with care to focus on special issues only.

Factory orders include goods shipments, which, given some assumptions about the strength of domestic demand, can offer clues on export performance.

The National Association of Purchasing Management's (NAPM) export orders index points to the trend in exports. However as discussed in Chapter 4 and Appendix A this is a 'diffusion index' based on the percentage of respondents reporting higher/lower/unchanged export orders and gives no quantitative guide.

What is their impact on financial markets?

The impact of the trade deficit on financial markets has been subject to violent changes of fashion. Currently its impact is less significant than it was in the 1970s and 1980s.

A decline in the trade deficit is usually good news for the US dollar, as one must buy dollars to purchase US exports and sell dollars to buy imports. However, generally speaking, if the dollar has been trading within a well-defined range, the monthly trade figures tend to be ignored beyond a few hours. Conversely if the dollar has just broken out of its recent trading range, data on trade flows have a greater impact.

The case for bond investors is a little subtler. Suppose the trade deficit comes in less than expected. Bond investors are torn between two factors. First, a smaller deficit triggers a dollar rally, which is good news for bond market participants.

But, if the trade deficit is shrinking, it simultaneously adds to GNP growth. A faster pace of economic activity is negative for bonds. What should an investor do? It is not always clear and the market reaction seems to be determined by the mood of the moment.

The stock market response depends on whether the trade deficit is deemed a 'problem' at the time. Currently it is not and the stock market would, in most circumstances, ignore the trade numbers – a situation that could easily change, given that the US trade deficit now represents 4 per cent of GDP.

7

So how do consumer confidence and consumer sentiment indicators help in interpreting financial market volatility?

As well as relying on 'hard' economic data financial market analysts also pay a great deal of attention to non-economic factors such as consumer attitudes towards spending. Whilst such data is, by its nature, more qualitative rather than quantitative it is no less important in providing valuable information as to the future behaviour of the economy. Household sentiment which turned adverse in early 1990 has frequently been cited as a major cause of the US 1990/91 recession.

Attitudes, expectations and sentiment are terms that are frequently used when people refer to the psychological mood of consumers. These are distinct concepts. Attitudes reflect the feelings that consumers have about current conditions, and expectations are attitudes which have been projected to some point in the future. Both attitudes and expectations are subsumed into the larger category called consumer sentiment or confidence.

Intuitively, it is clear that confidence or sentiment is an important causal factor in any one person's spending. If, for example, an individual feels that the government is mismanaging the economy and that this will lead to a recession and possibly cause him to be laid off, he will be less likely to purchase a new car than if he is optimistic about the future.

This chapter discusses the different indicators designed to measure consumer and consumer sentiment. The indicators discussed here are:

● Michigan Index of Consumer Sentiment
● Conference Board Consumer Confidence Index
● National Association of Purchasing Managers Index
● Business Outlook Survey of the Philadelphia Fed
● Help-Wanted Advertising Index
● Sindlinger Household Liquidity Index

Appendix D surveys some of the characteristics of the key consumer sentiment indicators.

Two organizations provide indicators of US consumer attitudes. They focus on consumer perceptions of general business conditions and of their personal financial well being, plus their attitudes toward purchasing big-ticket items, i.e., purchases that last a relatively long time, e.g. homes, cars, furniture and major household appliances.

These attitude indicators are the 'Consumer Sentiment Index' of the University of Michigan and the 'Consumer Confidence Index' of the Conference Board. Both indexes measure similar phenomena, but because the methodologies differ and the concepts are not identical, there are periods when their movements differ.

Michigan index of consumer sentiment (ICS)

Each month, the University of Michigan conducts a representative, cross-section sampling of 700 respondent households by telephone. In general, the sampling for a given month takes about four weeks. The interviewers are paid employees who ask the five questions which comprise the index along with other questions which are designed for the business clients who pay for the survey. While these other questions (which could, for example, ask about the respondent's attitude toward a tax cut) do vary, the five questions comprising the ICS never change. Table 7.1 lists the five questions that are asked.

Questions 1 and 5 highlight attitudes, while questions 2, 3 and 4 emphasize expectations. Although question 4 asks about the next five years, the time horizon in general is 12

Table 7.1 Index of Consumer Sentiment Questions

1 We are interested in how people are getting along financially these days. Would you say that you and your family are better off or worse off financially than you were a year ago?

2 Now – looking ahead – do you think that a year from now you people will be financially better off or worse off or just about the same as now?

3 Now turning to business conditions in the country as a whole – do you think that during the next 12 months we'll have good times financially or bad times or what?

4 Looking ahead, which you would say is more likely – that in the country as a whole, we'll have continuous good times during the next five years or so, or that we'll have continuous good times during the next five years or so, or that we will have periods of widespread unemployment or depression, or what?

5 About the big things people buy for their homes – such as furniture, house furnishings, refrigerator, stove, television, and things like that – for people in general – do you think that now is a good or bad time to buy major household items?

months. The survey also asks whether this is a 'good' or a 'bad' time to make a purchase. It does not query the actual intention to buy. Each question is equally weighted in the ICS. All positive replies are given a weight of two, a neutral response receives a one and a negative reply, zero. Therefore, if all respondents in the survey sample gave positive responses to all questions, the ICS would have a value of 200. Alternatively, one can calculate the index level by subtracting the number of negative responses from the number of positive and adding the constant 100.

The Index of Consumer Sentiment is recognized by the National Bureau of Economic Research and is included as one of the components of the Index of Leading Economic Indicators, discussed in Chapter 5.

Conference board consumer confidence index

The Conference Board survey is 10 times larger than the University of Michigan's Survey covering a representative sample of 5000 households. The survey is conducted by NFO

Research, Inc., of Connecticut, which mails a questionnaire to an entirely different sample of individuals each month, representing all geographic regions, age groups, and income levels.

The consumer confidence index is calculated from the responses to the questions posed in Figure 7.1. These questions are divided into two categories: the present situation (questions 1 and 2), and consumer expectations (remaining questions). The survey questionnaire also asks about actual intentions to purchase a home, car, and other durable goods. These data are used to calculate a buying plans index.

---

1. How would you rate the present general business conditions in your area:

☐ Good?   ☐ Normal?   ☐ Bad?

(a) 6 months from now, do you think they will be:

☐ Better?   ☐ Same?   ☐ Worse?

2. What would you say about the available jobs in your area right now:

☐ Plenty?   ☐ Not so many?   ☐ Hard to get?

(a) 6 months from now do you think there will be:

☐ More?   ☐ Same?   ☐ Fewer?

3. How would you guess your total family income to be six months from now:

☐ Higher?   ☐ Same?   ☐ Lower?

Figure 7.1 Consumer confidence index questions.

For each question, the respondent is given a choice of three reply options. To compute the CCI, neutral responses are discarded, while the positive and negative replies are added together. The positive responses are then expressed as a percentage of this total for each question. Each series, or question, is then adjusted for seasonal variation.

The logic of asking consumers whether they will buy durable goods is that these are infrequent purchases and presumably would not be made unless consumers were reasonably confident about their economic prospects.

How should you interpret them?

Consumer spending and consumer confidence indices rarely move in tandem. It is essential to look at the trend in the index rather than a one-month picture. Moreover, both the Index of Consumer Sentiment (Michigan Survey) as well as the Consumer Confidence Index (Conference Board) tend to move in similar directions over time but may diverge in any 1 month. The Conference Board series tends to increase more rapidly at business cycle peaks when employment prospects improve. Also, the Conference Board surveys an entirely different group of individuals each month. The consistency would not be the same as in the Michigan Survey, which talks to the same group each month.

One advantage of the Michigan Index is its earlier availability. However, one should bear in mind that the Michigan Index's preliminary figures are based on a much smaller sample size (about 250) than the Conference Board Index (about 2500), and are thus subject to somewhat greater measurement error.

What is their impact on financial markets?

Consumer confidence is a coincident indicator of the economy. Typically, consumers feel confident about the economy during an expansion and pessimistic about the economy during a recession.

The consumer confidence series were quite fashionable in the financial markets in 1990 and 1991. Most likely, this was because Federal Reserve Chairman, Alan Greenspan, cited them once or twice as indicators that he monitors. When a Federal Reserve chairman talks, market participants listen.

In the past few years, the markets have reacted strongly to consumer confidence surveys. This reaction is similar to that of actual consumer spending. Bond traders favour a drop in consumer confidence because it signals a weaker economy and points to lower bond yields (but higher bond prices). Conversely, the bond prices will drop (and yields will rise) if consumer confidence increases.

Participants in the stock market do not favour a drop in consumer confidence because it means lower corporate profits. Lower corporate earnings should lead to a dip in the stock market.

A pessimistic consumer won't make a foreign exchange market participant happy either. Pessimism signals a weak economy and low interest rates, leading to a drop in the value of the dollar. An optimistic consumer is favourable in that interest rates will rise and the demand for dollars will rise, pushing up the foreign exchange value of the dollar.

National association of purchasing managers index (NAPM)

Definition

The NAPM is a composite index of five series:

- new orders
- production
- supplier deliveries (also known as vendor deliveries/performance, discussed in Chapter 5)
- inventories
- employment

The NAPM is derived from the Report on Business. This is based on data compiled from monthly replies to questions asked of purchasing executives in more than 300 industrial companies.

The purchasing executives are asked eight questions, which then make up the Index. Separate seasonally-adjusted diffusion indices are created for the responses to each question. Five of these indices, listed above, are weighted together to produce the composite Purchasing Managers Index (PMI). The indices and their weights are: new orders (30 per cent); production (25 per cent); employment (20 per cent); supplier deliveries (15 per cent); and inventories (10 per cent).

The Report on Business survey is designed to measure the change (i.e., whether there has been an improvement or deterioration), if any, in the current month compared to the previous month for the eight questions.

The NAPM get these figures based on answers to rather straightforward questions. Purchasing managers are asked if their business situation is 'better', 'same', or 'worse' than the previous month. Sometimes, the terms 'higher' or 'faster' are substituted for 'better'; sometimes, 'slower' is substituted for 'worse'. In any case, the questionnaire is not asking for actual levels, just a subjective assessment of the company's business prospects. The results are compiled into a diffusion index. See Appendix A for a discussion of diffusion indexes.

Diffusion indices, which fluctuate between zero and 100 per cent, include the percentage of positive responses plus half of those responding the same (considered positive). They have the properties of leading indicators and are convenient summary measures showing the prevailing direction and scope of change.

The most important indicators, in terms of economic activity, receive most weight. New orders, which tends to be the most leading indicator and drives the others, has greatest weight, while inventories, which tends to lag in the economic cycle, has least weight.

Membership of the Business Survey Committee, from which the companies surveyed are drawn, is composed of 20 industries in 50 states. The composition of the committee membership is designed to parallel closely each manufacturing industry's contribution to gross domestic product (GDP). The responses from each member, or company, are treated as having equal weight regardless of the size of the company.

Who publishes it and when?

The NAPM is a purchasing, education and research organization in the US with over 35 000 members. The data are reported on the first day of the subsequent month (May figures are reported on 1 June), making this the most timely of all monthly indicators – its appearance could predate the employment situation by as much as a week. The figures are available on a seasonally-adjusted basis (as well as unadjusted). Unlike most other economic data, these figures are never revised from month to month.

The NAPM family

The NAPM is divided into 10 regions, some of which issue their own reports (see Table 7.2). There are also cities within the regions which issue separate reports. As the level of disaggregation grows, however, these reports may be a more useful indicator of local conditions (which are reflective of particular industries or the weather) than of the national economy.

Financial markets do give attention to the Chicago area's Purchasing Managers Index (Chicago PMI). Chicago is considered to be the industrial heartland and its PMI release also precedes the NAPM index.

How should you interpret it?

The NAPM indexes are different from most other indexes. Instead of setting a base year equal to 100 and measuring

Table 7.2 The NAPM Family

Purchasing Managers' Regions
Arizona
Austin, Texas
Buffalo, New York
Chicago, Illinois
Cleveland, Ohio
Detroit, Michigan
Grand Rapids, Michigan
Toledo, Ohio
Oregon
Rochester, New York
Milwood, Milwaukee

growth from there, the NAPM series are set at a trigger rate of 50 per cent. According to the NAPM, an index level of 50 per cent or more indicates that the economy as well as the manufacturing sector is expanding; an index level less than 50 per cent but greater than 45 per cent suggests that the manufacturing sector has stopped growing, but the economy is still expanding; a level less than 45 per cent signals a recession both in the economy and in the manufacturing sector.

The farther the index is away from 50 per cent, the stronger the economy when the index value is more than 50, and the weaker the economy when the index value is less than 50.

The basis for using the 50 per cent level as the point at which the economy is neither expanding nor declining is a function of diffusion indices. Basically, it eliminates the need to use a plus or minus with an index that uses zero as the dividing point between expansions and contraction. The evidence that a reading above 50 per cent generally indicates an expanding economy, and below 50 per cent a declining one, is based on analysis by the Commerce Department.

The rationale for incorporating the five components in the NAPM is fairly straightforward. New orders are a leading indicator of economic activity. Manufacturers' orders lead to increases in production. Production reflects the current state of affairs and is a coincident indicator of the economy. As output expands, producers hire additional workers to meet the increased demands. Employment is also a coincident indicator. Inventories are typically a lagging indicator of economic activity.

Inventory build-ups usually continue into a cyclical downturn as manufacturers are not sure whether the decline in demand is temporary or permanent. Inventories may continue to decline early in a recovery as producers unload stocks that were built up during the recession. Supplier deliveries, also known as vendor performance, work in much the same way as unfilled orders. When producers slow down their deliveries, it means they are busy and cannot fill all the orders quickly. Slower deliveries mean rapid economic growth. In contrast, faster deliveries suggest a moderating economy. When orders can be filled rapidly, it means producers aren't as busy. Vendor performance, as discussed in Chapter 6, is included in the Commerce Department's Index of Leading Indicators.

The number 45 on this index is important. In the past, whenever the Purchasing Managers Index has dropped below 45, a recession has occurred. Note that recessions have occurred without the index falling below the 45 level. The first oil shock in 1974, for example, precipitated a recession before the index fell below 50. The 1969 recession began before the index actually dropped below 45. However, whenever the index did fall below 45, a recession did unfold. There is one exception: the 'growth recession' of 1966/7. After two years of real GDP growth near 6 per cent, growth fell to 2.6 per cent and the unemployment rate rose. An actual recession, however, never developed, and the Purchasing Manager Index rebounded quickly to the mid-50s range.

There are a number of drawbacks associated with the compilation of the NAPM.

- It is concentrated on the industrial sector because that is the one that changes direction most quickly and is therefore of most interest to economists. The service sector, representing over 50 per cent of GDP, is thereby excluded.
- The purchasing managers' survey does not use a scientific sample (unlike official surveys). Instead, responses are taken from handpicked, established firms.
- There is no attempt to take into account the growing importance of some industries by increasing the number of firms in that sector. Newer, fast-growing firms are added to the sample only after they have become established in the business, while contracting firms stay in the sample until they fold.
- The sample covers less than 1 per cent of the NAPM's membership. The response rate varies from month to month

(although the NAPM says it is 'exceptionally high') and, compared with the entry and exit of members, firms answering the survey questionnaire can vary between samples.

What is its impact on financial markets?

Financial market participants have anxiously anticipated the NAPM ever since Federal Reserve Chairman Alan Greenspan once claimed that he placed great emphasis on this report. As usual, stock and foreign exchange market players look forward to healthy figures, whereas the fixed income professionals prefer weakness. As the NAPM moves in an upward direction, signalling economic strength, bond market participants will anticipate inflationary pressures or the end of a favourable environment for Federal Reserve easing conditions. Conversely, a declining trend in the NAPM will lead to a bond market rally.

Business outlook survey of the Philadelphia Federal Reserve

The Federal Reserve Bank of Philadelphia began to conduct monthly surveys of manufacturers in May 1968 to monitor business conditions in its district. The Business Outlook Survey (BOS) was based on the premise that surveying businesses about recent activity is one of the least costly methods of gathering economic data. Recent activity is available before other indicators reported by the government or private agencies. The trade-off is that most other economic data are quantitative whereas this survey is qualitative. Therefore, it is helpful in indicating trends in the Philadelphia Fed region as well as the country.

This survey is limited to manufacturing firms with plants in the area that employ at least 350 workers. It covers durable and non-durable industries. About 100 of the 550 eligible establishments agreed to participate in the monthly survey. Each month, the managers of the plants receive the survey questionnaire in the mail. On average, the response rate is just better than 50 per cent each month.

The survey produces a seasonally-adjusted diffusion index that represents the percentage of respondents indicating an increase in general business activity minus the percentage indicating a decrease. The survey also compiles data on a broad spectrum of questions meant to parallel the items in the NAPM including orders, shipments, delivery time, inventories, employment, and prices. Since the Philadelphia Survey includes questions about the workweek and capital expenditures, but not production, it cannot be used to duplicate the NAPM precisely, but forecasters do use it to refine their NAPM estimates.

Help-wanted advertising index

Definition

The help-wanted advertising index tracks employers' advertisements for job openings in the classified section of newspapers in 51 labour market areas. The index represents job vacancies resulting from turnover in existing positions, such as workers changing jobs or retiring, and from the creation of new jobs. It excludes non-advertised job vacancies and jobs advertised in non-classified sections. Many analysts believe it provides the most reliable long-term measure of pressures in the labour market and it is for this reason that it is so market sensitive.

The help-wanted advertising figures cover jobs in many fields, e.g. professional, technical, crafts, office, sales, farm, custodial, etc. They include a higher proportion of all junior and middle level vacancies than managerial, executive, or unskilled levels. In addition to the national help-wanted index, local indexes for 51 labour markets are provided. The index is currently based on 1967 = 100.

The help-wanted advertising figures are obtained from classified advertisements in one daily (including Sunday) newspaper in each of 51 labour markets (51 cities including their suburbs). Newspapers are selected according to how well their ads represent jobs in the local labour market area. The labour markets accounted for approximately one-half of non-agricultural employment in 1987.

Who publishes it and when?

Measures of the Help-Wanted Advertising Index are provided monthly by the Conference Board. The figures are published in a press release and in the Conference Board's monthly Statistical Bulletin. Secondary sources include Business Conditions

Digest. The Conference Board publishes the Index of Help-Wanted Advertising Index about four weeks after the end of the month.

How should you interpret it?

The Help-Wanted Advertising Index indicates the direction of employers' hiring plans. In theory, it provides an advance signal of future changes in employment and cyclical turning points. In practice, the Help-Wanted Index leads the downturn from the expansion peak to a recession, but it lags the turning point in moving from recession to expansion, based on analyses conducted as part of the leading, coincident and lagging indexes. The lag in timing as the economy is in recovery from a recession results from the tendency of employers to increase average weekly hours of existing workers when business improves or call back workers on layoff before advertising for new workers. Consequently it lags average weekly hours worked as an indicator of the economy moving from recession to expansion.

The Help-Wanted Index is inversely related to unemployment. When help-wanted advertisements increase, unemployment declines, while a decline in help-wanted advertisements is accompanied by a rise in unemployment. The help-wanted movements sometimes are sharper than the unemployment movements because of changing advertising practices. For example, during periods of low unemployment, employers may rely more heavily on help-wanted advertisements than on alternative means of finding workers. During high unemployment, employers may find workers easily through alternative means such as through workers initiating the contact on their own or on the advice of friends.

Some advertised jobs may not be filled because employers are not satisfied with the applicants, there is an overall shortage of applicants, or employers decide not to fill the jobs.

What is its impact on financial markets?

Most economic releases are reported when the financial markets are open. The Help-Wanted Index is released after markets have already closed. Usually, the financial press will bury the story in a corner and the local press may not even carry it. As a result, financial market participants do not normally react aggressively to this indicator. Economists who work with traders may not have much to say about these figures because they cannot use them to predict non-farm payrolls or the unemployment rate for the upcoming month. Although the Help-Wanted Index is not really necessarily useful to day traders who react to current news events, the series will have greater significance to those traders who take a longer perspective of the economy and it is closely watched around business cycle turning points.

Sindlinger household liquidity index

Definition

Sindlingers Household Liquidity Index is constructed from its findings on Current Income, Expected Income, Expected Employment and Expected Business. These are combined together to derive the index. Data are gathered through a continuous nation-wide telephone survey of America's household heads.

Who publishes it and when?

The privately produced Sindlinger Household Liquidity Index is published bi-weekly each Tuesday and Friday.

How should you interpret it?

Significant changes in consumer attitudes are apt to show up first in expectations for future employment conditions. Virtually all working Americans are sensitive to changing working conditions and information about changes in the local labour market is quickly transmitted through formal channels or by word of mouth. This component of confidence in future employment prospects tends to be sensitive to production, export sales, and stock market performance.

Expectations for local business conditions generally tend to follow the same pattern as expectations for employment. Declines in this component will show up in the early stages of an economic downturn. As household current income or expected income starts to diminish, expectations of local business conditions driven by consumer demand eventually falter. Changes in this component are less pronounced than the changes which occur in job and income expectations due to the fact that fewer people (in the total population) have a genuine awareness of business conditions.

The component which deals with expected household income is very sensitive to interest rates, US Federal monetary policy, US fiscal policy, as well as foreign monetary and fiscal policies. If tighter monetary policy is implemented to slow the economy, or a looser monetary policy is implemented, this influences the direction of expected income. In turn, the stock market is highly influential in determining whether there will be a tighter or looser monetary policy. If consumers perceive the trend in stock market prices, this directly affects the 'wealth effect', which in turn significantly changes expectations of income. By and large, American household heads expect their income to be the 'same' or 'higher', except for those persons engaged in seasonal employment or those who are leaving the labour market. On the negative side, a sustained decline in expected income will signify the economy is in an advanced phase of contraction and on the positive side an acceleration in expected income will signify an expansion in the pace of economic activity.

All household liquidity indicators are derived from responses to four questions that are asked of thousands of household heads each week. The four questions deal with:

- Current household income compared to the level of household income six months ago. Responses are recorded as 'Up', 'Down', 'Same', or 'Don't Know'.
- Expected household income in six months. Responses also are recorded as 'Up', 'Down', 'Same', and 'No Opinion'.
- Expected local employment situation in six months. Responses are recorded as 'More Jobs', 'Fewer Jobs', 'Same', or 'No Opinion'.
- Expected local business condition in six months. Categories of response are 'Better', 'Worse', 'Same' and 'No Opinion'.

Total Household Liquidity is expressed as a percentage and as a numerical projection of all US household heads. As a percentage, it represents the proportion of household heads in the US sample who provide either a positive or neutral answer to all four component questions. Respondents who provided a negative answer to any of the four questions are not included in the Household Liquidity Index sample percentage.

Because the sample size is sufficiently large and is representative of all US household heads, the Household Liquidity

Index percentage provides a broad trend as to consumers' spending patterns.

What is its impact on financial markets?

Household liquidity is an important determinant of future economic activity. When household liquidity is high consumers' willingness to spend or preparation to spend provides a stimulus to the economy. Low levels of household liquidity signal household decisions to cut back on spending and to increase saving. Although not a highly sensitive market indicator its main value is in reinforcing consumer confidence indicators at times when market sentiment is changing rapidly.

8

The global foreign exchange rate system and the 'Euroization' of the currency markets†

What is the ideal exchange rate system that a country should adopt?

The economics literature has identified a number of factors relating to an economy's structural characteristics, its susceptibility to external shocks, and macroeconomic and institutional conditions that influence the relative desirability of alternative exchange rate regimes.

The early literature on the choice of exchange rate regime, which was based on the theory of optimum currency areas, focused on the characteristics that determine whether a country would be better off, in terms of its ability to maintain internal and external balance, with a fixed or a flexible exchange rate arrangement. That literature generally indicated that small open economies, meaning economies where trade represents a large proportion of GNP, are better served by a fixed exchange rate. The less diversified a country's production and export structure is and the more geographically concentrated its trade, the stronger also is the case for a fixed exchange rate. The attractiveness of a

† The contents of this chapter are discussed in more detail in Kettell, B. (2000) *What Drives Currency Markets?* Financial Times–Prentice Hall.

fixed exchange rate is also greater, the higher the degree of factor mobility is, the less a country's inflation rate diverges from that of its main trading partners, and the lower the level of economic and financial development is (see Table 8.1).

Another approach to the choice of exchange rate regime has focused on the effects of various random disturbances on the domestic economy. The optimal regime in this framework is the one that stabilizes macroeconomic performance, that is, minimizes fluctuations in output, real consumption, the domestic price level, or some other macroeconomic variable. The ranking of fixed and flexible exchange rate regimes depends on the nature and source of the shocks to the economy, policy makers' preferences (i.e., the type of costs they wish to minimize), and the structural characteristics of the economy. An extension of this approach assumes that the choice of exchange rate regime is not simply one between a perfectly fixed or a freely floating exchange rate. Rather, it is suggested that there is a range of regimes of varying degrees of exchange rate flexibility reflecting different intensities of official intervention in the foreign exchange market. The typical finding is that a fixed exchange rate (or a greater degree of fixity) is generally superior if the disturbances impinging on the economy are predominantly domestic nominal shocks, such as sudden changes in the demand for money. A flexible rate (or a greater degree of flexibility) is preferable if disturbances are predominantly foreign shocks or domestic real shocks, such as shifts in the demand for domestic goods.

Credibility versus flexibility

A more recent strand of analysis has emphasized the role of credibility and political factors in the choice of exchange rate regime. A point that emerges from this analysis is that when the domestic rate of inflation is extremely high, a pegged exchange rate (by providing a clear and transparent nominal anchor) can help to establish the credibility of a stabilization programme. An exchange rate anchor may also be preferable because of instability in the demand for money as inflation is reduced sharply. This contrasts with the traditional view that the less a country's inflation rate diverges from that of its main trading partners the more desirable is a fixed exchange rate.

In some cases, a fixed exchange rate can help to discipline a country's economic policies, especially fiscal policy. This is particularly relevant for developing countries that do not have the same capacity as advanced economies to separate fiscal and monetary policy. A fixed exchange rate constrains the authorities' use of what is known as the 'inflation tax' as a source of revenue, the more so if the exchange rate is rigidly fixed as in a monetary union or a currency board.

The idea that inflation is a form of tax is based on the principle that we need to hold more cash when inflation rises. For example, when inflation is 10 per cent per year, a person who holds currency for a year loses 10 per cent of the purchasing power of that money and thus effectively pays a 10 per cent tax on the real money holdings. The beneficiary here being the government as they have purchased goods and services, which was the cause of the inflation in the first place. The advantage of the fixed exchange rate here is that if the commitment not to use the inflation tax implied by the adoption of a rigidly fixed exchange rate is credible, it allows the authorities to tie down private sector expectations of inflation. In contrast, a flexible exchange rate provides the authorities with greater scope for revenue from seigniorage, i.e., the revenue that the government raises by printing money, but at the expense of a lack of precommitment as regards future inflation. An adjustable peg provides the authorities with the option to devalue and tax the private sector by generating unanticipated inflation. The risk here, however, is that the peg may become unsustainable if confidence in the authorities' willingness, or ability to maintain it, is lost.

In this framework, the choice of regime involves a trade-off between 'credibility' and 'flexibility', and may depend not only on the nature of the economy and the disturbances to which it is subject but also on political considerations. For instance, it may be more costly politically to adjust a pegged exchange rate than to allow the nominal exchange rate to move by a corresponding amount in a more flexible exchange rate arrangement. This is because the former is clearly visible and involves an explicit government decision, while the latter is less of an event and can be attributed to market forces. When the political costs of exchange rate adjustments are high, it is therefore more likely that a more flexible exchange rate arrangement will be adopted, the more so the larger and more frequent the expected adjustment under a pegged regime.

Choice of peg: single currency or basket?

When the choice of regime has been made in favour of a pegged exchange rate, a further choice arises between pegging to a single currency and pegging to a basket of currencies. When the peg is to a single currency, fluctuations in the anchor currency imply fluctuations in the effective (trade-weighted) exchange rate of the currency in question. By pegging to a currency basket instead, a country can reduce the vulnerability of its economy to fluctuations in the values of the individual currencies in the basket. Thus, in a world of floating exchange rates among the major currencies, the case for a single currency peg is stronger if the peg is to be the currency of the dominant trading partner. However, in some cases, a significant portion of the country's debt service may be denominated in other currencies. This may complicate the choice of currency to which to peg. For instance for a number of East Asian countries the United States is the major export market, but debt is often serviced largely in Japanese yen. With their currencies typically pegged to dollar-denominated baskets, movements in the yen–dollar rate in recent years have thus posed difficulties for some of these countries.

Macroeconomic characteristics of exchange rate regimes

Traditionally a distinction in discussing exchange rate arrangements is to differentiate between 'pegged' and 'flexible' exchange rate systems. The former comprises arrangements in which the domestic currency is pegged to a single foreign currency or to a basket of currencies, including the Special Drawing Right, discussed below. The latter consists of arrangements in which the exchange rate is officially classified as 'managed' or 'independently floating'.

The major difference in economic performance between these two groupings of exchange rate arrangements is with respect to inflation. Inflation in countries with pegged exchange rates has historically been consistently lower and less volatile than in countries with more flexible exchange rate arrangements, but the difference has narrowed substantially in the 1990s. In contrast to the marked difference in inflation performance across regimes, there is no clear relationship between exchange rate regime and output growth over the past two decades as a whole. During the 1990s, however, the median growth rate in countries with flexible exchange rate arrangements appears to have been higher than in countries with pegged exchange rates between the two sets of exchange rate arrangements.

Countries that have officially declared flexible exchange rate regimes are on average larger economies. They are also less open, where openness is measured by the ratio of trade to output, which partly reflects the fact that larger economies tend to be more self-sufficient. These findings accord with the theory of optimal currency areas, which predicts that, all else being equal, the smaller and more open is an economy, the stronger is the case for a fixed exchange rate.

So what are the lessons with respect to the choice of an exchange rate regime?

In an era when countries are becoming increasingly linked to one another through trade and capital flows, the functioning of a country's exchange rate regime is a critical factor in economic policy making. At issue is the extent to which a country's economic performance and the mechanism whereby monetary and fiscal policies affect inflation and growth are dependent on the exchange rate regime.

There is no perfect exchange rate system. What is best depends on a particular economy's characteristics. A useful analysis in the IMF's May 1997 *World Economic Outlook* considers some of the factors which affect the choice. These include the following.

- **Size and openness of the economy**. If trade is a large share of GDP, then the costs of currency instability can be high. This suggests that small, open economies may be best served by fixed exchange rates.
- **Inflation rate**. If a country has much higher inflation than its trading partners, its exchange rate needs to be flexible to prevent its goods from becoming uncompetitive in world markets. If inflation differentials are more modest, a fixed rate is less troublesome.
- **Labour market flexibility**. The more rigid wages are, the greater the need for a flexible exchange rate to help the economy to respond to an external shock.
- **Degree of financial development**. In developing countries with immature financial markets, a freely floating exchange rate may not be sensible because a small number of foreign exchange trades can cause big swings in currencies.
- **The credibility of policymakers**. The weaker the reputation of the central bank, the stronger the case for pegging the exchange rate to build confidence that inflation will be

controlled. Fixed exchange rates have helped economies in Latin America to reduce inflation.

- **Capital mobility**. The more open an economy to international capital, the harder it is to sustain a fixed rate.

Table 8.1 summarizes many of these ideas.

Dollarization and the choice of an exchange rate regime

Dollarization, the holding by residents of a significant share of their assets in foreign currency-denominated form, in this case the US dollar, is a common feature of developing and transition economies. It is a response to economic instability and high inflation, and to the desire of domestic residents to diversify their asset portfolios. In countries experiencing high inflation dollarization is typically quite widespread as the public seeks protection from the cost of holding assets denominated in domestic currency.

To best understand the role of dollarization in influencing the choice of exchange rate regime, it is useful to distinguish between two motives for holding foreign currency assets: currency substitution and asset substitution. Currency substitution occurs when assets denominated in foreign currency are used as a means of payment, while asset substitution occurs when assets denominated in foreign currency serve as stores of value. Currency substitution typically arises during high inflation, when the cost of holding domestic currency for transactions purposes is high. Asset substitution results from portfolio allocation decisions and reflects the relative risk and return characteristics of domestic and foreign assets. In many developing countries, assets denominated in foreign currency have often provided residents with the opportunity to insure against major domestic macroeconomic risks.

Dollarization introduces additional complications into the choice of exchange rate regime. A key implication of currency substitution is that exchange rates will tend to be more volatile. One reason for this is that there may be frequent and unexpected shifts in the use of domestic and foreign money for transactions, given the ease of switching between domestic money and the dollar. Another is that demand for the domestic currency-denominated component of the money, stock will be

Table 8.1   Considerations in the Choice of Exchange Rate Regime.

Characteristics of Economy	Implication for the Desired Degree of Exchange Rate Flexibility
Size of the economy	The larger the economy, the stronger is the case for a flexible rate.
Openness	The more open the economy, the less attractive is a flexible exchange rate.
Diversified production/ export structure	The more diversified the economy, the more feasible is a flexible exchange rate.
Geographic concentration of trade	The larger the proportion of an economy's trade with one large country, the greater is the incentive to peg to the currency of that country.
Divergence of domestic inflation from world inflation	The more divergent a country's inflation rate from that of its main trading partners, the greater is the need for frequent exchange rate adjustments. (But for a country with extremely high inflation, a fixed exchange rate may provide greater policy discipline and credibility to a stabilization programme.)
Degree of economic/ financial development	The greater the degree of economic and financial development, the more feasible is a flexible exchange rate regime.
Labour mobility	The greater the degree of labour mobility, when wages and prices are downwardly sticky, the less difficult (and costly) is the adjustment to external shocks with a fixed exchange rate.
Capital mobility	The higher the degree of capital mobility, the more difficult it is to sustain a pegged-but-adjustable exchange rate regime.
Foreign nominal shocks	The more prevalent are foreign nominal shocks, the more desirable is a flexible exchange rate.
Domestic nominal shocks	The more prevalent are domestic nominal shocks, the more attractive is a fixed exchange rate.
Real shocks	The greater an economy's susceptibility to real shocks, whether foreign or domestic, the more advantageous is a flexible exchange rate.
Credibility of policymakers	The lower the anti-inflation credibility of policymakers, the greater is the attractiveness of a fixed exchange rate as a nominal anchor.

Source: IMF

more sensitive to changes in its expected opportunity cost. Using the jargon of economics, the interest elasticity of domestic money demand will be higher when there is significant currency substitution, meaning that as domestic and foreign interest rates change investors will switch between assets, with the choices depending on expected returns.

In a floating exchange rate regime, this higher elasticity and instability of money demand is likely to result in greater exchange rate volatility. This strengthens the argument for the adoption of a pegged exchange rate when currency substitution is extensive. Nevertheless, the broader considerations, discussed earlier in this chapter, that should guide the choice of exchange rate system, still apply. In particular, if shocks originate mostly in money markets, then fixed exchange rates provide more stability, but if shocks are mostly real in nature, floating rates are superior in stabilizing output.

There is a clear case for fixing the exchange rate when a highly dollarized economy is stabilizing from very high inflation or hyperinflation. Under these circumstances currency substitution is likely to be important, and monetary shocks are likely to predominate, especially as successful stabilization may result in a large but unpredictable increase in the demand for domestic currency. Moreover, during hyperinflation, foreign currency may assume the role of a unit of account, and the exchange rate may also serve as an approximate measure of the price level, making it a powerful guide for influencing expectations in the transition to a low inflation equilibrium. Argentina in 1991 is an example of a country where an exchange rate anchor helped to stop hyperinflation in the context of extensive currency substitution.

Dollarization in the sense of asset substitution also has implications for the choice of an exchange rate regime. The most important may be that the availability of foreign currency deposits in domestic banks increases capital mobility, as the public can potentially shift between foreign currency deposits held with domestic banks to those abroad, as well as between foreign currency-denominated and domestic currency-denominated deposits held in domestic banks. These various assets are likely to be close substitutes for savers, which strengthens the link between interest rates on dollar deposits at home, international dollar interest rates, and domestic currency interest rates. This would limit the control that the central bank can exert on monetary conditions, such as the level of interest rates on domestic currency. In contrast to the implications of currency substitution dollarization, in the sense of asset substitution, may thus increase the usefulness of a flexible exchange rate arrangement in enhancing monetary autonomy.

Why do currencies face speculative attacks?

Krugman's dilemma

Why are currencies repeatedly subject to speculator attacks? In searching for answers to this question Krugman (1998) draws on what he calls his matrix of opinion, which is defined by the different answers to two questions.

The first question is whether flexibility of the exchange rate is useful. A country that fixes its exchange rate, in a world in which investors are free to move their money wherever they like, essentially gives up the opportunity to have its own monetary policy. Interest rates must be set at whatever level makes foreign exchange traders willing to keep the currency close to the fixed target rate. A country that allows its exchange rate to float, on the other hand, can reduce interest rates to fight recessions and raise them to fight inflation. So the first question Krugman asks, is whether this extra freedom of policy is useful or is it merely illusory?

The second question is whether, having decided to float the currency, one can trust the foreign exchange market not to do anything crazy. Will the market set the currency at a value more or less consistent with the economy's fundamental strength and the soundness of the government's policies? Or will the market be subject to alternating bouts of irrational exuberance, to borrow the famous phrase of Federal Reserve Chairman Alan Greenspan, and unjustified pessimism?

The answers one might give to these questions define four boxes, all of which have their adherents. The matrix is illustrated in Figure 8.1.

Suppose that you believe that the policy freedom a country gains from a floating exchange rate is actually worth very little, but you also trust the foreign exchange market not to do anything silly. Then you will be a very relaxed individual. You will not much care what regime is chosen for the exchange rate. You may have a small preference for a fixed rate or better yet a

		Is exchange rate flexibility useful?	
		No	Yes
Can the forex market be trusted?	Yes	Relaxed guy	Serene floater
	No	Determined fixer	Nervous wreck

Figure 8.1 Krugman's matrix.

common currency, on the grounds that stable exchange rates reduce the costs of doing business, Krugman suggests, but you will not lose sleep over the choice.

Suppose on the other hand that you believe that freedom gained by floating is very valuable, and that financial markets can be trusted. Then you will be, what Krugman calls, a serene floater. You will believe in freeing your currency from the constraints of a specific exchange rate target, in order that you can get on with the business of pursuing full employment. This was the view held by many economists in the late 1960s and early 1970s.

You will be equally sure of yourself if you believe the opposite, that foreign exchange markets are deeply unreliable, dominated by those irrational bouts of optimism and pessimism, while the monetary freedom that comes with floating is of little value. You will then be a determined fixer.

But what if you believe both that the freedom that comes from floating is valuable and that the markets that will determine your currency's value under floating are unreliable? Then you will be a nervous wreck, subject to stress-related disorders. You will regard any choice of currency regime as a choice between evils, and will always worry that you have chosen wrongly.

So, given this matrix in which quadrant do we find ourselves? Krugman believes that the nervous wrecks have it. Yes, the monetary freedom of a floating rate is valuable. No, the foreign exchange market cannot be trusted. This reasoning starts with the case for floating currencies. The classic case against floating rates is that any attempt to make use of monetary autonomy will quickly backfire. Assume that a country drops its commitment to a fixed exchange rate and uses that freedom to cut interest rates, which in turn would lead to a decline in the value of the currency. Fixed exchange rate defenders would argue that instead of an increase in employment the result would be a surge in inflation, wiping out both any gain in competitiveness vis-à-vis foreign producers and any stimulus to real domestic demand. The evidence of the United Kingdom, which exited the exchange rate mechanism and painlessly stimulated the economy afterwards, provides a counter argument to this view. So floating exchange rates, it can be argued, do work.

Krugman then turns to whether or not the foreign exchange market can be trusted. The evidence, he suggests, is that the currency markets are not 'efficient' and they are subject to all sorts of anomalies, speculative bubbles, etc. Foreign exchange markets do not exist in a vacuum. What creates an environment in which speculators can make money is the prevalence of finance ministers who decide to fix their currencies but are suspected of being less than total in their commitment to that policy. The original model of such attacks, Krugman stresses, imagined a country that was known to be following policies ultimately inconsistent with keeping its exchange rate fixed – for example, printing money to cover the budget deficit.

More recent research work, Krugman emphasizes, has drawn attention to three further concerns. First, some economists have argued for the importance of self-fulfilling currency crises. They imagine a country whose government is prepared to pay the cost of sticking to an exchange rate indefinitely under normal circumstances, but which is not willing and/or able to put up with the pain of keeping interest rates high enough to support the currency in the face of speculators guessing that it might be devalued. In that case the fixed rate will survive if investors think it will, but it will also collapse if they think it will!

Second, there is the obvious point that if markets are subject to irrational shifts in opinion, for example forgetting the 'fundamentals' and simply running with the herd, this applies as much to speculative attacks on fixed exchange rates as to gyrations in the value of flexible exchange rates. One remarkable fact is that there was no sign in the markets that the great currency crises of the nineties were anticipated. Until only a few weeks before Black Wednesday in Britain in 1992, or the Mexican crisis of 1994, investors were cheerfully putting their money into pounds or pesos without demanding any exceptional risk premium. Then quite suddenly everyone wanted out. Was this because of some real news, or was it simply the observation that everyone else suddenly wanted out?

Finally, there is the return of the gnomes of Zurich. Finance ministers whose currencies are under attack invariably blame their problems on the nefarious schemes of foreign market manipulators. Economists usually treat such claims with derision. But a casual perusal of business magazines in the last few years would suggest that there appear to be investors who not only move money in anticipation of a currency crisis, but actually do their best to trigger that crisis for fun and profit.

There are, of course, two ways to defeat all of these speculative pressures. One is to be basically indifferent to the exchange rate pressure. The other is to lock in the exchange rate beyond all question – something best done by simply creating a common currency, leaving nothing to speculate in.

Which of these is the better solution? This Krugman suggests, is a peculiarly difficult question to answer. The theory of optimum currency areas gives us a checklist of the things that ought to matter. But it is famously hard to turn that checklist into an operational set of criteria. What recent theorising backed by recent experience, Krugman goes on to argue, does seem to indicate, is that a country should make a choice one way or the other. That is, in a world in which hot money can move as easily as it now does, an imperfectly credible fixed exchange rate combines the worst of both worlds. You forsake the policy freedom that comes with a flexible rate, yet you remain open to devastating speculative attacks.

The IMF exchange rate arrangements

Every member of the International Monetary Fund is obliged to notify the IMF of its exchange rate arrangements within 30 days of becoming a member and promptly thereafter of any subsequent changes. Since 1973, exchange rate regimes adopted by members have covered a broad spectrum, ranging by degree of flexibility from single currency pegs to free floats. Most countries have adopted regimes that fall fairly readily into one or another of the major categories of the classification system adopted by the IMF in 1982. Countries with dual or multiple exchange markets normally have one market that is clearly the most important, and the IMF's classification refers to that market.

Within the group of fixed-rate arrangements, several deserve separate discussion. In the most pure form of a single currency peg, the currency of another country circulates as legal tender; for example, the Australian dollar in Kiribati, and the US dollar in Liberia, the Marshall Islands, the Federated States of Micronesia, Ecuador and in Panama. In these countries, the financial stability provided by unifying the currency with the currency of the larger country, and thereby reducing administrative costs, was judged to be more important than the loss of seigniorage and the absence of an independent monetary policy.

A closely related type of peg is a currency board arrangement, whereby the country in question pegs its currency to the currency of a larger country, and simultaneously its issue of domestic currency is fully backed by the foreign currency of the larger country. Argentina, Estonia, Hong Kong, Lithuania, and Singapore, amongst others, use modified versions of currency boards.

A currency union is an arrangement under which a common currency circulates at par among the members. The seven currencies that make up the West African Economic and Monetary Union (WAEMU) maintain a common currency, the CFA franc, which has a fixed exchange rate against the French franc/euro. The countries in the WAEMU are Benin, Burkina Faso, Côte d'Ivoire, Guinea-Bissau, Mali, Niger, Senegal and Togo. The CFA franc was, prior to the introduction of the euro, also issued at the same fixed exchange rate to the six member countries of the Central African Monetary Area in which the CFA franc was also the common currency. These countries are Cameroon, Central African Republic, Chad, Republic of Congo, Equatorial Guinea and Gabon. Similarly, six Caribbean countries also maintain fixed exchange arrangements and use a common currency, the Eastern Caribbean dollar, which is issued by the Eastern Caribbean Central Bank and is pegged to the US dollar. These countries are Antigua and Barbuda, Dominica, Grenada, St Lucia, and St Vincent and the Grenadines.

At the other end of the spectrum, the distribution between managed and independently floating arrangements reflects the policy stance for full, or limited, market determination of the exchange rate. In countries with managed regimes, as with pegged and other less flexible regimes, the foreign exchange market does not necessarily clear, even in the limited sense of equalizing supply and demand in the presence of restrictions on foreign exchange flows, and the result has often been the emergence of a parallel, or black market, exchange rate. In contrast, under independently floating regimes, supply and demand is in continuous equality, albeit in the very short run. Currency market intervention is limited in the independently floating group because, by definition, the authorities may intervene only to smooth the exchange rate and are not striving to establish a particular level for it.

The number of member countries that peg their currencies to a single currency or a basket of currencies has decreased in recent years. This decrease is even more marked if one excludes individual country peggers that adhere to some form of regional arrangement and thus have less true discretion regarding their choice of regime. At the other extreme, the number of countries with more flexible exchange rates (particularly independently floating) regimes has increased. In some cases a currency can be classified into more than one category.

What is the current worldwide exchange rate system? (October 2001)

The IMF sets out its exchange rate classifications using the following taxonomy.

Exchange arrangements with no separate legal tender (39 countries)

Under this system the currency of another country circulates as the sole legal tender or, alternatively, the member belongs to a monetary or currency union in which the same legal tender is shared by the members of the union. It is useful to break down this group into countries that use another currency than their own as legal tender. This includes the following countries.

Group One

Ecuador	Palau
Kiribati	Panama
Marshall Islands	San Marino
Micronesia	

Group Two
The East Caribbean Common Market (ECCM).[1] This includes the following countries:

Antigua & Barbuda	St Kitts & Nevis
Dominica	St Lucia
Grenada	St Vincent & the Grenadines

Group Three

The West African Economic and Monetary Union (WAEMU). This includes the following countries:

Benin	Mali
Burkina Faso	Niger
Côte d'Ivoire	Senegal
Guinea-Bissau	Togo

Group Four

The Central African Economic Monetary Community (CAEMC). This includes the following countries:

Cameroon	Congo, Republic of
Central African Republic	Equatorial Guinea
Chad	Gabon

Group Five

Euro area. The classification of the Euro area in this category is based on the fact that, until they are withdrawn in the first half of 2002, national currencies will retain their status as legal tender within their home territories.[2] This classification includes the following countries:

Austria	Ireland
Belgium	Italy
Finland	Luxembourg
France	Netherlands
Germany	Portugal
Greece	Spain

Currency board arrangements (8 countries)

A currency board is defined by the IMF as a monetary regime based on an implicit legislative commitment to exchange domestic currency for a specified foreign currency at a fixed exchange rate, combined with restrictions on the issuing authority to ensure the fulfilment of its legal obligation. Countries applying a currency board arrangement are:

Argentina	China, P.R.: Hong Kong
Bosnia and Herzegovina	Djibouti
Brunei Darussalam	Estonia
Bulgaria	Lithuania

Other conventional fixed peg arrangements (44 countries)

Under this system the country pegs its currency (formally or de facto) at a fixed rate to a major currency or a basket of currencies where the exchange rate fluctuates within a narrow margin of at most ±1 per cent around a central rate. Countries adopting this system can be broken down into countries that adopt a single peg against a single currency, and those that adopt a single peg against a currency composite. Countries applying a fixed peg against a single currency are:

Aruba	Malaysia
Bahamas, The[3]	Maldives[4]
Bahrain[4,5]	Namibia
Barbados	Nepal
Belize	Netherlands Antilles
Bhutan	Oman
Cape Verde	Pakistan
China, P.R. Mainland[4]	Qatar[4,5]
Comoros[6]	Saudi Arabia[4,5]
El Salvador[4]	Syrian Arab Republic[3]
Iran[3,4]	Swaziland
Iraq	Trinidad & Tobago
Jordan[4]	Turkmenistan[4]
Lebanon[4]	United Arab Emirates[4,5]
Lesotho	Zimbabwe
Macedonia, FYR[4]	

Countries applying a fixed peg arrangement against a composite currency, defined below, are:

Botswana[3]	Myanmar[3]
Burundi	Samoa
Fiji	Seychelles
Kuwait	Solomon Islands
Latvia	Tonga
Malta	Vanuatu
Morocco	

The special drawing right (SDR)

The Special Drawing Right (SDR), also known as a currency composite, is an international reserve asset created by the IMF in 1969 and allocated to its members to supplement existing reserve assets. The value of the SDR, determined daily on the basis of a basket of currencies, tends to be more stable than that of any single currency in the basket. Movements in the exchange rate of any one component currency will tend to be partly or fully offset by movements in the exchange rates of the other currencies.

The composition of the basket is reviewed every five years to ensure that the currencies included in it are representative of those used in international transactions and that the weights assigned to the currencies reflect their relative importance in the world's trading and financial systems. Between 1981 and 1999, the currencies of five countries, France, Germany, Japan, the United Kingdom, and the United States, were included in the basket because successive reviews had determined that these were the five countries with the largest exports of goods and services. The reviews also specify the initial weights of the currencies in the basket, reflecting their relative importance in international trade and reserves, as measured by the value of exports of goods and services of the countries issuing them and the balances of the currencies held as reserves by members of the IMF.

With the introduction of the euro on 1 January 1999, the currency amounts of the Deutschmark and the French franc in the SDR basket were replaced with equivalent amounts of euros, based on the fixed conversion rates between the euro, the Deutschmark and the French franc announced by the European Council on 31 December 1998.

With effect from 1 January 2001, the IMF has determined that four currencies meet the selection criteria for inclusion in the SDR valuation basket. The weights assigned to the different currencies and the SDR valuation are given in Table 8.2.

Pegged exchange rates within horizontal bands (5 countries)

Under this arrangement the value of the currency is maintained within margins of fluctuation around a formal or de facto fixed peg that are wider than ±1 per cent around a central rate. Countries applying this system can be broken down into two groups: those within a co-operative arrangement usually referred to as ERM II, discussed in detail below, or those falling under what the IMF calls 'Other Band Arrangements'[4].

Table 8.2 SDR Valuation on 1 January 2001

Currency	Currency Amount*	Exchange rate on January 1st†	US Dollar equivalent‡
Euro	0.426	0.9302	0.396265
Japanese yen	21.0	114.87	0.182815
Pound sterling	0.0984	1.4922	0.146832
US dollar	0.577	1.00000	0.577000
		Total	1.30291

SDR 1 = US$1.30291
US$1 = SDR 0.767512§
* The currency components of the SDR basket.
† Exchange rates in terms of currency units per US dollar, except for the euro and the pound sterling, which are expressed in US dollars per currency unit.
‡ The US dollar equivalents of the currency amounts.
§ The official SDR value of the US dollar, which is the reciprocal of the total of the US dollar equivalents

Countries falling into ERM II are:

Denmark.

Countries falling into Other Band Arrangements are:

Cyprus   Suriname
Iceland   Vietnam
Libyan A.J.

Crawling pegs (5 countries)

Under this arrangement the currency is adjusted periodically in small amounts at a fixed, preannounced rate or in response to changes in selective quantitative indicators. Countries applying this system are:

Bolivia   Turkey
Costa Rica   Zimbabwe
Nicaragua

Exchange rates within crawling bands (6 countries)

Under this arrangement the currency is maintained within certain fluctuation margins around a central rate that is adjusted periodically at a fixed preannounced rate or in response to changes in selective quantitative indicators. Countries applying this system are:

Honduras	Sri Lanka
Hungary	Uruguay
Israel	Venezuela

Managed floating with no preannounced path for the exchange rate (33 countries)

Here the monetary authority influences the movements of the exchange rate through active intervention in the foreign exchange market without specifying, or precommitting to, a preannounced path for the exchange rate. Countries applying this system are:

Algeria	Mauritania
Azerbaijan	Nigeria
Belarus[3]	Norway
Burundi	Pakistan
Cambodia[3]	Paraguay
Croatia	Romania
Czech Republic	Russian Federation
Dominican Rep[3]	Rwanda
Egypt	Singapore
Ethiopia	Slovak Republic
Guatemala	Slovenia
India	Sudan
Jamaica	Tajikistan
Kazakhstan	Tunisia
Kenya	Ukraine
Kyrgyz Republic	Uzbekistan
Lao PDR[3]	

Independent floating (45 countries)

Here the exchange rate is market determined, with any foreign exchange intervention aimed at moderating the rate of change and preventing undue fluctuations in the exchange rate, rather than at establishing a level for it. Countries applying this system are:

Afghanistan[3]	Brazil
Albania	Congo, Democratic Republic of
Angola	Canada
Armenia	Colombia
Australia	Chile

Eritrea

Gambia, The

Georgia

Ghana

Guinea

Guyana

Haiti

Indonesia

Japan

Korea

Liberia

Madagascar

Mauritius[4]

Mexico

Moldova

Mongolia

Mozambique

New Zealand

Papua New Guinea

Peru

Philippines

Poland

São Tomé and Principe[3]

Sierra Leone

Somalia[3]

South Africa

Sweden

Switzerland

Tanzania

Thailand

United Kingdom

United States

Uganda

Yemen, Rep. of

Zambia[3]

The 'Euroization' of the foreign exchange market

The introduction of the euro on 1 January 1999 has meant that relationships between members of the euro bloc, the former EMS currencies, have now altered. In this section we describe the impact of the euro on the exchange rate regimes applied in both non-participating European countries and on other countries affected by the change. Finally, we describe the operational features of the European Exchange Rate Mechanism (ERM II), a mechanism which will be applied to the countries formally applying for membership of the European Union.

The introduction of the euro has meant that changes to the pegging arrangements formerly in place have had to be made. These changes range from the introduction of the euro as their own currency to the adoption of exchange rate regimes involving the use of the euro. Some of these arrangements are a legacy of past links to the former euro area national currencies. Besides these ad hoc monetary agreements there are also approximately 50 countries around the euro area that currently have exchange rate regimes involving the euro.

We discussed earlier the group of countries whose currency is pegged to the euro. Between January 1999 and January 2001 two European Union member states, Denmark and Greece, participated in the new exchange rate mechanism (ERM II), discussed below, that links the currencies of the EU member states to the euro on a bilateral and voluntary basis. The Greek drachma was formally linked to the euro with effect from 1 January 2001.

The exchange rate regimes, involving a link to the euro or to a basket of currencies including the euro, are illustrated in Table 8.3. These can be broken down into five groups.

- The first group consists of the various ad hoc arrangements that have been introduced largely relating to French territorial communities, to the Vatican City, The Republic of San Marino, and to the Principality of Monaco.
- The second group (Bosnia-Herzogovina, Bulgaria and Estonia) have adopted euro/Deutsche Mark-based currency boards. The formal substitution of the euro for the Deutsche Mark in these exchange rate regimes is planned to take place, at the latest, upon the introduction of the euro banknotes in 2002.
- A third group have peg arrangements where the pegs are either only to the euro (19 countries), pegging to the SDR (9 countries), or pegging to other currency baskets including the euro (9 countries). This group includes those countries with currencies pegged to the Special Drawing Right (SDR). When it was introduced the euro, as discussed earlier, automatically replaced the fixed currency amounts of the Deutsche Mark and the French franc in the SDR basket. The components of the SDR are illustrated in Table 8.2.
- A fourth group, Hungary, Turkey, Chile and Israel, have crawling fluctuation bands.
- A fifth group, Croatia, Czech Republic, FYR Macedonia, Poland, Slovak Republic and Slovenia, have managed floating with the euro used as reference currency. This group has adopted a system of managed floating with the euro used informally as the reference currency.

The European Exchange Rate Mechanism: ERM II

On 1 January 1999, at the start of stage three of European Economic and Monetary Union (EMU), the currencies of 11 EU member states merged into the euro, forming a common and

Table 8.3 Exchange rate regimes involving a link to the euro or to a basket of currencies including the euro (*)

Exchange rate regime	Number of countries/ Territorial communities	Countries/Territorial communities
Exchange rate arrangements with no separate legal tender	4	French territorial communities of Saint-Pierre-et-Miquelon and Mayotte. The Republic of San Marino, the Vatican City and the Principality of Monaco *will* be entitled to use the euro as their official currency subject to an agreement with the European Union. Negotiations are currently in place with Monaco, and have been recently concluded with San Marino and Vatican City
Currency board arrangements	3	Bosnia-Herzegovina, Bulgaria, Estonia
Peg arrangements (including pegging to the SDR and other currency baskets including the euro)	18	*Pegging only to the euro*: Cyprus, Denmark, 14 African countries of which the CFA franc is the legal tender, Cape Verde, Comoros
	9	*Pegging to the SDR(*)*: Latvia, Bahrain, Botswana, Jordan, Libyan Arab Jamahiriya, Myanmar, Qatar, Saudi Arabia, United Arab Emirates
	9	*Pegging to other currency baskets including the euro*: Iceland, Malta, Bangladesh, Botswana, Burundi, Chile, Morocco, Seychelles, Vanuatu
Crawling fluctuation bands	5	Hungary, Turkey (basket), Chile (basket), Israel (basket)
Managed floating with the euro used as a reference currency	6	Croatia, Czech Republic, FYR Macedonia, Poland, Slovak Republic, Slovenia

Total: 53

* Besides exchange rate regimes, the phenomenon of *direct currency substitution* deserves also a mention. Deutsche mark banknotes have been recognized by the UN administration as preferred means of payment for official transactions in Kosovo.
This weight has been adjusted to 29% as of 1.01.2001, as a result of the quinquennial revision of the SDR basket.
Source: ECB monthly bulletins.

independent currency. Previously, those 11 currencies had been linked by the exchange rate mechanism (ERM) of the European Monetary System (EMS). On that date, the euro superseded the European Currency Unit (ECU), which was defined in principle as a basket currency, in the ratio of 1:1, as provided in the EC Treaty. At the same time, the EMS ceased to exist. However, in order to foster the convergence process in the member states that are not yet participating in the single monetary policy, and to strengthen and underpin the single market, some member states that were not introducing the euro from the outset (Denmark and Greece) were given an opportunity to prepare themselves for full integration into the euro area by linking their currencies to the euro in the context of a new, modified exchange rate mechanism. As discussed earlier, Greece joined the euro arrangements with effect from 1 January 2001.

This section provides an overview of the structural and operational features of the new exchange rate mechanism, known as ERM II for short. Although only Denmark now participates in ERM II, as membership of the European Union increases (as discussed below) it can be expected that many of the potential new members will be obliged to accede to ERM II type arrangements.

Legal basis

In legal terms the new exchange rate mechanism rests on two pillars. The first is the 'Resolution of the European council on the establishment of an exchange rate mechanism in the third stage of economic and monetary union' of June 1977, which defines the principles and objectives of the system and its main structural features. Second, the decision-making bodies of the European Central Bank (ECB), i.e., the Governing Council and the General Council, agreed on 1 September 1998 on the text of an agreement between the ECB and the central banks of the EU member states outside the euro area, which specifies the operating procedures of ERM II. Subsequently, that agreement was signed by the relevant parties, i.e., by the ECB President and the Governors of the central banks of the four non-euro area member states.

Objectives

The introduction of the euro in 12 of the 15 EU member states has given rise to a fundamentally new situation for European monetary policy. The vast majority of the member states have transferred their monetary policy sovereignty to the European central bank, while Denmark, Sweden and the United Kingdom will continue to pursue autonomous monetary and foreign exchange policies for the time being. Even so, Article 109 of the EC Treaty requires those member states to treat their exchange rate policy as a matter of common interest.

Linking the currencies of the member states that are not participating in the euro area from the outset (known as the 'pre-ins') to the euro will, it is hoped, give those countries a strong incentive to pursue stability-oriented economic and monetary policies. That is particularly important for those EU member states which are seeking to join the euro area in the foreseeable future but which have not yet reached the degree of economic convergence required by the EC Treaty. Equally, it is hoped that the new reference system will counteract possible speculative exchange rate fluctuations that are unwarranted, given the economic fundamentals. Thus it is hoped that foreign exchange market turmoil within the European Union, such as has often occurred in the past, can be largely avoided.

Principles

In much the same way as in the previous EMS, 'pre-ins' are, in principle, free to participate actively in the new exchange rate mechanism. Countries that do not participate from the outset can do so at a later stage. However, the European Council has drawn attention to the fact that member states with a derogation, which is not participating in the full euro arrangement, will be expected to join ERM II. Participation is compulsory for those EU member states that are seeking to introduce the euro in the foreseeable future, since the convergence criterion spelt out in Article 109 of the EC Treaty requires their participation in the exchange rate mechanism for at least two years without devaluation and within the 'normal' fluctuation margins.

At their own request, Denmark and Greece participated in the new exchange rate mechanism from 1 January 1999. This was the outcome of an informal agreement between the ministers of the euro-area member states, the ECB and the ministers and central bank governors of Denmark and Greece, involving the European commission and after consulting the Monetary Committee, in September 1998. The Greek drachma joined the euro arrangement with effect from 1 January 2001. A fluctuation band of ±2.25 per cent has been agreed for Denmark.

Against the background of the experience gained with the existing EMS, the new exchange rate mechanism has been designed to be more flexible in a number of areas. The underlying motive here was that the objective of maintaining price stability, which has been given priority by the ECB and by the national central banks, must in no circumstances be jeopardized. Thus, the generally automatic and quantitatively unlimited obligation to intervene in support of exchange rates, once the limits of the fluctuation bands have been reached, may be suspended, if there is a risk of conflict with the European System of Central Banks (ESCB's) primary objective.

In addition, all the parties involved in central exchange rate decisions, including the ECB, have the right to initiate a confidential procedure aimed at reconsidering central rates, in order that necessary adjustments can be carried out in good time. Furthermore, it is now possible for different degrees of progress in convergence on the part of the 'pre-ins' to be taken into consideration. There is a fixed procedure enabling member states whose economic performance has converged very closely with that of the euro-area member states to agree with the ECB on fluctuation bands for their currencies that are narrower than the standard bands envisaged in the Central Bank Agreement.

Structural features: central rates and fluctuation bands

Unlike the situation in the former EMS, which provided for reciprocal central and intervention rates in the form of a parity grid for all the participating currencies, in the new exchange rate mechanism, the euro has expressly been given the role of the anchor currency. Central and intervention rates are all defined in terms of the euro. Hence, the new system is sometimes likened to a 'hub and spokes' approach. Around the central rate of the currency of every 'pre-in' country vis-à-vis the euro, a ±15 per cent standard band for exchange rate fluctuations is fixed. In the case of the standard fluctuation band, the intervention rates are determined by simply adding the 15 per cent margin to, or subtracting it from, the bilateral central rates, and subsequently rounding the result to six significant digits. The central and marginal rates are quoted as the countervalue of one euro and are announced in the markets.

For future participants, a further implication of the new system is that the assessment of their currency's exchange rate stability within ERM II depends only on the relation to the euro. Under the old system, a currency's exchange rate stability was assessed by reference to what was termed a 'divergence indicator', which was based on the deviation of the ECU market rates from the ECU central rates, and therefore incorporated weighted deviations from all other participants in the system.

According to the Resolution of the European Council, decisions on central rates and the standard fluctuation band are taken by mutual agreement between the ministers of the euro-area member states, the ECB, and the ministers and central bank governors of the 'pre-in' member states participating in the new exchange rate system.

Interventions and central rate adjustments

As a matter of principle, the central banks concerned will automatically intervene when the upper or lower intervention points are reached. In the euro area, such operations are normally carried out by the central banks of the 'ins', acting on behalf of the ECB. In each individual case, the initiative for such support measures, which are generally unlimited in amount, proceeds from the market participants who offer their central bank, at which they are required to maintain an account, the weak currency at the marginal rate or seek to buy the strong currency at the intervention rate. However, the notion underlying the Resolution of the European Council and the Central Bank Agreement makes it clear that foreign exchange market intervention to defend central rates are only designed to bolster other policy measures. A stability-orientated monetary and fiscal policy must be at the heart of any central rate stabilization. In particular, the interest rate instrument has to be employed flexibly, in this context, in order to stabilize exchange rates. As described above, the central banks involved may suspend intervention if the overriding objective of maintaining price stability appears to be at risk. Any decision to suspend compulsory intervention would have to take due account of the particular circumstances and of the credible functioning of ERM II.

In the event of shifts in the economic fundamentals between participants in the system (such as changes in the purchasing-power parities), thereby applying pressure to the currencies participating in ERM II, central rates are to be adjusted to the new economic situation faster than had been the case in the EMS. Thus, all the parties involved in decision-making have the right to initiate a confidential procedure aimed at reconsidering central rates. This new element of granting initiator rights to the ECB and national central banks is designed to help de-politicize central rate adjustments and to accelerate adjustment procedures, which are thought to have been sluggish in the past.

Very short-term financing

To enhance the credibility of the intervention commitments assumed automatically accessible, 'very short-term financing facilities' have been established between the ECB and the central banks of the 'pre-ins' participating in the exchange rate mechanism. They serve to ensure that all participants in the system have access to a sufficiently large amount of partner currencies so as to be able to intervene in the foreign exchange market in favour of their currencies, if necessary. However, central banks which seek recourse to short-term financing are required to make appropriate use of their own foreign reserve holdings for their support operations before taking up such loans. In the event of compulsory intervention, the financing is in principle unlimited in amount, has an initial maturity of three months and is denominated in the currency of the creditor central bank. In much the same way as the interventions, it may be suspended if the target of stability would otherwise be at risk.

This very short-term financing facility may also be used in the event of intramarginal interventions, but only up to specified ceilings fixed for the central banks of the 'pre-in' member states. These ceilings for cumulative borrowing are defined as twice the amount formerly made available to the respective national banks in the context of the short-term monetary support mechanism. Under this arrangement, the ceilings for the central banks amount to euro 520 million for Denmark, euro 990 million for Sweden and euro 3480 million for the United Kingdom. These amounts are notional for the central banks of the member states that are not participating in ERM II – the United Kingdom and Sweden. The ceilings for the ECB and the central banks of the 'ins' have been set at zero, which also indicates that the ECB, as the anchor central bank, and the other central banks of the 'ins' will not engage in intramarginal intervention as a matter of principle.

Monitoring

The General Council of the European Central Bank (which comprises the central bank governors of the 'ins', the ECB's president and vice president, and the central bank governors of the 'pre-ins') monitors the functioning of the new exchange rate mechanism. Equally, the General Council serves as a forum for monetary and exchange rate policy co-ordination between all EU central banks, and for assessing the administration of the intervention and financing mechanisms specified in the Agreement. In addition, it has to monitor, on a permanent basis, the sustainability of exchange rate relations between every currency participating in ERM II and the euro.

The future

The new exchange rate mechanism is also likely to be of significance in the light of the expected enlargement of the European Union to include a number of countries in central and eastern Europe. Once these countries have joined the EU, they will be able, in principle, to adjust their currencies to the euro by participating in the exchange rate mechanism. It remains to be seen how fast the individual countries will be able to adapt their economic and monetary policies to conditions in the euro area, thus meeting the requirements for adopting the euro at a later stage.

Notes relating to IMF exchange rate classifications (pp. 187–193).

(1) These countries also have a currency board arrangement within the common market.
(2) Until they are withdrawn in the first half of 2002, national currencies will retain their status as legal tender within their home territories.
(3) Member maintained exchanged rate arrangement involving more than one market. The arrangement shown is that maintained in the major market.
(4) The indicated country has a de facto arrangement under a formally announced policy of managed or independent floating. In the case of Jordan, it indicates that the country has a de jure peg to the SDR but a de facto peg to the US dollar. In the case of Mauritius, the authorities have a de facto policy of independent floating, with only infrequent intervention by the central bank.
(5) Exchange rates are determined on the basis of a fixed relationship with the SDR, within margins of up to ±7.25 per cent. However, because of the maintenance of a relatively stable relationship with the US dollar these margins are not always observed.

(6) Comoros has the same arrangement with the French Treasury as do the CFA Franc Zone countries.

(7) The band width for these countries is, Cyprus (±2.25 per cent), Denmark (±2.25 per cent), Iceland (±9 per cent), Libya (±77.5 per cent), and Vietnam (0.1 per cent daily movement, one sided).

(8) The band for these countries is Honduras (±7.0 per cent), Hungary (±2.25 per cent), Israel (±19%), Sri Lanka (±14 per cent), Uruguay (±3 per cent), and Venezuela (±7.5 per cent).

9

Why are exchange rates so volatile? The fundamental and the asset market approach†

'There is no sphere of human thought in which it is easier to show superficial cleverness and the appearance of superior wisdom than in discussing questions of currency and exchange.'
(Winston Churchill, 1925)

Exchange rate determination over the long term: the fundamental approach

The fundamental approach to the determination of exchange rates refers to those factors that render a given path for exchange rate as being sustainable over time. It is useful to break down these long run factors into various categories.

- International competitiveness
- Macro-economic balance
- Tariffs and Quotas
- Preference for Domestic versus Foreign Goods
- Productivity.

† The contents of this chapter are discussed in more detail in Kettell, B. (2000) *What Drives Currency Markets?* Financial Times-Prentice Hall.

The law of one price

The starting point for understanding how exchange rates are determined is a simple idea called the law of one price. This states that if two countries produce an identical good, the price of the good should be the same throughout the world no matter which country produces it. Suppose American steel costs $100 per ton and Japanese steel costs 10 000 yen per ton and that the steel is identical. The law of one price suggests that the exchange rate between the yen and the dollar must be 100 yen per dollar ($0.01 per yen) in order for one ton of American steel to sell for 10 000 yen in Japan (the price of Japanese steel) and one ton of Japanese steel to sell for $100 in the United States. If the exchange rate were 200 yen/$, then Japanese steel would sell for $50 per ton in the United States or $50 less than the American steel, while American steel would sell for 20 000 yen per ton in Japan (10 000 yen more than Japanese steel). Because American steel would be more expensive than Japanese steel in both countries and, as it is identical to Japanese steel, the demand for American steel would go to zero. Given a fixed dollar price for the American steel, the resulting excess supply of American steel will be eliminated only if the exchange rate falls to 100 yen/$, making the price of American steel equal to Japanese steel in both countries.

International competitiveness

This is the Purchasing Power Parity (PPP) approach, which focuses on the analysis of the real exchange rate. In line with PPP theory, when prices of American goods rise (holding prices of foreign goods constant), the demand for American goods falls and the dollar tends to depreciate so that American goods can still sell well. On the other hand, if prices of Japanese goods rise so that the relative prices of American goods fall, the demand for American goods increases and the dollar tends to appreciate, because American goods will continue to sell well even with a higher value of the domestic currency. In the long run, a rise in a country's price level (relative to the foreign price level) causes its currency to depreciate, while a fall in the country's relative price level causes its currency to appreciate.

The attraction of PPP lies in its relative simplicity. Once one has identified the relevant indicators and basket of goods, one can apply the principle. While providing useful inputs to any assessment of the fundamentals, PPP, however, suffers from a number of drawbacks that reduces its value when measuring a currency's fundamentals. Two of the most significant are as follows.

- The need for careful choice of the base period for comparison. Not only does the external account of the economy in questions have to be in equilibrium but it also needs to be a good base period for partner countries – a condition seldom fulfilled.
- The approach is also based on an unchanging equilibrium exchange rate, which may in fact alter through time to reflect a myriad of factors, from changing technologies to changes in the propensity to save and invest. Hence while the signals from PPP are an important part of the fundamentals, a more comprehensive approach is required to get a full assessment of the appropriate level of the exchange rate.

Macroeconomic balance

Sustainability lies at the heart of this macroeconomic balance approach, which focuses on both the internal and external balance within an economy.

Internal balance is inextricably linked with the concepts of productive potential and the natural rate of unemployment. An economy can be said to be in internal balance when, against a background of full employment, it is expanding at the fastest rate possible without threatening a rise in inflation over the medium term. In Figure 9.1 internal balance is represented by **YY**, which slopes upward because as the real exchange rate rises more domestic demand is diverted to imports, the foreign demand for exports falls, and this then necessitates an increase in domestic demand in order to sustain the same level of output. The area to the right of **YY** shows an economy above its long-run productive potential with inflation pressure building. To the left of **YY** an economy is operating below productive capacity with spare resources.

An economy that is operating with a high level of capacity utilization and with a very low level of unemployment will run an inflation risk if it continues to grow at a rate faster than its productive potential. This would be characterized by point P in Figure 9.2.

External balance can be broadly defined as the net flow of international capital that corresponds to the equilibrium levels

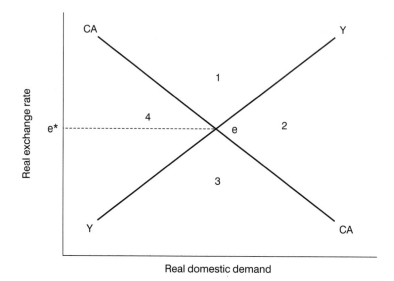

Figure 9.1 Macroeconomic balance and the real exchange rate.

of national savings and investment over the longer term. Assessing external balance will therefore not only necessitate a view on the structural state of a country's current account of the balance of payments but also on its ability to attract sufficient capital to finance the deficit on a sustainable basis.

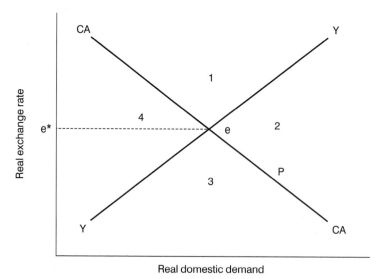

Figure 9.2 Inflation impulse requires rise in real exchange rate.

This will depend, to some extent, on currently existing debt levels as well as rates of return in the domestic economy relative to those available abroad. A country that is a significant net debtor may find it much more difficult to sustain a current account deficit than one that is a substantial creditor. External balance is represented by **CACA** in Figure 9.2. **CACA** slopes downwards because the higher the domestic demand is the lower the external balance is, which then necessitates a lower real exchange rate to offset the deterioration. The area to the left of **CACA** signifies a current account surplus and to the right a current account deficit.

The equilibrium real exchange rate **e*** which sustains both internal and external balance, is determined by the intersection **YY** and **CACA** at point **e**. Hence at **P** in Figure 9.2 the economy is not only above full capacity and therefore in inflation territory, it is also running a current account deficit because **P** is above **CACA**. Internal and external balance are restored at **e** by the real exchange rate rising, reducing the demand for exports and hence domestic employment. As unemployment slows, domestic demand will slow faster than exports, and output will slow sufficiently quickly to relieve the inflation pressure thus restoring internal balance. The slowing in domestic demand will also reduce the demand for imports and external balance will also be re-established at **e**, and with it the equilibrium exchange rate.

The equilibrium real exchange rate in this approach may well vary over time and with structural changes to the domestic economy. German reunification, for instance, led to a large transfer of resources from West Germany to rebuild the economy of the east, and thus a redirection of German savings from abroad to the domestic economy. The implicit reduction in the equilibrium current account moved the **CACA** line to the right which points to a higher equilibrium exchange rate at **e**** (see Figure 9.3).

It is fairly easy to identify episodes from recent economic history, which correspond to the four different quadrants in these diagrams. Some examples, applied to Figure 9.2, are:

Point 1. Depressed output, external deficit – UK and Sweden, 1987–92
Point 2. Inflation pressure, external deficit – United States, 1985
Point 3. Inflation pressure, external surplus – Italy 1995
Point 4. Depressed output, external surplus – Japan 1993

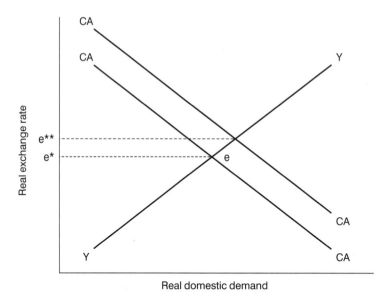

Figure 9.3 A shift in the equilibrium exchange rate.

The macroeconomic balance approach has significant advantages over PPP by providing a framework in which to assess whether movements in the exchange rate are in line with the fundamentals. However, it should be pointed out from the outset that while the framework may be used to identify currency misalignment, other shorter term factors, discussed below, may determine actual movements in the currency. Also while providing an analytical framework, the macroeconomic balance approach inevitably involves a high degree of judgement. Nonetheless it provides a particularly useful means of assessing whether significant shifts in exchange rates are in line with the fundamentals or represent a potentially damaging misalignment.

Tariffs and quotas

Barriers to free trade, such as tariffs (taxes on imported goods) and quotas (restrictions on the quantity of foreign goods that can be imported), can affect the exchange rate. Suppose that the United States imposes a tariff or a quota on Japanese steel. These trade barriers increase the demand for American steel, and the dollar tends to appreciate because American steel will still sell well even with a higher value of the dollar. Tariffs and quotas cause a country's currency to appreciate in the long run.

Preferences for domestic versus foreign goods

If the Japanese develop an appetite for American goods, say for Florida oranges and American movies, then the increased demand for American goods (exports) tends to make the dollar appreciate because the American goods will continue to sell well even with a higher value of the dollar. Likewise, if Americans decide that they prefer Japanese cars to American cars, the increased demand for Japanese goods (imports) tends to depreciate the dollar. Increased demand for a country's exports causes its currency to appreciate in the long run, while increased domestic demand for imports causes its currency to depreciate.

Productivity

If one country becomes more productive than other countries, businesses in that country can lower the prices of domestic goods relative to foreign goods and still earn a profit. As a result, the demand for domestic goods rises and the domestic currency tends to appreciate because domestic goods will continue to sell well with a higher value of the currency. If its productivity lags behind other countries, on the other hand, its goods become relatively more expensive and the currency tends to depreciate. In the long run, as a country becomes more productive relative to other countries, its currency appreciates.

The factors that affect exchange rates in the long run are summarized in Table 9.1.

Table 9.1 Factors That Affect Exchange Rates In the Long Run

Factor	Response of the Exchange Rate (E)†
Domestic price level* ↑	$E \downarrow$
Tariffs and quotas* ↑	$E \uparrow$
Import demand ↑	$E \downarrow$
Export demand ↑	$E \uparrow$
Productivity[a] ↑	$E \uparrow$

Note: Only increases (↑) in the factors are shown; the effects of decreases in the variables on the exchange rate are the opposite of those indicated in the second column.
*Relative to foreign countries
†E is defined so that $E \uparrow$ means that the currency has appreciated. For the United States, this means that E represents units of foreign currency per dollar.
Source: Mishkin and Eakins. *Financial Markets and Institutions*, Addison Wesley, 1998.

Determination of exchange rates in the short run: the asset market approach

Central to understanding the short-run behaviour of exchange rates is to recognize that an exchange rate is the price of domestic bank deposits (those denominated in the domestic currency) in terms of foreign bank deposits (those denominated in the foreign currency). The modern asset approach to explaining exchange rate determination (exemplified by Krugman and Obstfeld (1997) drawn on in this section) does not emphasize the flows of purchases of exports and imports over short periods, because these transactions are quite small relative to the amount of domestic and foreign bank deposits at any given time. Foreign exchange transactions are very large as compared with the flows associated with foreign trade and foreign direct investment. The effect of this is that over short time periods decisions to hold domestic versus foreign assets play a much greater role in exchange rate determination than does the demand for exports and imports.

Assumptions in the asset market approach

To grasp fully the central role that the asset market approach makes to understanding short-term currency movements, we have to make several assumptions. Assume that the United States is the domestic or home country with the implication that domestic bank deposits are denominated in dollars. Also assume that the foreign country is France and that foreign bank deposits are denominated in euros. The theory of asset demand suggests that the most important factor affecting the demand for domestic (dollar) deposits and foreign (euro) deposits is the expected return on these assets relative to one another. When Americans or foreigners expect the return on dollar deposits to be high relative to the return on foreign deposits (euros), there is a higher demand for dollar deposits and a correspondingly lower demand for euro deposits.

To understand how the demands for dollar and foreign deposits change, we need to compare the expected returns on dollar deposits and foreign deposits (euros). First, make the following assumptions:

$i^{\$}$ = Return on dollar deposit

$i^{\euro}$ = Return on euro deposit

E_t = Spot exchange rate, dollar/euro

E_{t+1}^{e} = Expected exchange rate

$\dfrac{(E_{t+1}^{e} - E_t)}{E_t}$ = Expected rate of appreciation of dollar

How would investment returns be seen from a French perspective? To compare the expected returns of dollar deposits and foreign deposits (euros), investors must convert the expected return into the currency they use. Therefore a French investor would see the returns in terms of euros and would go through the following reasoning.

Question: What is the return on a dollar deposit in terms of euros for a French investor (RET$^{\$}$)?

Answer: $RET^{\$} = i^{\$} + \dfrac{(E_{t+1}^{e} - E_t)}{E_t}$

Question: What is the return to a French investor of investing in euros (RET$^{\euro}$)?

Answer: $(RET^{\euro}) = i^{\euro}$
This is simply the return in his local currency.

Question: What is the relative return to French investor, holding euros, of investing in dollars (relative RET$^{\$}$)?

Answer: Relative $RET^{\$} = i^{\$} - i^{\euro} + \dfrac{(E_{t+1}^{e} - E_t)}{E_t}$

So as the relative expected return on dollars (increases) investors will seek to hold more (fewer) dollar deposits and fewer (more) euro deposits.

How would investment returns be seen from an American perspective? An American investor would see any investment return in terms of dollars, so expected returns in euros have

to be converted into dollars. The American investor will be
aware that:

$$\mathrm{RET}^{\mathfrak{E}} = i^{\mathfrak{E}} - \frac{(E^e_{t+1} - E_t)}{E_t}$$

Now assume $i^{\mathfrak{E}} = 5$ per cent. Also assume that the dollar is
expected to appreciate by 4 per cent. Inserting this into the
above formula gives us $5 - 4 = 1$ per cent.

$$\mathrm{RET}^{\$} = i^{\$}$$

Relative return on dollar $\mathrm{RET}^{\$} = i^{\$} - \left[i^{\mathfrak{E}} - \frac{(E^e_{t+1} - E_t)}{E_t} \right]$

$$= i^{\$} - i^{\mathfrak{E}} + \frac{(E^e_{t+1} - E_t)}{E_t}$$

This is the same as the earlier result. So the relative expected
return on dollar deposits is the same whether calculated in
terms of euros or dollars. As the relative expected return on
dollar deposits increases (decreases), both foreigners and
domestic residents respond in exactly the same way – both will
want to hold more (fewer) dollar deposits and fewer (more) euro
deposits. Where does this now take us?

The interest parity conditions

Assume, as is the case, that capital is highly mobile and that
bank deposits are perfect substitutes. Under these circumstances if US dollar returns rise both American and French
investors will demand dollars (and vice versa). Under the asset
market approach in order for the demand for assets (domestic
and foreign) to equal the supply of asset (domestic and foreign)
there must be no difference in their expected returns. This can
be restated in that their relative expected returns must equal
zero. This condition is know as the interest parity condition and
is restated below.

$$i^{\$} = i^{\mathfrak{E}} - \frac{(E^e_{t+1} - E_t)}{E_t}$$

The interest parity condition states that the domestic interest
rate equals the foreign interest rate minus the expected

appreciation of the domestic currency. Alternatively stated this also means that the domestic interest rate equals the foreign interest rate plus the expected appreciation of the foreign currency. For the interest parity conditions to hold it must be the case that if the domestic interest rate is above the foreign interest rate then there must be a positive expected appreciation of the foreign currency, which compensates for the lower foreign interest rate.

So if the domestic interest rate is 15 per cent and the foreign interest rate is 10 per cent, then the domestic currency (foreign currency) is expected to depreciate (appreciate) by 5 per cent.

The importance of the interest parity condition is that only when the exchange rate is such that expected returns on domestic and foreign deposits are equal, i.e., interest parity holds, will the outstanding domestic and foreign deposits be willingly held. Otherwise something must give. Exactly what gives is discussed in the next section.

To illustrate how the interest parity condition affects the foreign exchange market we need to describe how the expected return on euro and dollar deposits change as the current exchange rate changes. Figure 9.4 is used to illustrate the discussion below.

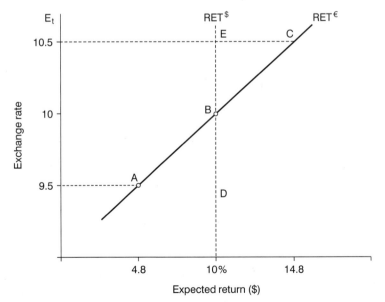

Figure 9.4 The interest parity condition. (Adapted from Mishkin, F.S. and Eakins, S.G. (1998) *Financial Markets and Institutions*. Addison Wesley.)

Expected return on the euro deposit

Earlier we demonstrated that the expected return in terms of dollars on the foreign deposit is

$$RET^€ = i^€ - \frac{(E^e_{t+1} - E_t)}{E_t}$$

Assume that

$i^€$ = 10 per cent
E^e_{t+1} = 10 euros/\$
E_t = 9.5 euros/\$

The expected appreciation of dollar

$$= \frac{10 - 9.5}{9.5} = 0.052 = 5.2\%$$

$RET^€$ = 10% – 5.2% = 4.8% (Point A in Figure 9.4)

Now assume that E_t = 10 euros/\$, then the expected dollar appreciation

$$= \frac{10 - 10}{10} = 0\%$$

$RET^€$ = 10% (Point B in Figure 9.4)

Now assume that E_t = 10.5, then expected dollar appreciation

$$= \frac{10 - 10.5}{10.5} = 0.048\%$$

$$= -14.8\% \text{ (Point C in Figure 9.4)}$$

$RET^€$ = 10% – (–4.8%) = 14.8%

A change in the current exchange rate results in a movement along the expected return schedule for euro deposits ($RET^€$).

$RET^€$ is positively sloped. As E_t rises the expected return on euro deposits rises. The reasoning behind this is that as the current exchange rate of the dollar rises there is less expected appreciation of the dollar. Thus a higher current exchange rate means a greater expected appreciation of the foreign currency (euro) in the future, which increases the expected return on foreign currency deposits in dollars. This is summarized in Figures 9.5 and 9.6.

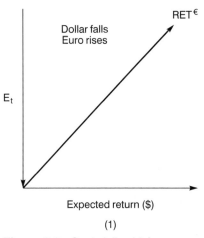

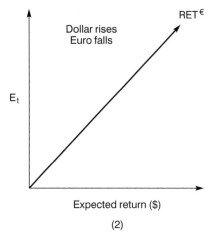

Figure 9.5 Spot dollar high, expected to fall.

Figure 9.6 Spot dollar low, expected to rise.

Expected return on dollar deposits

The expected return on dollar deposits in terms of dollars must be RET$^\$$. Say RET$^\$$ = $i^\$$ = 10 per cent. If E_t = 9.5 then RET$^\$$ = 10 per cent (point D in Figure 9.4). If E_t = 10.0 then RET$^\$$ = 10% (point B in Figure 9. 4). But where is the spot rate?

Say

$$\text{RET}^\$ = \text{RET}^\euro = (\text{point B}) = 10.0$$

$$\text{RET}^\$ < \text{RET}^\euro = (\text{point E}) = 10.5$$

then the market will sell \$/buy euros and the effect is that the dollar falls/euro rises.

Say

$$\text{RET}^\$ > \text{RET}^\euro = (\text{point D}) = 9.5$$

then the market will buy \$/sell euros and the effect is that the dollar rises/euro falls.

Why do exchange rates change?

They change so that the exchange rate settles at the intersection of RET$^\euro$ and RET$^\$$. Naturally if either of these expected return schedules shift then so will the exchange rate. Let us examine the effects of these changes in turn.

Shifts in expected return schedule for foreign deposits

Earlier we established that

$$RET^{\epsilon} = i^{\epsilon} - \frac{(E_{t+1}^e - E_t)}{E_t}$$

A change in E_t will result in a movement along the expected return schedule for euros. Factors that shift the whole schedule will be the remaining terms in this formula, namely the foreign interest rate i^{ϵ} and the expected future exchange rate.

Changes in the foreign interest rate (i^{ϵ})

If i^{ϵ} rises the RET^{ϵ} also rises. In Figure 9.7 RET_1^{ϵ} moves to RET_2^{ϵ}. The dollar falls from E_1 to E_2 as investors sell euros and buy dollars. Naturally if i_{ϵ} falls, RET^{ϵ} moves to the left and the domestic currency, the dollar, appreciates and the euro depreciates.

Changes in the expected future exchange rate E_{t+1}^e

If the future exchange rate of the dollar is expected to fall this decreases the expected appreciation of the dollar and hence

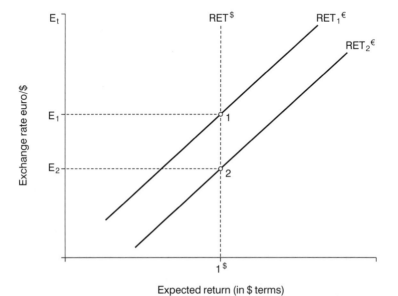

Figure 9.7   Changes in the foreign interest rate.

raises the expected return in euros, moving from $RET_1^{\in}$ to $RET_{2\in}$. The dollar falls from E_1 to E_2. An expectation that the dollar will rise shifts the schedule with the dollar rising and the euro falling.

On the other hand, a rise in E_{t+1}^e raises the expected appreciation of the dollar, lowers the expected return on euro deposits, shifts the $RET^{\in}$ schedule to the left, and raises the exchange rate.

To summarize: a rise in the expected future exchange rate shifts the expected return on foreign (euro) deposits schedule to the left and causes an appreciation of the domestic currency (dollar). A fall in the expected future exchange rate shifts the $RET^{\in}$ schedule to the right and causes a depreciation of the domestic currency (dollar).

Shifts in the expected return schedule for domestic deposits

Since the expected return on domestic (dollar) deposits is just the interest rate on these deposits, $i^{\$}$, this interest rate is the only factor that shifts the expected return on the dollar deposits schedule. This can be seen from Figure 9.8.

Shifts in the expected return on domestic deposits schedule ($RET^{\$}$). An increase in the expected return on dollar deposits ($i^{\$}$),

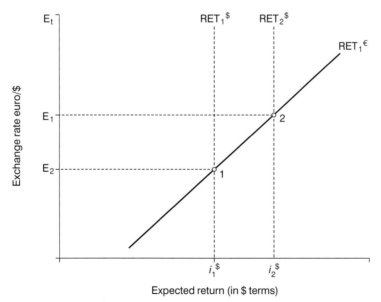

Figure 9.8 Changes in the expected return schedule for foreign deposits.

shifts the expected return on domestic (dollar) deposits from $RET_1^\$$ to $RET_2^\$$ and the exchange rate falls from E_1 to E_2.

Changes in the domestic interest rate ($i^\$$)

A rise in $i^\$$ raises the expected return on dollar deposits, shifts the $RET^\$$ schedule to the right, and leads to a rise in the exchange rate, as shown in Figure 9.8. Another way of seeing this is to recognize that a rise in $i^\$$, which raises the expected return on dollar deposits, creates an excess demand for dollar deposits at the original equilibrium exchange rate, and the resulting purchases of dollar deposits causes an appreciation of the dollar. A rise in the domestic interest rate ($i^\$$) shifts the expected return on domestic deposits to the right and causes an appreciation of the domestic (dollar) currency: a fall in $i^\$$ shifts the $RET^\$$ schedule to the left and causes a depreciation of the dollar.

Our earlier analysis of the long-run determinants of the exchange rate indicated that the factors that influence the expected future exchange rate are: the relative price level, relative tariffs and quotas, import demand, export demand, and relative productivity. The theory of purchasing power parity suggest that if a higher American price level relative to the foreign price level is expected to persist, the dollar will depreciate in the long run. A higher expected relative American price level should thus have a tendency to raise the expected return on euro deposits, shift the $RET^€$ schedule to the right, and lower the current exchange rate.

Similarly the other long-run determinants of the exchange rate we discussed earlier can also influence the expected return on euro deposits and the current exchange rate.

Briefly the following changes will increase the expected return on euro deposits and the current exchange rate. The following changes will increase the expected return on euro deposits, shift the $RET^€$ schedule to the right, and cause a depreciation of the domestic currency, the dollar.

- Expectations of a rise in the American price level relative to the foreign price level;
- Expectations of lower American tariffs and quotas relative to foreign tariffs and quotas;
- Expectations of higher American import demand;
- Expectations of lower foreign demand for American exports; and

- Expectations of lower American productivity relative to foreign productivity.

These effects are summarized in Table 9.2.

Why are exchange rates so volatile?

The answer to this question is provided by the asset market approach to exchange rate determination outlined above. Because an expected appreciation of the domestic currency affects the expected return on foreign deposits, then expectations about the price level, inflation, tariffs and quotas, productivity, import demand, export demand, and the money supply play an important role in determining the exchange rate.

When expectations about any of these variables change, there will be an immediate effect on the expected return of foreign deposits and therefore on the exchange rate. Since expectations on all these variables change with just about every bit of news that appears it is not surprising that exchange rates are so volatile. See Kettell (1998, 1999, 2000) for details of exactly which news moves the currency markets.

An illustration of the effect of changing the assumptions about the factors applied in the asset market approach is given in Table 9.3.

In case 1 the interest differential in favour of dollar deposits is 4 per cent per year ($i^\$ - i^€ = 0.10 - 0.06 = 0.04$) and at the same time no change in the exchange rate is expected [$(E^e_{t+1} - E_t)/E_t = 0.00$]. This means that the expected annual real rate of return on dollar deposits is 4 per cent higher than that on euros so that, other things equal, investors would prefer dollars rather than euro deposits.

In case 2, the interest differential is the same (4 per cent), but it is just offset by an expected depreciation rate of the dollar of 4 per cent. The two assets therefore have the same expected rate of return.

In case 3, a 4 per cent interest differential in favour of dollar deposits is more than offset by an 8 per cent expected depreciation of the dollar, so euro deposits are preferred by market participants.

Table 9.2 Factors that Shift the RET$^€$ and RET$^\$$ schedules and cause exchange rates to change

Factor	Change In Factor	Response of Exchange Rate, E_t	
Domestic interest rate, $i^\$$	↑	↑	RET$_1^\$$ RET$_2^\$$ · RET$^\$$ · E_t, E_2, E_1 · RET in $
Foreign interest rate, $i^€$	↑	↓	RET$^\$$ RET$_1^€$ RET$_2^€$ · E_t, E_1, E_2 · RET in $
Expected domestic price level*	↑	↓	RET$^\$$ RET$_1^€$ RET$_2^€$ · E_t, E_1, E_2 · RET in $
Expected tariffs and quotas*	↑	↑	RET$^\$$ RET$_2^€$ RET$_1^€$ · E_t, E_2, E_1 · RET in $
Expected import demand	↑	↓	RET$^\$$ RET$_1^€$ RET$_2^€$ · E_t, E_1, E_2 · RET in $
Expected export demand	↑	↑	RET$^\$$ RET$_2^€$ RET$_1^€$ · E_t, E_2, E_1 · RET in $
Expected productivity	↑	↑	RET$^\$$ RET$_2^€$ RET$_1^€$ · E_t, E_2, E_1 · RET in $

Source: Adapted from Mishkin and Eakins *Financial Markets and Institutions*. Addison Wesley, 1998.

Note: Only increases (↑) in the factors are shown; the effects of decreases in the variables on the exchange rate are the opposite of those indicated in the third column.

Table 9.3 Comparing rates of return on dollar and euro deposits

Case	Dollar interest rate (%) $i^\$$	Euro interest rate (%) i^ϵ	Expected rate of dollar depreciation against euro (%) $\dfrac{E^e_{t+1} - E_t}{E_t}$	Rate of return difference between dollar and euro deposits (%) $i^\$ - i^\epsilon + \dfrac{E^e_{t+1} - E_t}{E_t}$
1	0.10	0.06	0.00	0.04
2	0.10	0.06	0.04	0.00
3	0.10	0.06	0.08	−0.04
4	0.10	0.12	−0.04	0.02

Source: Adapted from Mishkin and Eakins *Financial Markets and Institutions*. Addison Wesley, 1998.

In case 4, there is a 2 per cent interest differential in favour of euro deposits, but the dollar is expected to appreciate against the euro by 4 per cent over the year. The expected rate of return on dollar deposits is therefore 2 per cent per year higher than that on euros, so dollar deposits are preferred by market participants.

10

How can investors predict the direction of US interest rates? What do 'Fed watchers' watch?

A 'Fed watcher' is an economist who specializes in predicting and analysing the actions of the Federal Reserve, the US central bank. They try to understand the basic thrust of policy and to detect any signs that objectives are changing by predicting the variables that the Federal Reserve follows and anticipating future policy developments. In particular the Fed watcher tracks the Federal Open Market Committee (FOMC), the activities of the Fed open market desk at the Federal Reserve Bank of New York, and the behaviour of the economy overall. We have set out below some rules of thumb that a Fed watcher should apply. As with any rule-of-thumb approach these rules must be adapted as the circumstances demand. Given that the FOMC plays such a central role in determining the path of US interest rates, towards the end of the chapter we discuss the problem of 'decoding' the FOMC minutes. Table 10.1 sets out the golden rules for Fed watching.

Rule 1: remember the central role of nominal/real GNP quarterly growth

The Fed watcher must project and interpret developments other than Federal Reserve policy that are likely to affect

Table 10.1 FED Watching Rules

Rule 1	Remember the central role of nominal/real GNP quarterly growth.
Rule 2	Track the shape of the yield curve if you want to predict business cycle turning points.
Rule 3	Watch what the Fed watches – not what you think it should watch.
Rule 4	Keep an eye on the 3-month eurodollar futures contract.
Rule 5	Use the Taylor rule as a guide to changes in Fed policy.
Rule 6	Pay attention to what the Fed does – not to what it says.
Rule 7	View potential Fed policy shifts as a reaction to rather than a cause of undesired economic/monetary conditions.
Rule 8	Remember that ultimately the Fed is a creature of congress.
Rule 9	Follow the trends in FOMC directives.
Rule 10	Fears of inflation provoke faster changes in monetary policy than do fears of unemployment.

future economic conditions and interest rates. A Fed watcher will produce advance estimates of key economic statistics to give market traders a benchmark for evaluating the statistics when they are released. Statistics published monthly on the economy, e.g. retail sales, production, employment, and prices, are all forecast. There are fashions in what data receive the most attention, some of which were discussed in Chapters 5, 6, and 7. Whenever the Federal Reserve is perceived to be shifting its focus, market attention and forecasting efforts shift as well.

To forecast economic behaviour, financial economists examine recent trends and consider components that might be changing. Some analysts make comprehensive forecasts of the supply and demand for funds associated with different sectors of the economy, e.g. consumer, business, government and foreign. The modelling involved relies heavily on both individual judgement and econometric techniques.

The semi-annual Humphrey–Hawkins Testimony sets out the Federal Reserve central targets and projections for nominal GDP, real GDP and the Personal Consumer Expenditure (PCE) Price Index. To illustrate this, the economic projections for 2002 are set out in Table 10.2.

If the nominal GDP growth appears to be overshooting the target there is pressure for the Fed funds rate to rise. Similarly

Table 10.2 Economic projections for 2002

Percent Indicator Change fourth quarter to fourth quarter	Federal Reserve governors' and Reserve Bank presidents	
	Range	Central tendency
Nominal GDP	$4\frac{3}{4}$–6	5–$5\frac{1}{2}$
Real GDP	3–$3\frac{1}{2}$	3–$3\frac{1}{4}$
PCE prices	$1\frac{1}{2}$–3	$1\frac{3}{4}$–$2\frac{1}{2}$
Civilian unemployment rate	$4\frac{3}{4}$–$5\frac{1}{2}$	$4\frac{3}{4}$–$5\frac{1}{4}$

Source: Humphrey–Hawkins Testimony 2001

if there appears to be undershooting there is pressure for the Fed funds rate to fall. The job of a Fed watcher is to track the economic cycle with a view to projecting the next quarter GDP growth and thus to have some view as to the likely trend of interest rates.

Read the Beige Book

Boards of Directors of the Reserve Banks and branches provide the Federal Reserve System with a wealth of information on economic conditions in virtually every corner of the United States. This information is used by the FOMC and the Board of Governors in reaching major decisions about monetary policy. Information from directors and other sources gathered by the Reserve Banks is also shared with the public in a special report (informally called the Beige Book) which is issued about two weeks before each meeting of the FOMC.

The Beige Book, called this because of the colour, provides a useful summary of the current state of the economy representing the regions of the 12 reporting banks. It is this broad representation and coverage that is its great strength and the reason why the FOMC will analyse it carefully.

A typical schedule of publication is published annually and the schedule follows the format of Table 10.3.

The FOMC will also have access to the Green Book and the Blue Book. The Green Book provides an analysis of domestic economic indicators and projections, whilst the Blue Book examines the monetary policy options of the status quo, easing or tightening. From a Fed watchers point of view these are unhelpful as they are only published after a five-year time lag.

Table 10.3 Key dates in 2002

Beige Book Released	FOMC Meetings	Release of Minutes
January 15	January 29/30	These are made available
March 7	March 19	within a few days after the
April 26	May 7	next regularly scheduled
June 13	June 25/26	meeting.
July 23	August 13	
September 10	September 24	
October 24	November 6	
November 28	December 10	

Rule 2: track the yield curve if you want to predict business cycle turning points

Economists often use complex mathematical models to forecast the path of the US economy and the likelihood of recession. But simpler indicators such as yield curves, defined below also contain valuable, simple to analyse, insights into likely future economic activity.

Historical experience shows that on several occasions prior to recessions, long-term interest rates dipped below prevailing short-term rates, a phenomenon known as an inverted or negative yield curve. Since 1960 the yield curve has been inverted prior to all five recessions. The extent to which the yield curve is tilted away from its normal 'shape' has been identified by many researchers as a valuable indicator of forthcoming recession.

It is well understood that the macroeconomic effects of monetary policy occur with significant lags. Consequently, having an early predictor of economic developments is useful in helping monetary authorities to determine the appropriate policy stance. It has been recognized for some time that the yield curve, which shows the term structure of interest rates prevailing in an economy at any point in time, contains information that can be used as an indicator of economic prospects. This is because the term structure reflects both the settings of the instruments of monetary policy, as shown in the level of short-term interest rates, and the market's expectation of future short-term rates, and hence of future growth and inflation.

An easing of monetary conditions, by lowering short-term rates, will both tend to steepen a normally upward-sloping yield curve and raise prospective growth and inflation. The opposite would occur for a tightening of monetary conditions. Similarly, a shift in market expectations toward higher inflation or growth, for given settings of short-term interest rates, will tend to raise long-term rates and steepen the yield curve. The difference between long-term and short-term rates can often be a useful leading indicator of macroeconomic developments.

To appreciate the importance of yield curves we must first turn to the theory and then to the empirical evidence.

What is the theory behind the shape of the yield curve?

Monetary policy works most directly, as discussed in earlier chapters, by changing reserve availability. Such changes affect the overnight Fed funds rate and other short-term rates, which in turn affect the monetary aggregates.

Expectations of future interest rates influence the shape of the yield curve as long as potential investors and borrowers have choices about the maturity of the instruments they purchase or issue. For instance, potential investors can compare their expected returns from buying either a long-term security or a succession of short-term securities. They will buy the longer-term security if their expectations about the course of interest rates over the security's lifetime support their view that the longer-term instrument is more attractive. Investors will continue to switch to longer-term issues until those rates fall, relative to shorter rates, by enough to remove the expected interest rate advantage of the longer-term issues. Investors form their expectations on the basis of the outlook for inflation and for real interest rates, which will, in turn, be influenced by expectations about economic activity, monetary policy and fiscal policy.

When business cycles follow what is considered the traditional pattern, the shape of the yield curve may do the same, because the traditional business cycle is accompanied by cycles in inflation and credit demands. A 'normal' upward-sloping yield curve would emerge when a major acceleration or deceleration in inflation was not expected (Figure 10.1, yield curve

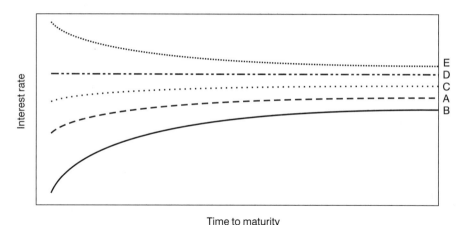

Time to maturity

Figure 10.1 Yield curves over a 'normal' business cycle. (Source: US Monetary Policy and Financial Markets (1998) Ann-Marie Meulendyke. Federal Reserve Bank of New York.)

A). Towards the latter part of a recession, the yield curve would be expected to slope upwards more sharply than 'normal' (yield curve B). Short-term rates would fall more than long-term rates, since the recession would not be expected to persist throughout the life of the long-term debt instruments.

As a recovery got underway, the yield curve would initially remain steep. At some stage it would be likely to flatten somewhat as short-term interest rates rose, but it would generally remain upward-sloping (yield curve C). If significant inflationary pressures become evident, however, the Fed funds rate and other short-term rates would be likely to rise substantially, prompted by tighter monetary policy and changes in the market's expectations about inflation. The yield curve would then tend to shift upward and flatten (yield curve D). An inverted or downward-sloping yield curve (yield curve E) would reflect market views that short-term interest rates were already high enough to reduce real GNP growth and inflation and that a slowing in economic activity and inflation should lead to a decline in interest rates.

What is the empirical evidence to support the use of yield curves as business cycle turning points?

Arthur Estrella and Frederick Mishkin, in their model discussed below, estimate the probability of a recession as being dependent on the yield curve spread, defined as the difference between interest rates on the 10-year US Treasury note and the three-month US Treasury Bill for the period 1960–1995. The model estimates the probability of recession four quarters in the future as a function of the current value of the yield curve spread.

As Table 10.4 shows the estimated probability of a recession four quarters ahead estimated from the model is 10 per cent when the spread averages 0.76 percentage points over the quarter, 50 per cent when the spread averages –0.82 percentage points, and 90 per cent when the spread averages –2.40 percentage points. Consequently the more negative the yield spread the higher the likelihood of recession.

The usefulness of the model can be illustrated through the following examples. Consider that in the third quarter of 1994, the spread averaged 2.74 percentage points. The corresponding predicted probability of recession in the third quarter of 1995 was only 0.2 per cent, and indeed, a recession did not materialize. In contrast, the yield curve spread averaged –2.18 percentage points in the first quarter of 1981, implying a probability of recession of 86.5 per cent four quarters later. As predicted, the first quarter of 1982 was in fact designated a recession quarter by the National Bureau of Economic Research.

Table 10.4   Estimated Recession Probabilities for a Probit Model Using the Yield Curve Spread

Four quarters ahead

Recession probability (per cent)	Value of spread (percentage points)
5	+1.21
10	+0.76
15	+0.46
20	+0.22
25	+0.02
30	–0.17
40	–0.50
50	–0.82
60	–1.13
70	–1.46
80	–1.85
90	–2.40

Source: Estrella, A. and Mishkin F. *Current issues in Economics and Finance*. Federal Reserve Bank of New York, 1996.

So what is the advantage of using yield curves?

First, forecasting with the yield curve has the distinct advantage of being quick and simple. With a glance at the 10-year note and three-month bill rates on the computer screen, anyone can compute a probability forecast of recession almost instantaneously by using Table 10.4.

Second, a simple financial indicator such as the yield curve can be used to double-check both econometric and judgmental predictions by flagging a problem that might otherwise have gone unidentified. For example, if forecasts from an econometric model and the yield curve agree, confidence in the model's results can be enhanced. In contrast, if the yield curve indicator gives a different signal, it may be worthwhile to review the assumptions and relationships that led to the prediction.

Third the expectation theory of the term structure, discussed in Chapter 3, provides a theoretical foundation for the predictive power of the yield curve.

Rule 3: watch what the Fed watches – not what you think it should watch

In tracking and anticipating the Federal Reserve's trading desk actions, financial market economists begin with a close reading of the most recently released FOMC minutes. The Fed watcher will try to understand the Committee's concerns and the balance of opinion among its members. They will identify those factors that the FOMC chose to emphasize in its guidelines to the Fed open market desk in order to predict a change in reserve pressures that might be made between meetings. Before the policy record is released, the economists must interpret developments in the light of their understanding of the committee's primary emphasis, be it the different measures of inflation such as non-farm payroll employment or the consumer price index, different monetary aggregates or the behaviour of nominal gross domestic product. Then they must gauge the likely behaviour of those variables that the Federal Reserve appears to be following most closely.

In tracking desk operations and evaluating whether reserve pressures have been modified, analysts try to distinguish between the defensive and dynamic aspects of open market operations. An open market operation may represent a change in stance toward the policy objective or it may merely be designed to offset the movement in some other balance sheet item or to address normal seasonal movement in required reserves. To interpret open-market actions properly, Fed watchers must analyse a variety of statistics. They essentially duplicate the Federal Reserve's daily estimation of reserve supplies and demands. The outside forecasters operate under a handicap during the period since they do not have the daily flow of reserve information available to their Federal Reserve counterparts.

Each Thursday afternoon, after the Federal Reserve's 4:15 release of a variety of statistics (including weekly data on the Federal Reserve balance sheet, known in the markets as Tables H.3 and H.4.1), the Fed watchers analyse the borrowing at the discount window, excess reserves, and other factors to try to assess the Federal Reserve's policy stance. Under most circumstances, the analysts will expect borrowing and reserve pressures to continue near the level recently prevailing. They will also estimate what range for the Fed funds rate appears to be consistent with such borrowing.

Figure 10.2 provides a summary of how changes in free reserves affect the Fed funds rate. Federal Reserve money supply targets are really non-borrowed reserves targets.

Open market operations are designed to change free reserves. A contractionary monetary policy involves the sale of securities, forcing Fed funds up, and an expansionary monetary policy involving the purchase of securities brings down rates.

The Federal Reserve focuses on the ratio of non-borrowed reserves to required reserves and to discount window borrowing as measures of the strength of monetary policy. If the ratio of

Figure 10.2 How do you measure the strength of monetary policy.

non-borrowed reserves to required reserves falls and there is increased discount window borrowing there are pressures for free reserves to fall and Fed funds to rise. If the ratio of non-borrowed reserves to required reserves rises and there is a fall in discount window borrowing, there are pressures for free reserves to rise and Fed funds to fall.

Rule 4: keep an eye on the three-month Euro–Dollar futures contract

This contract is amongst those financial instruments most sensitive to Fed funds rate changes and indicates what investors think three-month deposits will cost when the market expires. It is expressed as: 100 minus the annualized interest rate. So if the three-months euro–dollar futures contract is priced at 95.00 this indicates an expected three-month interest rate of around 5 per cent. Clearly if the contract price rises above 95.00 interest rates are expected to fall and if the contract price falls below 95.00 then interest rates are expected to rise.

The reasoning behind why three-month euro–dollar futures contracts are so market sensitive is based on the relationship behind the determinants of futures prices. The prices of short-term interest rate futures are influenced, for the nearer maturities at least, by arbitrage based on forward/forward calculations.

Suppose that the three-month interest rate is 14 per cent p.a. whilst the six-month rate is 15 per cent p.a. A trader could borrow for three months and lend for six months and thereby guarantee a profit from the 1 per cent margin during the first three months. However, a trader is at risk from a rise in the three-month interest rate by the commencement of the second three-month period. There is a three-month rate for the second period above which the loss on the second period will push the whole operation into a loss. That is the forward/forward rate.

Suppose that the trader lends $1 million for six months at 15 per cent p.a. and borrows it for three months at 14 per cent p.a. He will receive $1,072,380.50 at the end of the six-month period. Meanwhile he must pay $1,033,299.50 at the end of the first three months and must borrow $1,033,299.50 in order to repay the debt. A $39,081 interest payment on this second loan would mean that the trader breaks even on the exercise, since the second debt could be repaid with the $1,072,380.50 from the $1 million originally lent. On a three-month loan of $1,033,299.50, $39,081 corresponds to a rate of interest of 16.01 per cent p.a.

This is the forward/forward rate and arbitrage tends to ensure that the futures rate approximates closely to it. If the futures rate were significantly below the forward/forward rate, arbitrageurs would lend long and borrow short, using the futures market to guarantee future short-term interest rates. This would involve selling futures (commitments to future borrowing) and the increased sales would push down their prices. The fall in futures prices corresponds to a rise in futures interest rates. This increase in futures interest rates will tend to eliminate the scope for further arbitrage profits.

Rule 5: use Taylor's rule as a guide to changes in Federal Reserve policy

If you wanted to set interest rates to achieve stable prices while avoiding large fluctuations in output and employment, how would you do it? This is exactly the question that Alan Greenspan and other governors of the Federal Reserve must ask themselves every day. As we discussed in Chapter 1 the short-term policy instrument that the Federal Reserve now sets is the Fed funds rate – the short-term interest rate at which banks make loans to one another. Whenever the Federal Open Market Committee meets, it chooses a target for the Fed funds rate. The Federal Reserve's bond traders are then told to conduct open-market operations in order to hit the desired target.

The hard part of the Federal Reserve's job is choosing the target for the Fed funds rate. Two guidelines are clear. First, when inflation heats up, the Fed funds rate should rise. An increase in the interest rate will mean a smaller money supply and, eventually, lower investment, lower output, higher unemployment, and reduced inflation. Second, when real economic activity slows, as reflected in real GDP or unemployment, the Fed funds rate would be expected to fall. A decrease in the interest rate will mean a larger money supply and, eventually, higher investment, higher output, and lower unemployment.

The Federal Reserve needs to go beyond these general guidelines, however, and decide how much to respond to changes in inflation and real economic activity. To assess Federal Reserve potential behaviour many Fed watchers are applying a rule known as the Taylor rule, named after John Taylor, an economist formerly at Stanford University. Mr Taylor's argument (1994) is that central banks ought to 'lean against the wind' when setting interest rates. He suggested, therefore, that short-term nominal interest rates should be equal to the sum of four elements.

The first is the real short-term rate that is consistent with 'neutral' monetary policy, i.e., one that is neither expansionary nor contractionary. The second is the expected inflation rate. Third, in the simplest and commonest version of the Taylor rule, 0.5 percentage points should be added to, or subtracted from, short-term rates for every percentage point by which the current inflation rate is above or below its target. And fourth, the same adjustment should be made for the 'output gap', i.e., for every percentage point by which GDP is above or below its long-term trend level. The idea is that output above trend is a signal of inflation on the way; output below trend is a signal of the reverse. Several studies have found that central banks have, in effect, been following the Taylor rule for some time.

As with any simple rule it is subject to obvious limitations. First, it is heavily dependent on the estimation of trend GDP, where there is plenty of scope for disagreement. Second, the

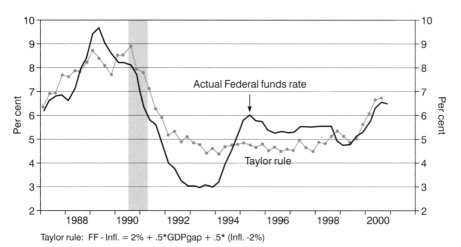

Taylor rule: FF - Infl. = 2% + .5*GDPgap + .5* (Infl. -2%)

Figure 10.3 What the Taylor rule tells us about the stance of monetary policy. (Source: Federal Reserve Bank of New York and authors own calculations.)

appropriate level of interest rates suggested by the rule depends on the chosen measure of inflation, e.g. PCE price index, GDP deflator, CPI, core CPI, wage inflation – the list is long.

Despite these limitations the Taylor rule, as can be seen from Figure 10.3, does provide a useful predictor of the stance of monetary policy which Fed watchers would be advised to keep a close eye on. Notice how closely together the two series move. John Taylor's monetary rule may be more than an academic suggestion.

Rule 6: pay attention to what the Federal Reserve does – not to what it says

This may sound rather obvious but it is not necessarily the case that the Federal Reserve does what it says it will. Former Federal Reserve Chairman Arthur Burns (1970–1978) and G. William Miller (1978–1979) both talked of the need for restrictive action but did very little. It must be said, however, that the same charge cannot be made against either Paul Volcker (1979–1987) or Alan Greenspan (1987–).

Rule 7: view potential Federal Reserve policy shifts as a reaction to, rather than a cause of, undesired economic/monetary conditions

Alan Greenspan has frequently referred to the economy being the patient whilst the Federal Reserve is the doctor. If the patient is hyperactive the doctor should take the appropriate action. As former Federal Reserve Chairman William McChesney Martin (1951–1970) famously commented 'the role of the Fed chairman is to take away the punch bowl just as the party is starting'.

Rule 8: remember that ultimately the Federal Reserve is a creature of Congress

Although insulated in the short-term from partisan political pressures it is not insulated in the longer term. The limits of its independence are clearly delineated. The Federal Reserve was created by an act of Congress and, like any agency so created, can be changed or terminated altogether by Congress. What Congress creates it can also destroy! So although the Federal Reserve receives its mandate from Congress regarding what it should try to achieve with monetary policy over time, these decisions are subject to Congressional Review. Former Chairman Martin liked to describe the Federal Reserve as 'independent within the government, not of the government'.

Federal Reserve governors are appointed to 14-year terms. However, most Federal Reserve governors do not serve a full 14-year term. Many are appointed in the middle of a term to replace a departing governor. Among the governors who have served since 1946, terms varied from the three months served by Paul E Miller, who died in office, to the 28 years served by M.S. Szymczak, who was appointed in 1933 and remained a governor until 1961, having been reappointed twice. There is some evidence to suggest that the average length of a governor's term has decreased since World War II. Governors appointed before 1960 stayed an average of 11 years, while those appointed in or after 1960 averaged only seven years.

A new US president is likely to be able to choose several governors for the Federal Reserve during his or her term of office. Through the choice of nominees, the president can influence the direction of monetary policy. President George W. Bush is in the unusual opportunity of influencing the selection of a large number of governors.

Rule 9: follow the trends in FOMC directives: how to interpret Fed speak?

The FOMC directive prior to August 1997

At each meeting the FOMC issued a policy directive, the language of which determined whether the directive was symmetric or asymmetric. While the FOMC never formally stated the purpose of an asymmetric policy directive it was often interpreted as indicating the likely direction of the FOMC's next policy action.

One of the most important decisions reached at Federal Open Market Committee meetings is whether to ease or tighten monetary policy. The FOMC transmits its decision to the Federal Reserve Bank of New York (where open market operations are actually executed) in a domestic policy directive that guides monetary policy in the subsequent weeks. One of the key roles of a Fed watcher is to decode the FOMC policy directive. This did not use to be as straightforward as it currently is.

The domestic policy directives issued by the FOMC in recent years have contained two parts. The first part summarizes available information about the economy that provides a context for the actions taken. The second part is a discussion of policy and the actual directive. Up until July 1997 the directive used the following key wording.

'In the implementation of policy for the immediate future, the Committee seeks to:

(1)   the existing degree of pressure on reserve positions. In the context of the Committee's long-run objectives for price stability and sustainable economic growth, and give careful consideration to economic, financial and monetary developments.

(2)   somewhat greater reserve restraint   or

(3)   slightly lesser reserve restraint   be acceptable in the intermeeting period.'

The implication of the wording in the blank spaces is discussed below.

Policy directives express the preference of the FOMC for the implementation of monetary policy during the period until the next FOMC meeting. Symmetrical directives express no bias toward either greater ease (a lower Fed funds rate) or toward greater restraint (a higher Fed funds rate). Asymmetrical directives do express a policy bias. By writing an asymmetrical directive, the FOMC empowers the chairman to raise or lower the Fed funds rate target during the intermeeting period.

When the wording about tightening or easing reserve conditions was identical, then the directive was symmetric. A combination of wording that used 'slightly' or 'somewhat' with 'would' or 'might' indicated an asymmetric directive. For example, if the directive stated that 'somewhat greater reserve restraint would or slightly lesser reserve restraint might be acceptable' the chairman had the authority, but not the obligation to direct the Fed open market desk to increase pressure on reserves in the banking system, thereby setting a higher Fed funds rate target. In practice, the chairman exercised this authority very infrequently, and typically involved the other members of the FOMC in the process. The terms 'somewhat' and 'slightly', 'would' and 'might', helped to express the strength of the Committee's bias.

Looking at the blank spaces above, a symmetric directive would indicate for space (1):

'Decrease' – meaning an easing of monetary policy or
'Increase' – meaning a tightening of monetary policy or
'Maintain' – meaning no immediate change in monetary policy.

This then indicated whether interest rates were rising, falling or staying the same in the near future. So it was the second two blank spaces that determined the so-called bias of the directive and were particularly important when the first blank space indicated that the main thrust is 'maintained'.

The choices for both the second (2) and the third (3) blanks are the words 'would' and 'might'. The key insight is that 'would' is stronger than 'might'. If the main thrust of the directive is 'maintain' and the directive says that slightly greater reserve restraint might or slightly lesser reserve restraint would be acceptable, the directive was referred to as biased or asymmetric towards ease. Pairing might with might or would with would gave a symmetric directive. Pairing would and might was known as biased or asymmetric toward restraint. A directive that was biased towards ease was intended to give the Chairman somewhat more leeway in the direction of ease in the day-to-day implementation of policy between meetings.

The FOMC directives change of wording

With effect from the FOMC August 1997 minutes, the wording has been altered as follows.

> 'In the implementation of policy for the immediate future, the committee seeks conditions in reserve markets consistent with maintaining the Federal funds rate at an average of around $5\frac{1}{2}$ per cent. In the context of the Committee's long-run objectives for price stability and sustainable economic growth, and giving careful consideration to economic, financial and monetary developments, a somewhat higher Federal funds rate would or a slightly lower federal funds rate might be acceptable in the intermeeting period. The contemplated reserve conditions are expected to be consistent with moderate growth in M2 and M3 over coming months.'

An explicit target, 5.5 per cent here, is now formally stated. The wording now, 'a somewhat higher Fed funds rate would or a slightly lower Fed funds rate might be acceptable in the intermeeting period', as before, indicates a preference for tightening interest rates.

Rule 10: fears of inflation provoke faster changes in monetary policy than do fears of unemployment

The reasoning behind this rule comes from Alan Blinder, former Vice Chairman of the Board of Governors of the Federal Reserve, in his publication *Central Banking in Theory and Practice* (1998). He discusses the extent to which monetary policy should take the form of a 'pre-emptive strike' when faced with fighting either inflation or unemployment. Blinder argues that the lags in monetary policy could be longer for inflation-fighting than for unemployment-fighting, calling for earlier pre-emption in the former case. He then cites empirical evidence that supports his views.

Blinder then goes on to highlight that given the nature of committee decision-making, systematic policy errors can continue which then induce the central bank to maintain its policy stance too long. In Blinders words 'monetary policy decisions tend to regress towards the mean and to be inertial.' Given that Blinder combines practical Federal Reserve experience with being a distinguished academic, Fed watchers would be advised to heed his views.

11

Derivatives: what do you need to know about economics to understand their role in financial markets?†

What are derivatives?

Derivatives are contracts which give one party a claim on an underlying asset (derived from the cash value of an underlying asset) at some point in the future, and bind a counterparty to meet a corresponding liability. The contract might describe an amount of currency, a security, a physical commodity, a stream of payments, or a market index. It might bind both parties equally, or offer one party an option to exercise it or not. It might provide for assets or obligations to be swapped. It might be a bespoke derivative combining several elements. Whether derivatives are or are not traded on exchanges, their market price will depend in part on the movement of the price of the underlying asset since the contract was created.

The rapid growth of derivatives trading around the world in recent years has been propelled by the internationalization of capital markets in general, by technological advances in computers and telecommunications, and by the increasingly fierce competition among big banks and securities houses to devise and sell products.

† The contents of this chapter are discussed in more detail in Kettell, B. (2001) *Financial Economics*. Financial Times–Prentice Hall.

Where did derivatives come from?

Trading in derivative contracts has a long history. The first recorded accounts of derivative contracts can be traced back to the philosopher Thales of Miletus in ancient Greece, who, during winter, negotiated what were essentially call options on oil presses for the spring olive harvest. De la Vega reported in 1688 that options and futures, or 'time bargains' as they were then known, were trading on the Amsterdam Bourse soon after it was opened. Evidence also suggests that futures contracts for rice were traded in Japan in the 17th and 18th centuries.

The first formalized futures exchange in the United States was the Chicago Board of Trade, which opened in 1848 with 82 members. In March 1851, the first futures contract was recorded. The contract called for the delivery of 3000 bushels of corn in June at a price of one cent per bushel below the March price. Listed stock options began trading in April 1973 on the Chicago Board Options Exchange (CBOE). Other exchanges began offering stock call options in 1975 and put options in 1977.

The recent revolution in option pricing theory also dates to 1973 with the publication by Fischer Black and Myron Scholes of their classic paper on option valuation. Since the publication of that paper the valuation of options and various other derivative contracts has been one of the primary areas of research among financial economists.

Some terminology

Derivatives are often described as being complex instruments that defy understanding for the mathematically unsophisticated. Despite their intimidating appearance they are in fact constructed from simple elements, known to the financial markets for literally centuries.

Take the most basic of derivative transactions, a **forward contract**. One party agrees to buy, say, $1 m in three months' time, at a price fixed today in sterling terms. The mathematics of the transaction are well within the capacity of a pocket calculator. If prevailing interest rates are higher for the dollar than for sterling, somebody who wants to buy dollars forward for payment in sterling will be quoted a price lower than the one that is prevailing for transactions that are settled immediately.

Futures contracts differ from forward contracts by virtue of being traded on official exchanges. To make trading easier, their terms will be standard ones set by the appropriate exchange; they will be for a fixed quantity (of bonds, or pork bellies or whatever instrument is being traded) and will run for a fixed period.

Options are a form of forward contracts in which the buyer can decide whether or not to exercise a right to buy (or sell) the underlying asset within an agreed time. The seller of the option then has to work out how to price the probability that the option will or will not be exercised. Only in 1973 did two American financial economists, Myron Scholes and Fischer Black, provide a plausible answer to the option pricing problem by devising a mathematical model with several inputs, the most important of which was the volatility of the price of the underlying asset.

Swaps complete the simple taxonomy. Albeit on a rather larger scale, an interest-rate swap works just as if, for sound financial reasons, person A with a fixed-rate mortgage, and person B with a floating-rate mortgage of the same size, agree to assume responsibility for one another's interest payments. Person A will take over the floating-rate payments and person B will take over the fixed-rate payments. In real life, big borrowers may swap interest-rate or currency obligations because they disagree over interest-rate trends, or because they find it cheaper to borrow money in foreign markets. A Japanese company wanting long-term Japanese yen may find it cheaper to borrow US dollars, then swap them into yen.

Table 11.1 provides a formal definition of the principal derivatives contracts traded, forwards, futures, options and swaps.

What is an option?

Options are one of the most powerful derivative contracts. An option is a contract between two parties that gives the buyer the right but not the obligation to buy or sell a specific quantity of a commodity or instrument at an agreed price for a specified

Table 11.1 Derivatives Defined

Forward Contract:	A contract to buy or sell a specified amount of a designated commodity, currency, security, or financial instrument at a known date in the future and at a price set at the time the contract is made. Forward contracts are negotiated between the contracting parties and are not traded on organized exchanges.
Futures Contract:	A contract to buy or sell a specified amount of a designated commodity, currency, security, or financial instrument at a known date in the future and at a price set at the time the contract is made. Futures contracts are traded on organized exchanges and are thus standardized. The contracts are marked to market daily, with profits and losses settled in cash at the end of the trading day.
Option Contract:	A contract that gives its owner the right, but not the obligation, to buy or sell a specified asset at a stipulated price, called the strike or exercise price. Contracts that give owners the right to buy are referred to as call options and contracts that give the owner the right to sell are called put options. Options include both standardized products that trade on organized exchanges and customized contracts between private parties.
Swap Contract:	A private contract between two parties to exchange cash flows in the future according to some prearranged formula. The most common type of swap is the 'plain vanilla' interest rate swap, in which the first party agrees to pay the second party cash flows equal to interest at a predetermined fixed rate on a notional principal. The second party agrees to pay the first party cash flows equal to interest at a floating rate on the same notional principal. Both payment streams are denominated in the same currency. Another common type of swap is the currency swap. This contract calls for the counterparties to exchange specific amounts of two different currencies at the outset, which are repaid over time according to a prearranged formula that reflects amortization and interest payments.

period. The option buyer pays the seller a premium for the privilege of being able to buy or sell the instrument, at a fixed price, without having the commitment to do so.

To take an example, consider an option to buy gold at US$400 per ounce. Let us say the market price of gold is currently US$395. The option buyer pays the option seller a premium of US$3.50. The option buyer has the right, but not the obligation to buy gold at US$400. It will be profitable for the option buyer to exercise this right if the price of gold rises above US$403.50. However, if the price of gold falls in the market then the option buyer has no commitment to buy gold at US$400, and the option buyer can then allow the option to expire unexercised, and purchase gold at the cheaper market price.

It is important to become familiar with the terminology of the option market. A summary of the principal terms is illustrated below.

- The option buyer becomes the Holder. The option seller is called the Writer.
- A Call option gives the owner the right to buy a specified quantity of a commodity at an agreed price over a given period.
- A Put option gives the owner the right to sell a specified quantity of a commodity at an agreed price over a given period.
- The Premium is the price paid for the option.
- The Strike Price or Exercise Price is the rate at which the option may be exercised; in other words, it is the price that has been agreed under the option contract.
- The Expiry Date is the final date on which the option can be exercised.
- A European-style option can be exercised only on the expiry date, whereas an American-style option can be exercised at any date prior to and including the expiry date. (Note these terms have no geographical significance.)

Exchange-traded versus over-the-counter (OTC) options

Options may be traded on exchanges, i.e., in a physical location, or on the over-the-counter (OTC) market, in which dealing takes place between two counterparties, usually over the telephone. Exchange-traded options have the following characteristics.

- Fixed expiry dates, generally at three-monthly intervals for the third Wednesday in March, June, September and December.
- Maturities generally up to two years.
- Strike/exercise prices at fixed intervals.
- Fixed contract sizes.
- Standardization of contracts. This means that markets tend to be liquid. In other words, bid-offer spreads (the difference

between the buying and selling price) tend to be narrow, and large orders can usually be transacted fairly easily.

- Given that these options are traded on regulated exchanges, trading is closely monitored. The clearing-house of the exchange acts as the counterparty to every trade, thus the credit risk, i.e., the risk of default on a trade, is standardized and limited.
- Prices are publicly quoted, i.e., trading takes place by open outcry between traders on the floor of the exchange. Prices are reported by information vendors, such as Bloomberg and Reuters, and prices and volumes are reported in the financial press.

Over-the-counter options have the following characteristics.

- Strike rates, contract sizes and maturity are all subject to negotiation.
- They can be longer term than exchange-traded options; some banks will write them for up to 10 years.
- The holder has a direct credit risk on the writer. The writer has no credit risk on the holder provided the premium is paid up front.
- The price at which the option is dealt is known only to the counterparties.

Where do option prices come from?

In order to understand option prices it is essential to understand two key concepts: arbitrage and forwards/futures markets. Arbitrage is discussed below. Forwards and futures are financial instruments that relate present and future prices, and they are critical in understanding option pricing.

Arbitrage

Arbitrage is a powerful market force that helps to establish the value of many financial instruments. When discussing arbitrage it is important to distinguish between deterministic arbitrage and statistical arbitrage.

What is deterministic arbitrage?

Deterministic Arbitrage is the classic technique of simultane-ously buying and selling the same or equivalent products at different prices to achieve a riskless profit. For example, what do we do if gold trades at $400 in New York and $410 in London? The answer is quite simple: we buy low and sell high. Specifically, we buy low for $400 in New York, and we sell high at $410 in London – and we make $10 risklessly. By 'risklessly' we mean there is no risk of prices moving against us. If we can execute these two trades simultaneously, there is no gold price risk, and we can be confident of a profit as long as other factors do not intervene.

One of the best ways to illustrate arbitrage opportunities is to use examples based on simple raffles. Raffles define and clarify some of the ideas of profit and probability that will be discussed further in this chapter. Let us assume that a daily raffle sells exactly 100 tickets each morning. At the end of the day, one of these 100 tickets is chosen, and the holder of that ticket wins $1000. What is the fair price or expected value of one ticket? To solve this problem, we divide the $1000 prize by 100 tickets for a fair price of $10.

If we pay $10 for the ticket and we do not win, we will not feel we were cheated because we paid too much. We will attribute it to, say, the luck of the draw. Similarly, if we win, we will be ecstatic, but we will not think we bought a cheap ticket because, by the accident of probability, we won the prize. When we divide the value of the prize by the number of tickets, we are able to derive the fair value or, in statistical terminology, the expected value or mean value of each ticket.

What do we do if tickets sell for $9 instead of $10? At $9, the ticket is cheap – so cheap that it is worth buying every ticket in the raffle. When the winning number is drawn at the end of the day we stand to make a riskless profit of $100. If we hold all the tickets, we win the $1000 prize, having paid only $900. We can arbitrage a deterministic $100 profit – meaning we are certain to make that $100 – as long as the person who created the raffle does not disappear after collecting our money.

What do we do if tickets sell for $11? Because $11 is too much to pay for a ticket, we want to sell raffle tickets instead of buying them if we can. We might hold our own raffle selling tickets at $10.50. After selling 100 tickets, we will take in $1050. The prize we have to pay the raffle winner is $1000, so we have $50 left in our pockets. If any raffle ticket sells for less than fair value it is worth buying it. If it is overvalued, it is worth selling it.

The effect of these raffle scenarios is similar to the effect of gold trading at $400 in New York and at $410 in London. When there are many buyers of gold in New York, their demand forces the price up. When there are many sellers of gold in London, their supply forces the price down. Nobody can say exactly where the price will end up, but we presume it will finish up somewhere between $400 and $410. Eventually, we know that the price will equilibrate to a fair value – the same price to buyers and sellers in all markets. The fair value of gold does not necessarily mean this is the price gold will trade at; it means it is the efficient market value or the expected value. Locking in a sure profit by taking advantage of mis-pricing is known as deterministic arbitrage.

What is statistical arbitrage?

Let us assume for purposes of illustration that raffle tickets sell for less than their fair value. Let us look at a different, but related, kind of arbitrage: statistical arbitrage.

What do we do if raffle tickets sell for $9 but we are permitted to buy only one ticket a day? Do we: (1) never buy a ticket, (2) buy a ticket once in a while, or (3) buy a ticket every day? In this case, the ticket should be selling for $10 but only costs $9, so we have a $1 'edge', or expected profit per ticket. If we buy only one ticket a day, we are engaged in statistical arbitrage.

We do not have a certain profit if we cannot buy all the tickets in an underpriced raffle. We have to decide what is the best thing to do in an uncertain situation. In fact, the correct choice for someone who can accept the risk of a string of losses before he wins the prize is not one, two, or even three tickets. The full answer is: buy one ticket every day until the universe ends. What do we expect to happen after buying a ticket every day until the end of time? We expect our fortune to grow without limit!

The key word in this scenario is expect. We are not certain to win this money, but we expect to win this money. We expect to earn an average of $1 a day on this raffle, because our 'edge', the expected value of our position, is $1. We expect to make that edge on average after repeated trials. This is called statistical arbitrage because it is not certain or determined that we will make this profit, but we expect to make this profit over time.

What do we expect to happen after 100 days when we have spent $900 on raffle tickets? We expect to win one time. Are we assured of winning one time? Absolutely not – we could lose every time or we could win two, three, or even 99 times.

What do we expect to happen after 1000 days? There will be 1000 winners after 1000 days. With 1000 winners and a one in 100 chance of winning each day, we expect to win 10 times. We may not win 10 times, we may win only eight times, or we may win 12 times. In fact, there is about a 70 per cent chance that we will win between seven and 13 times. If we play 1000 times, we will be very surprised if we do not win at all, because the probability of not winning at all in 1000 tries is extremely small, if the raffle is fair.

The more times we play, the closer we should come to the number of times we expect to win and to the average of $1 a day we expect to make. If we play 1 000 000 times, we expect to make close to $1 000 000. Our profit might fall a few hundred dollars short of $1 000 000 or rise a few hundred dollars beyond $1 000 000, but that is a fairly small percentage variation compared to the percentage variation we might see after 100 days.

After 1 000 000 raffles, we expect to win about 10 000 times (1/100 of 1 000 000). Statisticians tell us we have about a 70 per cent chance of winning between 9900 and 10 100 times. The larger number of raffles brings us closer to our expected average of one win for every 100 times. The longer the period, the closer we expect to come to the average payoff. To apply these principles to the pricing of derivatives we now need to turn to probability distributions.

Probability distributions

Suppose gold is trading at $400 an ounce today. What price will gold be in one year? If we ask many different people this question, we will probably get many different answers. Some people will be very pessimistic, predicting a dramatic drop in gold prices. Others will be very optimistic, predicting a large rise in gold prices. A number of people will fall in between the two extremes. After we accumulate all of the responses, we will get a picture of where people think gold is going to trade in a year. The picture might look something like Figure 11.1.

The numbers at the top of each bar represent the percentage of people who predict that the price of gold will reach that price category in a year. Our first bar, centred at $350 an ounce,

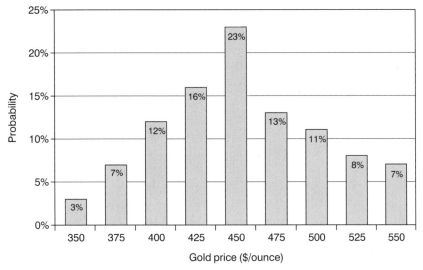

Figure 11.1 Survey of expectations about the future gold price.

indicates that 3 per cent of the people surveyed think gold will be around $350; about 7 per cent of the people think it will be around $375; 12 per cent predict a price near $400, and so forth. Many people are clustered in the middle, around $450. This picture is called a distribution. A distribution is characterized by its mean or average – its expected value. A distribution will always be centred at the expected value.

When we add up and average the different responses from the people surveyed, we find that, for this particular example, the mean is centred around $450. (The mean calculated from the actual responses is $453.50.) On average, the people in this group feel that the future price of gold, that is the price of gold a year from now, should be approximately $450.

A distribution is also characterized by its width or dispersion, which is sometimes expressed as the standard deviation or the volatility. You can see in this distribution that, even though it is centred around $450, there is a great deal of variation in the responses. Some people estimate a price as low as $350, and some people estimate a price as high as $550. The standard deviation measures the dispersion in the distribution, and for our gold price survey distribution this measure of dispersion is around $50.

The mean and the standard deviation are two important quantitative characteristics of the distribution. Many distributions we encounter in nature and in the financial markets have a particular shape called a normal or bell-shaped distribution.

Returns for commodities, such as gold, or for currencies or stocks or bonds have underlying distributions that are often approximately normal. A normal distribution is characterized in part by its symmetry about the mean and by the fact that it is high in the middle and low at the ends. We will assume, for purposes of the illustration that follows, that gold prices are approximately normally distributed.

The normal distribution has some very useful characteristics and these are illustrated in Figure 11.2. In a normal distribution of gold price forecasts, we have 68 per cent confidence that the future price will be within one standard deviation of the mean. In our forecast distribution, the mean is about $450, and the standard deviation is about $50. Assuming this distribution is normal, we are 68 per cent confident that the future price will fall somewhere between $400 and $500 – $450 minus $50 and $450 plus $50. Adding the percentage responses in the price range between $400 and $500 on our bar chart in Figure 11.1, we find that about 75 per cent of our forecasters feel that the future price will be within one standard deviation of the mean.

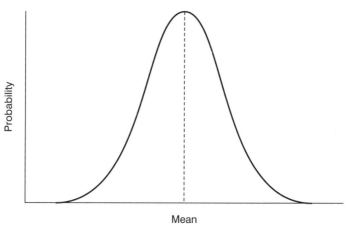

Figure 11.2 A normal distribution.

From the normal distribution we know that we have 95 per cent confidence that the future price will be within two standard deviations of the mean in a normal distribution. Two standard deviations down from the mean is about $350, and two standard deviations up from the mean is about $550 so we have about 95 per cent confidence that the future price of gold will be somewhere between $350 and $550. In our forecast distribution, all the responses are within that interval.

Finally, we are 99 per cent confident that the future price will be within three standard deviations of the mean in a normal distribution. Three standard deviations from the mean is $150. We are 99 per cent confident, or almost completely confident, that the future price of gold will be within a range of $300 to $600, that is $150 down from the mean and $150 up from the mean. These properties of the normal distribution provide powerful assistance in the pricing of derivatives.

Who are the market participants in the derivatives markets?

In order to understand how to apply these arbitrage principles and ultimately understand how option prices are determined, we need to examine the actions of the different participants in the markets. In this case we chose the gold market but any other market could easily have been chosen.

The expected future price of gold is important to anyone who uses the gold spot markets, that is the market for immediate delivery or receipt of gold, and to the gold futures and forward markets, the markets for delivery at some future time period. These users would include:

A. investors
B. long speculators
C. short speculators
D. long hedgers
E. short hedgers
F. arbitrageurs.

It is useful to describe each of these market participants, discuss what motivates their market behaviour, and look at how their actions affect the spot and the future or forward price of an underlying commodity or security.

Let us look first at A, our investor. A thinks that gold is a good investment, a gold bug in the terminology of the market. He wants to buy gold and hold it long term. When A buys gold, he forces up the spot price of gold. When the spot price of gold rises, the future or forward price tends to rise as well.

B, our long gold speculator, is not a long-term investor, like A, but she thinks gold is going up and would like to take a position that is going to be profitable if she is right. B can accomplish this in a couple of different ways. First, B can buy spot gold. If gold goes up in a short period of time, she can sell that gold at a higher price and make a profit. Alternatively, B can buy a future or forward contract on gold. B's purchase of forward gold tends to make the future or forward price go up; and, just as demand for spot gold tends to raise future or forward prices, demand for forward gold tends to raise spot prices. As we will see later, when B buys a future or a forward, she does not have to pay out much money. When A buys spot gold, say 100 ounces at $400, he has to pay $40 000, immediately.

Our short speculator, C, thinks that the gold price is going down. She is very pessimistic about the outlook for gold. Like A and B, C has two choices. She can sell gold spot, or she can sell a future or forward contract on gold. If C happens to own gold she can simply sell it. Alternatively, if she is in a position to borrow gold relatively easily and sell it short, i.e., to sell gold she does not physically own, she might do that. But if she does not have direct access to gold, she will probably find it easier to sell a future or forward contract on gold.

Short speculators like C affect the price of spot gold. The effect on the spot price is clear if the short speculators own gold and want to shift their investment to something else. If they are not trading in the spot market, the direct effect of their sale will be on the forward or future price, making it trade at a lower price.

D is someone who needs gold a year from now. D might be a dentist or a jeweller, someone who has all the gold he needs right now but who wants to be assured of the gold price a year from now. There is no advantage in buying the gold now and spending a large sum of money to store and insure it. D probably will want to buy a future or forward contract on gold, which will tend to push up the future or forward price.

E, our gold producer, is very busy digging gold out of the ground. He does not have much gold right now, but in a year he expects to have a large store of gold to sell. He wants to make sure his hard work pays off and that he can sell his gold at a good price. He cannot sell spot gold because he does not have it. However, he can sell a future or forward contract on gold now. E is likely to affect the future of forward price, and since he is selling, his actions will tend to make the future or forward price trade lower.

Our last market participant, the gold arbitrageur, is the most important in some ways. F has no opinion about gold's value and no opinion on the likely direction of gold prices, but she is very aware of gold price relationships. Even if F did have a personal opinion about the value of gold or the direction of gold prices, her opinion would not affect her financial transactions. F is an arbitrageur, and her actions in the market place tie the actions of all other market participants together. F makes sure that the spot price of gold and the future or forward price of gold are in their proper relationship. If the prices are not appropriate relative to one another, she will try to profit by buying in the cheap market and selling in the expensive market. The actions of arbitrageurs are extremely important in seeing that spot prices and future prices are kept in line.

The arbitrageur's role and the pricing of futures markets

One of the reasons for emphasizing the role of the arbitrageur in a discussion of options is that arbitrageurs are an important factor in determining the spot/forward price relationship, and the first step in finding the value of an option is finding the value of future or forward prices.

If gold is trading at $400 today, at what price will someone agree today to buy or sell it one year in the future? We used a survey, Figure 11.1, to forecast the price of gold in a year, but there is a rational, deterministic relationship between the spot price and the forward price of gold that does not rely on an opinion survey or on anyone's gold price forecast, it simply applies the arbitrage ideas discussed above.

Suppose that the carry cost of gold, that is, the cost of borrowing money, the cost of buying the gold and financing it for a year, is 10 per cent. Assume the spot gold price is $400. Holding the gold position will cost us 10 per cent for a year, because if we had to borrow the $400 to buy the gold we would have had to pay interest at 10 per cent. To own gold a year from now, it will cost us more than $400 now. In fact as shown by equation (11.1), it will cost us $440.

Spot price of gold + cost of carry = future or forward
price of gold   (11.1)

$400   + (10% × $400) = $440

If the present value of gold is $400, the future value of gold in one year should be $440. By future value, we do not necessarily mean the price gold will sell for in the future; it is the value that the future gold price has today because of the cost of carrying gold for a year.

Present value, spot value and the cash market refer to the same thing. We have been talking about spot gold, but we can also talk about the spot value, current market value or cash value of a stock, a bond, or some other underlying commodity or financial instrument, to broaden the futures pricing principles.

Future value refers to the value of the future or the forward. There is a difference between futures and forwards, but the difference is in how they are traded, not in how they are valued. At this point we will treat futures and forwards as though they were interchangeable. Later, we will discuss the practical differences between futures markets and forward markets.

What are the factors influencing the price of futures?

Traders in any commodity, say a wheat buyer (bread maker), or a wheat seller (wheat farmer), fearing wheat price volatility, are anxious to use a cash market hedge to hedge wheat price risk. A futures contract is a derivative of this spot market hedge. A seller of wheat will not wish the price to fall in the future when a sale is anticipated. A buyer of wheat will not wish the price to rise when a purchase is anticipated. If an agreement is made to deliver a quantity and grade of wheat in three months' time, how might the seller of the wheat arrange affairs so that there is no price risk? If they remain in an open position, i.e., not owning the wheat, there is no knowing what the price of wheat will be in three months' time. Therefore a cash market hedge can be constructed as follows. Wheat will already be held or can be purchased at today's spot price. Take today's spot price, which is known, and add to this the cost of carrying the wheat for three months. These carry costs will be:

● storage
● insurance

- transport costs involved in making delivery to a named place
- financing costs of the operation over the three months, i.e., interest foregone, or interest paid on funds used to purchase the commodity.

This gives us the following relationship between the spot and futures price:

> spot wheat price + the cost of carry = agreed price of wheat in 3 months' time (i.e., futures price)

Such a strategy will fix the price of wheat for both parties in 3 months' time. Regardless of what happens to the spot price during the 3 months, the agreed price will be received or paid.

Futures pricing

A price in the futures agreement or contract has to be agreed. The question arises what must/should this price be? The price, as indicated above, 'should' be today's spot price adjusted by the cost of carry for three months. If you agree this price with your counterparty this will become the entry price, as it is known. If the entry price is not 'correct', then an arbitrage can be made, as illustrated below, using the cash market hedge described above and the simultaneous mispriced futures agreement.

If the entry price of the futures contract (remember this will give the seller of wheat the right to sell the wheat at this agreed entry price in three months' time) is greater than spot plus cost of carry, then an arbitrage profit is possible. In this example, the futures price is said to be 'rich' to the cash price, so on the principle that you sell that which is overpriced (the future) and buy that which is underpriced (commodity at spot), it follows that if

> future (entry) price > spot plus cost of carry
> (e.g. $10   > $8 + $1.50)

then arbitrageurs in the spot market will take a long position, i.e., purchase wheat at the spot rate and carry this for three months.

Their total outlay = spot price plus the cost of carry

$9.50   = $8 + $1.50

In the futures market they will take a short position, i.e., sell a futures contract. In three months' time they will sell the goods held over the three months at a total outlay of original spot ($8) plus cost of carry ($1.50), for a sum greater than this, ($10) as enabled by the futures contract held, because:

future contract price > spot price plus cost of carry

$10   > $8 + $1.50

This arbitrage process is called a cash and carry transaction. In this example a risk-free profit is being made. The arbitrage opportunity will be eroded and disappear as such transactions are made. Demand at the spot price will raise the spot price so that this, when added to the cost of carry, equals the futures price. At the same time there will be a greater demand for short positions in futures and this will drive down the futures price. In both markets the tendency will be to equalize prices. If the futures price equals the spot price plus full carrying cost, then the futures price will be what is known as a full carry price.

If the futures price is 'cheap', then arbitrageurs buy what is cheap (the futures market) and sell that which is expensive (the spot price). This arbitrage again 'should' result in a full carry futures price. At the end of either of these transactions the futures entry price should equal the spot price plus the cost of carry.

The principle emerges therefore that spot and future prices differ due to the principle of cost of carry. However, at maturity spot and futures will be identical. If they are not identical it will be possible, a fraction of time before maturity, to take a futures position and an opposite cash market position, arbitrage and profit from the difference. A simple example illustrates this.

Say the futures price is $10 and the spot price is $8. Selling a futures contract (right to deliver at $10) and buying in the spot market at $8 obviously gives a profit of $2 per unit quantity. If prices are identical at maturity, but differ at the beginning of the period, it follows that even if the spot price were to remain constant (highly unlikely) the futures price would gradually have to change as the contract approached maturity. To illustrate this we must first define what in the derivatives market is known as 'basis'.

What is basis?

Basis is the difference between the forward or future value and the spot value. For many products, the basis is defined as the cost of undertaking the transaction minus the benefit of undertaking the transaction, i.e., holding the underlying security. This gives the following relationship:

basis = cost of transaction – benefit from the transaction

In our gold futures pricing example, we considered only the financial cost of carrying gold at 10 per cent, because there are no economic or financial benefits from owning gold. (It might give you a feeling of comfort to own gold, but we are not counting that.) In some other products, there are benefits to holding financial instruments as well as costs, as will be seen below.

Should we now consider the futures markets for stocks we must again consider the cost of carry, i.e., the cost of the money to buy the stock, but we must now also consider the possible benefit of holding stocks, i.e., the possibility of receiving a cash dividend. Not all stocks pay dividends, but if they do, the dividend is a benefit.

In currency markets, the cost of carrying a foreign currency is the investor's domestic interest rate. If a US dollar-based investor wants euros, she has to give up dollars to buy the euros. When she gives up the dollars, she either takes them out of an interest-bearing account, which means she loses the interest income, or she borrows the dollars from a bank and pays domestic interest. Either way she has a carry cost in the domestic currency, and that is the dollar cost. On the other hand, when she gets the euros, she can invest them in a euro account and earn interest at euro rates. The interest on the euro account is a benefit of owning the euros.

Let us now turn to the bond market. Often, traders or portfolio managers have to borrow money to carry bonds. They borrow money in the repo (repurchase agreement) market, posting the bonds as collateral for the loan. The repo rate is the term used for the interest rate charged on such a loan. On the other hand, while they own the bond they are entitled to any coupon interest that accumulates. For a bond, the repo rate is the carry cost of the bond, and the coupon interest is the benefit.

The basis in each of these examples consists of the cost of holding the instrument or commodity minus the benefit of owning the underlying instrument or commodity from the spot date to the forward date.

What is the basis for different instruments?

- For gold, the basis is simply the interest cost of carrying the gold.
- For a stock, the basis is the interest cost of carrying the stock minus the dividends earned from the stock.
- For a currency, the basis is the cost of the interest on the domestic currency minus the benefit of the interest earned on the foreign currency.
- For a bond, the basis is the cost of borrowing at the repo rate minus the benefit of the coupon payment.

Spot versus forward arbitrage

Applying the idea of basis to arbitrage examples will help to clarify some spot and forward pricing relationships. Suppose that gold is trading for $400, and the forward price, which we said earlier should be trading at $440, is trading at $450. It will cost us $400 plus 10 per cent of $400 to buy gold and carry it for one year. That means we can buy gold today by borrowing money from the bank, and in one year we have to repay the bank $440. With the gold forward trading today for $450, we can sell it and make a profit. In one year, we do two more transactions: (1) deliver gold for $450 an ounce to complete the forward contract, and (2) repay the bank $440 an ounce, giving a net difference of $10 profit.

With a spot price of $400 and a forward price of $450, we can buy gold today and sell it forward, making a certain profit of $10 per ounce. This is a riskless profit, an arbitrage profit, which we make by simultaneously buying and selling equivalent instruments.

Let us look at this transaction from a different perspective. It may seem as though we bought gold, but because we bought gold by borrowing money and carrying it for a year, we effectively bought the forward, paying $440 an ounce to own gold in one year. Simultaneously, we sold the actual forward, the one that is tradeable, for $450. These are equivalent instruments, and they should be priced identically. When equivalent instruments do not trade at the same price an arbitrage profit can be made.

Suppose that spot gold is trading at $400 and forward gold is trading at $420 – lower than the $440 forward price we calculated earlier. Forward gold at $420 sounds like a bargain; let us buy the forward and simultaneously sell the spot to make a certain profit of $20.

If we do not own gold, we must borrow it and sell it for $400, or sell short spot gold. We can then invest the $400 from the sale of the gold. The bank will pay us 10 per cent interest, and we will have $440 in the bank a year later. Then, we will do two more transactions to close out the arbitrage: (1) withdraw money from the bank at $440 an ounce, and (2) accept delivery of forward gold at $420 an ounce, giving a net difference of $20 profit.

We have to return the gold we borrowed, and our profit may be reduced if we have to pay a fee for borrowing the gold. In the first example, the gold forward was expensive compared to the $440 it would cost us to buy gold and carry it for a year. So we sold forward gold, bought spot gold, and carried it for a year. In the second example, the gold forward was cheap, so we bought forward gold, sold spot gold, and earned interest on a bank deposit.

In both cases, we arbitraged a profit with no price risk. In fact, we exchanged price risk for basis risk. It is important to emphasize that, in both cases, forward transactions were agreed on at the beginning of the period, and actual transactions were done at the end of the period.

Regardless of what any investor thinks the price of gold will be in a year, the actions of arbitrageurs, i.e., the people who monitor the relationships between the spot and the forward, will ensure that the spot price and the forward price have the appropriate cash and carry relationship to each other. That does not mean the arbitrageurs determine the value of the spot or the value of the forward. While hedgers, speculators, and investors affect the spot price or the forward price, arbitrageurs ensure that the cash and carry relationship between the spot and forward is preserved. We have emphasized this relationship because knowing how to value futures and forwards relative to the spot price is the first step towards knowing how to value options.

What are forward market contracts?

A forward contract is an agreement between two parties made independently of any organized exchange market. Nobody other than the parties to the forward agreement needs to be involved; there are no formal rules outside the agreement between the two parties. The forward contract is a stand-alone, customized contract. It can be based on any amount of any good. It can be written for settlement at any time and at any price. It can be, as an extreme example, for delivery of 37 000 gallons of vodka in 52 days at $2 a gallon. The terms can be virtually anything as long as both parties agree to them.

One party agrees to sell the vodka at the contract price, and the other party agrees to buy it at that price. Since the contract can be for any amount of any good, at any time and at any price, and since each party depends on the other party to meet contractual obligations, the forward contract cannot be traded freely with other potential counterparties. Forwards are not fungible, i.e., one forward contract is not inter-changeable with another contract that has similar terms, and the present value of the forward contract is not easily con-verted to a cash market value.

Each party has to be able to trust that the other party will uphold his side of the agreement, because the two counter-parties are exposed to each other's ability and willingness to perform on the contract. There is credit risk associated with a forward contract, which must be controlled. This is based in the fact that you cannot be sure that the counterparty will deliver as agreed. Often, the credit risk is controlled by banks, which act as intermediaries, assuring the performance of their clients. A very important point to remember about forward contracts is that no money is exchanged by the parties until the actual exchange of goods or financial instruments at settlement. There is normally no interim cashflow.

What are futures contracts?

A futures contract, in contrast to a forward, is an agreement between two parties made through their agents on an orga-nized futures exchange. The parties who trade on the exchange can represent themselves or they can represent customers. There are specific rules and regulations that set the terms of the contract and the procedures for trading. The contract is for a specific amount of a specific good to be delivered at a specific time determined by the exchange. The price discovery, as fixing the price is often referred to, is usually, but not always, determined by open outcry in a trading pit, i.e., by people yelling and screaming prices at each other in a room.

This is the way prices are discovered and goods are exchanged in many efficient markets. Some markets now use computer systems, known as screen-based trading, which expose bids and offers to a large number of potential traders at many locations, but the principle of bringing bids and offers together is the same. Several features of futures markets are worth noting.

- First, a futures contract is always for a specific amount of a specific good. We cannot set out our own contract amount, say 37 000 gallons of vodka. If the vodka contract set by the exchange is 20 000 gallons, we can trade any number of contracts, but each contract must be for 20 000 gallons. And we must specify the type of vodka; it must be Finlandia vodka or Stolichnaya vodka, or, more likely, simply 80-proof vodka. Since all terms are determined in the futures contract, the contracts can be retraded freely with other counterparties. We can buy the contract from one person, sell the contract to another, and wash our hands of the commitment. We can eliminate our obligation, because, with futures, the organized futures exchange handling the transaction takes the other side of the contract.
- The futures exchange is the ultimate counterparty for all futures trades, so the only credit risk is the credit worthiness of the exchange, which is normally very low. Once a trade is completed, the transaction is passed to some type of exchange clearing corporation. The futures contract buyers and sellers have agreement with the clearing corporation. Ultimately, if a trader takes delivery rather than offsets the contract, i.e., reverses it, the exchange will select someone who is short the contract, i.e., has agreed to sell, to make delivery. The party making delivery does not have to be the party who sold the contract originally. After the trade settles, the original parties to the trade lose any direct tie to each other based on the trade. No credit intermediary is necessary, but margin must be deposited to ensure each party meets its obligations.

The exchange clearing corporation has to stand behind the creditworthiness of its members, so it asks everyone for a deposit. Customers make a deposit with their broker, known as margin, and the broker passes the deposit to the clearing corporation. Futures margin is a good faith deposit,

Table 11.2   The advantages and disadvantages of futures and forwards

	Futures markets	Forward markets
Default risk	+ Low	− Greater than for futures
Transaction costs/ commissions	+ Low	− Higher than for futures
Standardization	+ Contracts are liquid; allows for secondary market	− No secondary market
	− Imperfect hedge	+ Tailor made hedge
Interest rate risk	− Daily cash flows from marking to market must be deposited at unknown interest rates	Not applicable
Contract sizes and underlying currencies	− Limited number of contracts and underlying securities makes hedging with futures less effective	
Maturities	− Short maturity only	+ Slightly longer to much longer maturities than for futures

demonstrating ability and willingness to meet contractual obligations. Table 11.2 illustrates the advantages and disadvantages of futures and forward contracts.

How are options priced?

The method used to price options depends on the type of option being priced. As can be seen from Table 11.3 the two pricing

Table 11.3   European versus American options

Type of option	Exercise date	Pricing model
American option	Any time up to maturity	Cox, Rubinstein and Ross
European option	At maturity date	Black–Scholes

models are the binomial model used for American options (which was designed by Cox, Ross and Rubinstein), and the Black–Scholes option pricing model, used for pricing European options. As we show below the binomial model can also be used to price European options.

The key to valuing options is to design a risk-free portfolio in which the value does not change when there is a change in the underlying asset. This risk-free element is achieved by designing a portfolio that replicates, i.e., one in which the pay-offs of the portfolio exactly match the pay-offs of the option. A good example of this is achieved by applying the binomial model.

The binomial model

One-period binomial model: the role of the replicating portfolio

To illustrate the binomial model it is necessary to look at what the effect of the prices of the underlying stock rising or falling in price should have on the option price. Our first example is a European call option on a stock, and assumes that the stock is currently valued at $100. In this example there is an option to purchase this stock and this expires in one year and the strike or exercise price is $100. The annual risk-free interest rate is 5 per cent, so that borrowing $1 today will mean having to pay back $1.05 one year from now. For simplicity, the assumption here is that there are only two possible outcomes when the option expires: the stock price can be either $120 (an up state), or $80 (a down state). Note that the value of the call option will be $20 if the up state occurs and $0 if the down state occurs as shown below (see Figure 11.3). In other words if the price falls to $80 the option becomes valueless.

Since there are only two possible states in the future it is possible to replicate the value of the option in each of these states by forming a portfolio of the stock and a risk-free asset. If Δ, an unknown number of shares of the stock are purchased and M, an unknown amount of dollars are borrowed at the risk-free rate, the stock portion of the portfolio is worth $120 \times \Delta$ in the up state and $80 \times \Delta$ in the down state, while $1.05 \times M$ will have to be paid back in either of the two states. Thus, to match, or replicate, the value of the portfolio to the value of the option in the two possible states, it must be the case that

$$\$120 \times \Delta - 1.05 \times M = \$20 \text{ (up state)} \qquad (11.2)$$

and

$$\$80 \times \Delta - 1.05 \times M = \$0 \text{ (down state)} \qquad (11.3)$$

By rearranging the formulae from equations (11.2) and (11.3) this gives us a value for Δ.

$$\$40 \, \Delta = 20$$

$$\therefore \Delta = 0.5$$

Inserting $\Delta = 0.5$ in equation (11.2) gives us

$$\$120 \times 0.5 - 1.05 \, M = \$20$$

$$\$40 = 1.05M$$

So $M = \$38.10$

The resulting system of two equations with two unknowns Δ and M, solved above, gives us $\Delta = 0.5$, and M is approximately $38.10. Therefore, one would need to buy 0.5 shares of the stock and borrow $38.10 at the risk-free rate in order for the value of the portfolio to be $20 and $0 in the up state and down state, respectively. Equivalently, selling 0.5 shares of the stock and lending $38.10 at the risk-free rate would mean pay-offs from that portfolio of $20 and $0 in the up and down state respectively, which would completely offset the pay-offs from the option in those states. This is a powerful finding as it enables us to replicate the risk-free portfolio and price the options accordingly. It is also worth noting that the current value of the option must equal the current value of the portfolio, which is $100 \times \Delta - M = 100 \times 0.5 - M = \$11.90$. In other words,

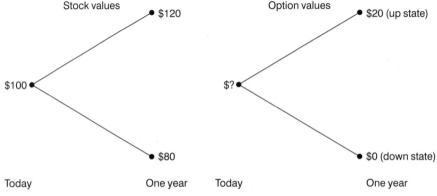

Figure 11.3 Stock and option values in the one-period model.

a call option on the stock is equivalent to a long position in the stock financed by borrowing at the risk-free rate.

The variable Δ is called the delta of the option. In the previous example, if C_u and C_d denote the values of the call option in the up and down states, with S_u and S_d denoting the price of the stock in the up and down states, respectively, then it can be verified that $\Delta = (C_u - C_d)/(S_u - S_d)$. The delta of an option reveals how the value of the option is going to change with a change in the stock price. For example, knowing both $\Delta = C_d$, and the difference between the stock prices in the up and down state, it makes it possible to know how much the option is going to be worth in the up state, i.e., C_u is also known.

The two-period binomial model

A model in which a year from now there are only two possible states of the world is certainly not realistic, but construction of a multiperiod model can alleviate this problem. The one-period model assumes a replicating portfolio for a call option on a stock currently valued at $100 with a strike price of $100 and which expires in a year. However, let us now assume that the year is divided into two six-month periods and the value of the stock can either increase or decrease by 10 per cent in each period. The semi-annual risk-free interest rate is 2.47 per cent, which is equivalent to an annual compounded rate of 5 per cent. The states of the world for the stock values are given in Figures 11.4 and 11.5. Given this structure, how does one build a portfolio of the stock and the risk-free asset to replicate the option? The calculation is similar to the one above except that it is done

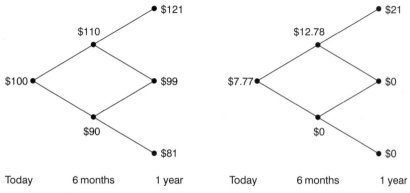

Figure 11.4 Stock values in the two-period model.

Figure 11.5 Option values in the two-period model.

recursively, starting one period before the option expires and working backwards to find the current position.

In the case in which the value of the stock over the first six months increases by 10 per cent to $110 (i.e., the up state six months from now), the value of the option in the up state is found by forming a replicating portfolio containing Δ_u shares of the stock financed by borrowing M_u dollars at the risk-free rate. Over the next six months, the value of the stock can either increase another 10 per cent to $121 or decline 10 per cent to $99, so that the option at expiration will be worth either $21 or $0. Since the replicating portfolio has to match the values of the option, regardless of whether the stock price is $121 or $99, the equations (11.4) and (11.5) must be satisfied.

$$\$121 \times \Delta_u - 1.0247 \times M_u = \$21 \qquad (11.4)$$

and

$$\$99 \times \Delta_u - 1.0247 \times M_u = \$0 \qquad (11.5)$$

Solving these equations results in $\Delta_u = 0.9545$ and $M_u = 92.22$. Thus the value of the replicating portfolio is $110 \times \Delta_u - M_u = \$12.78$. If instead, six months from now the stock declines 10 per cent in value, to $90 (the down state), the stock price at the expiration of the option will either be $99 or $81, which is less than the exercise price. Thus the option is worthless a year from now if the down state is realized six months from now, and consequently the value of the option in the down state is zero. Given the two possible values of the option six months from now, it is now possible to derive the number of shares of the stock that one needs to buy and the amount necessary to borrow to replicate the option pay-offs in the up and down state six months from now. Since the option is worth $12.78 and $0 in the up and down states, respectively, it follows that

$$\$110 \times \Delta - 1.0247 \times M = \$12.78 \qquad (11.6)$$

and

$$\$90 \times \Delta - 1.0247 \times M = \$0 \qquad (11.7)$$

Solving equations (11.6) and (11.7) results in $\Delta = 0.6389$ and $M = \$56.11$. Thus the value of the option price today is $100 \times \Delta - M = \$7.77$. The values of the stock option are shown graphically in Figures 11.4 and 11.5.

A feature of this replicating portfolio is that it is always self-financing. Once it is set up, no further external cash inflows or outflows are required in the future. For example, if the replicating portfolio is set up by borrowing $56.11 and buying 0.6389 shares of the stock, and in six months the up state is realized, the initial portfolio is liquidated. The sale of the 0.6389 shares of stock at $110 per share, nets $70.28. Repaying the loan with interest, which amounts to $57.50, leaves $12.78. The new replicating portfolio requires borrowing $92.22. Combining this amount with the proceeds of $12.78 gives $105, which is exactly enough to buy the required 0.9545 Δ_u shares of stock at $110 per share. Replicating portfolios always have this property: liquidating the current portfolio nets exactly enough money to form the next portfolio. Thus the portfolio can be set up today, rebalanced at the end of each period with no infusions of external cash, and at expiration should match the pay-off of the option, no matter which states of the world occur.

In the replicating portfolio presented above, the option expires either one or two periods from now, but the same principle applies for any number of periods. Given, in this example, that there are only two possible states over each period, a self-financing replicating portfolio can be formed at each date and state by trading in the stock and a risk-free asset. As the number of period's increases, the individual periods get shorter so that more and more possible states of the world exist at expiration. In the limit, continuums of possible states and periods exist so that the portfolio will have to be continuously rebalanced. The Black–Scholes–Merton model, discussed below, is the limiting case of these models with a limited number of periods.

What determines the value of call options?

A call option is the right to purchase the underlying asset for a specified exercise price until the expiration date. As discussed earlier, American options can be exercised at any time. European options can be exercised only at the expiration date. In the discussion below, which draws on Livingston (1995) the following notation is used.

- C is the market value of the call option
- P is the market value of the underlying asset
- E is the exercise price (strike price).

If the price of the underlying asset (P) is less than the exercise price ($P < E$), the call is described as being out-of-the-money. If P equals E, the call option is described as being at-the-money. If the price of the underlying asset exceeds the exercise price ($P > E$), the call option is described as being in-the-money.

What is the value of the call option at expiration?

At expiration, the value of the call option must be zero if the market value of the underlying asset is less than or equal to the exercise price. No rational investor would exercise a call option if the underlying asset sells for the exercise price or less since buying the underlying security in the open market would be cheaper than exercising the call option. For example, in Table 11.4, if a bond sells for $90 in the open market, a call option with an exercise price of $100 is valueless at expiration. Instead of exercising the call and paying the $100 exercise price, it is preferable to buy the bond directly for $90.

Table 11.4   Value of Call Option at Expiration (E = $100)

$P < E$	$P = E$	$P > E$
e.g. $P = 90$	$P = 100$	$P = 110$
$C = 0$	$C = 0$	$C = P - E$
		e.g. $C = 10$
out-of-the-money	at-the-money	in-the-money

Source: Livingstone (1995)

In Table 11.4, if the price of the underlying asset exceeds the exercise price, the call option is worth the price of the underlying asset minus the exercise price, i.e., $P - E$. The amount $P - E$ is called the intrinsic value of a call option. If the call option sells for less than $P - E$, an arbitrageur would buy the call, exercise it, and make an arbitrage profit. At expiration, buying the call option for $C and exercising it is equivalent to buying the underlying security directly for $P. Thus, $P = C + E$, or $C = P - E$.

At expiration, the value of a call option is:

$$C = 0 \qquad \text{if } P \leq E \quad \text{at- or out-of-the-money} \qquad (11.8)$$

$$C = P - E \quad \text{if } P > E \quad \text{in-the-money} \qquad (11.9)$$

What is the value of the call option before expiration?

With time left until expiration, an American call option has a value greater than an otherwise identical expiring call option. Table 11.5 illustrates the possibilities. Before expiration:

$$C > 0 \qquad \text{if } P \leq E \quad \text{at- or out-of-the-money} \qquad (11.10)$$

$$C > P - E \quad \text{if } P > E \quad \text{in-the-money} \qquad (11.11)$$

If these conditions do not hold, arbitrage opportunities are available to investors. For out-of-the-money call options, a zero price allows an arbitrageur to buy the call for nothing. If the call expires worthless, the arbitrageur loses nothing; if the call ends up in-the-money, the arbitrageur has a net profit. To eliminate profitable arbitrage, the market value of the call option must be positive.

Table 11.5 Value of Call Option before Expiration ($E = \$100$)

$P < E$	$P = E$	$P > E$
e.g. $P = 90$	$P = 100$	$P = 110$
$C > 0$	$C > 0$	$C > P - E$
		e.g. $C > 10$

Source: Livingstone (1995)

For in-the-money call options, a price less than the under-lying asset price minus the exercise price $(P - E)$ allows an arbitrageur to buy the call option for C and exercise it for E, for a total cost of $C + E$. The acquired security is then sold for its market value P, which, by assumption, is greater than $C + E$ for an arbitrage profit of $P - (C + E)$. To eliminate arbitrage profit opportunities, $C + E$ must be equal to or exceed P, meaning that C must be greater than or equal to $P - E$. For example, if a bond sells for $110 and if a call option with $100 exercise price sells for $5, anyone could buy the call for $5, exercise it for $100, and sell the resulting bond for $110 for a sure profit of $5.

The price of the underlying security is a logical upper bound for the price of a call option. No one should logically pay more for an option to buy a security than the price to purchase the security outright. If a bond is selling for $100, a logical person would never pay more than $100 for a call option. The investor is better off to buy the underlying asset directly in the market itself.

What is the profit profile for a call option?

The possible value of a call option can be seen from a profit profile. As a reference point, consider someone who buys a bond (for which options trade) currently selling at its exercise price of $100 and holds this bond for three months until the option expires. The possible profits and losses, overlooking coupon interest, are shown as a solid line in Figure 11.6.

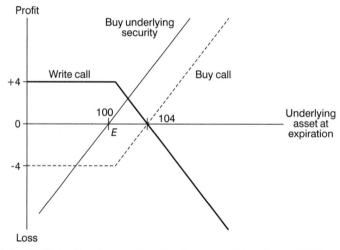

Figure 11.6 Profit profiles for a call option (source: Livingstone, 1995).

Consider the purchase of a call option for $4 with an exercise price of $100. The investor holds this call option for three months until expiration. The profit profile is shown as the dotted line in Figure 11.6. The first step in drawing the profit profile is to compute the profit and loss on the position for several levels of the price of the underlying at expiration. These prices should include the option's exercise price and several points on either side of the exercise price. The procedure is illustrated in Table 11.6.

Table 11.6 Profits of losses for a Call Buyer (*E* = $100)

	Price of Underlying Security at Expiration			
	98	100	102	104
Buy call (*C*)	−4	−4	−4	−4
Exercise call at expiration			−100	−100
Sell underlying bond acquired from exercising option			+102	+104
Net profit = +*C* −*E* +*P*	−4	−4	−2	0

Source: Livingstone (1995)

The call buyer suffers a loss of $4, the entire purchase, if the bond price is below the exercise price of $100. This $4 is the maximum loss for the buyer of a call option. If the bond price at expiration is above the exercise price, the profit equals *P* − *E* = $4. A net loss is incurred if the bond price is below $104 and a net profit if the bond price is above $104. The profit profile indicates that call buyers are anticipating a rising price for the underlying asset.

If the bond price is at or below the exercise price, the profit profile shows the call buyer's maximum loss to be the purchase price, *C*. Since this call purchase price is a small percentage of the bond price, the loss from buying a call is small in absolute dollars compared to the loss from purchasing the bond outright. On the other hand, the call buyer gains substantially if the bond does well.

For everyone who buys a call option, someone sells or writes the call. The call writer agrees to sell the underlying asset at the exercise price if the option is exercised by the call buyer. Call options are a zero-sum game, meaning that the call buyer's gains are the call writer's losses and vice versa. In effect, the buyer and the writer are betting against each other. The profits or losses for a call writer in the earlier example are shown in Table 11.7.

The profit profile for the call writer is shown in Figure 11.7. If the call is out-of-the-money at expiration, the call writer benefits by the original sale price of the call. For every dollar that the underlying asset rises above the exercise price, the call writer's profit is reduced by $1.

Table 11.7 Profits or Losses for Call Writer (E = $100)

	Price of Underlying Security at Expiration			
	98	100	102	104
Write call	+4	+4	+4	+4
Sell underlying bond at call price at expiration			+100	+100
Sell underlying bond in the open market			−102	−104
Net profit = $+C +E -P$	+4	+4	+2	0

Source: Livingstone (1995)

Put options

A put option is the right to sell a security at a stated exercise price E during a stated time interval.

What is the value of put options at expiration?

To see the value of a put option, consider the possible pay-offs at expiration for the buyer of a put (see Table 11.8). The price of a put is denoted by Pp.

At expiration, if the price of the underlying security equals or exceeds the exercise price $(P > E)$, the put has no value, since no investor would choose to sell the underlying asset at E when the higher market price of P is available. If a bond sells at $110 and if there is a put option with $100 exercise price, exercising the put

Table 11.8 Value of put option before expiration (E = $100)

$P < E$	$P = E$	$P > E$
e.g. $P = 90$	$P = 100$	$P = 110$
$Pp = P - E$	$Pp = 0$	$Pp = 0$
e.g. $Pp = 10$		

Source: Livingstone (1995)

option involves selling the bond at the exercise price of $100. For any rational investor, selling the bond at its current market price of $110 is preferable. No one would exercise the put option. At expiration, the put option expires worthless.

At expiration, if the underlying asset price is less than the exercise price, the put has value, since it represents the right to sell the underlying asset at E, which is above the current market price. Clearly, the put is worth the difference $E - P$. For example, if a bond sells for $80, a put option with a $100 exercise price is worth $20 at expiration. If the put sells for $15, an arbitrageur can buy the put for $15, buy the bond for $80, and sell the bond for $100 by exercising the put. There is a sure profit of $5.

At expiration, the value of a put, Pp, must be:

$$Pp = 0 \qquad \text{if } P \geq E \quad \text{at- or out-of-the-money} \qquad (11.12)$$

$$Pp = E - P \quad \text{if } P < E \quad \text{in-the-money} \qquad (11.13)$$

What is the value of a put option before expiration?

Before expiration, the value of a put option is shown in Table 11.9.

Before expiration:

$$Pp = 0 \qquad \text{if } P \geq E \quad \text{at- or out-of-the-money} \qquad (11.14)$$

$$Pp > E - P \quad \text{if } P < E \quad \text{in-the-money} \qquad (11.15)$$

Put option profit profile

The example in Table 11.10 illustrates a put option profit profile. Three months before expiration an investor buys a put option for a price (Pp) of $3 with an exercise price (E) of $100.

Table 11.9 Value of put option before expiration ($E = \$100$)

$P < E$	$P = E$	$P > E$
e.g. $P = 90$	$P = 100$	$P = 110$
$Pp > E - P$	$Pp > 0$	$Pp > 0$
e.g. $Pp = 10$		e.g. $C > 10$
in-the-money	at-the-money	out-of-the-money

Source: Livingstone (1995)

Table 11.10   Profits or Losses for Buying a Put Option ($E = \$100$)

	Price of Underlying Asset at Expiration			
	96	98	100	104
Buy put	−3	−3	−3	−3
Buy underlying at expiration	−96	−98		
Sell underlying in the open market	+100	+100		
Net profit = $-Pp + E - P$	+1	−1	−3	−3

Source: Livingstone (1995)

The profit profile for a put option is shown in Figure 11.7. The put buyer makes a net profit if the price of the underlying security is less than the exercise price minus the purchase price of the put (that is, if $P < E - Pp$). The profit profile clearly indicates that the put option purchaser expects falling prices for the underlying asset.

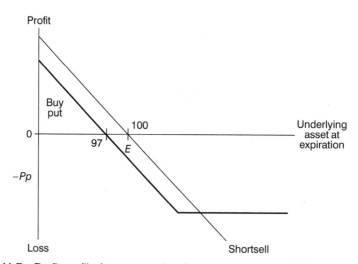

Figure 11.7   Profit profile for a put option (source: Livingstone, 1995).

The put writer (seller) enters into a contract to buy the underlying asset at the exercise price if the buyer of the put option chooses to exercise. The put writer is playing directly against the put buyer. The cash inflows to the one are the cash outflows to the other.

Put-call parity

There is a relationship between the price of a put option, the price of a call option with the same exercise price, the price of the underlying security, and the interest rate. This relationship is called put-call parity. For European options on non-dividend-paying or non-interest-bearing assets, the put-call parity relationship is given by:

Price of a call	=	Price of a put	+	Price of underlying asset	+	Borrowing the present value of the exercise price

Table 11.11 Put-Call Parity

Cash Flows at Expiration from:	$P < E$	$P = E$	$P > E$
Call	0	0	$P - E$
Put	$E - P$	0	0
Underlying	$+P$	$+P$	$+P$
Loan	$-E$	$-E$	$-E$
Net	0	0	$P - E$

Source: Livingstone (1995)

Table 11.11 shows that the purchase of a European call option results in the same cash flows at expiration as purchase of a European put option plus the purchase of the underlying asset plus borrowing the present value of the exercise price. Positions with the same value at expiration have the same value before expiration, assuming no intervening cash flows.

What are the determinants of the value of a call option?

The value of a call option is determined by the following six factors.

1. *The Price of the Underlying Asset.*
   The value of a call option is positively related to the price of the underlying security. The higher the value of the

underlying asset, the greater the value of the call option. This is not surprising, as a call buyer has bought the right to buy at a fixed price. The more the underlying asset rises the more the call option is worth, and vice versa.

2. *The Exercise Price.*

   The value of a call option is inversely related to the exercise price. The lower the exercise price, the higher the value of the call option. Other things being equal, a lower exercise price means that the call option is more in-the-money. Again this is not surprising as this is what the call option owner has to pay when he or she exercises the option.

3. *The Time until Expiration.*

   The value of a call option is a positive function of time until expiration. The longer the time until expiration, the greater the value of the call option. The reason for this is that the call owner has more time to allow his or her option to get in-the-money.

Table 11.12 illustrates the first three determinants of call option values. Look across any row of the table; the value of the call option decreases as the exercise price increases. Look down any column; as time to maturity increases and the value of the call option also increases.

Table 11.12 The Impact of Maturity and Exercise Price on Call Option prices

Maturity (months)	Price of Underlying = $110 Exercise Price		
	$90	$100	$110
3	$30	$16	$4
6	$34	$19	$6.50
9	$37	$21.50	$8.50

Source: Livingstone (1995)

4. *The Price Volatility of the Underlying Asset.*

   The greater the volatility of the underlying asset, the higher the value of the call option, since pay-offs to a call buyer are asymmetric. If the underlying asset does poorly, the call buyer loses everything. If the underlying asset does well, the call buyer does very well. Greater dispersion in the possible value of the underlying asset implies bigger call option pay-offs on the upside but the same pay-off (loss of everything) on the downside, making a call option more valuable. Obviously asset prices can fall as well as rise but if they fall the option holder has the option not to exercise his option

5. *The Risk-Free Interest Rate.*

   The higher the interest rate, the greater the value of a call option. This is based on the fact that if a call buyer has bought the option rather than the underlying asset then the funds saved can be invested at the now higher interest rate.

6. *Dividends or Interest on the Underlying Asset.*

   The higher the cash payments on the underlying asset the lower the value of a call option. The total return on an asset is the cash payment (dividends or coupon interest) plus price appreciation. For a given total rate of return, higher cash payments on an asset imply lower returns from price increases. Since the call buyer gains only if the price of the underlying asset increases, higher cash payments on the underlying asset tend to reduce the capital gains and the value of the call option.

From put-call parity, the price of a put can be shown to depend upon the call price, the price of the underlying asset, and the present value of the exercise price. It follows that the preceding six determinants of call prices also affect put prices. There are two major differences for put options. First, as the price of the underlying security increases, the value of the put goes down. That is, the value of a put is inversely related to the price of the underlying security. Second, a higher exercise price increases the value of the put. The value of a put option is directly related to the exercise price.

Table 11.13 provides an illustration of how both call options and put options respond to the factors influencing their price.

Table 11.13 Factors Affecting Option Prices

Variable increases	Call price	Put price
Share Price	Increases	Decreases
Time to Expiry	Increases	Increases
Share Volatility	Increases	Increases
Risk Free Rate	Increases	Decreases
Exercise Price	Decreases	Increases
Dividend	Decreases	Increases

Black–Scholes model

The binomial model discussed earlier, assumes a discrete-time stationary binomial stochastic process for security price movements. In the limit, as the discrete-time period becomes infinitely small, this stochastic process becomes a diffusion process (also called a continuous-time random walk, an Ito process, or geometric Brownian motion). This was the process assumed by Black and Scholes (1973) in their derivation of the option pricing formula. As with the binomial model, Black and Scholes begin by constructing a risk-less hedge portfolio, long in the underlying security and short in call options. This portfolio generates the risk-less rate of return, but the internal dynamics of the portfolio are driven by the diffusion process for the security price. The structure of the hedge portfolio can be put into a form that is identical to the heat equation in physics. Once this was recognized, the solution to the equation was easily derived.

In the case of a European call option with no cash payments on the underlying asset and with a certain, continuously compounded interest rate, Black and Scholes demonstrated that the value of a call option is an explicit function of the first five factors mentioned above. The Black–Scholes model is shown in equation (11.17).

$$C = PN(d_1) - Ee^{-rt} N(d_2) \qquad\qquad (11.17)$$

where C = the price of a call option, P = the current price of the underlying, E = the exercise price, e = the base of natural logarithms, r = the continuously compounded interest rate, and t = the remaining life of the call option.

$N(d_1)$ and $N(d_2)$ are the cumulative probabilities from the normal distribution of getting the values d_1 and d_2, where d_1 and d_2 are as follows:

$$d_1 = \frac{\ln(P/E) + (r + 0.5\sigma^2)t}{\sigma\sqrt{t}}$$

$$d_2 = d_1 - \sigma\sqrt{t}$$

where σ = the standard deviation of the continuously compounded rate of return on the underlying asset.

The term e^{-rt} is the present value of $1 received t periods from the present. It is the continuously compounded equivalent of what we have called d, the present value of $1.

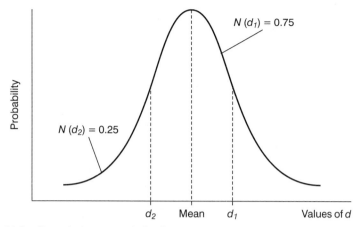

Figure 11.8 Cumulative normal distribution.

To understand the Black–Scholes model better, consider the case where $N(d_1)$ and $N(d_2)$ are both equal to 1. This is equivalent to assuming complete certainty. Then the model becomes equation (11.18).

$$C = P - Ee^{-rt} \qquad\qquad (11.18)$$

$N(d_1)$ and $N(d_2)$ represent cumulative probabilities from the Normal distribution. Figure 11.8 illustrates these cumulative probabilities, which must be numbers between 0 and 1. If they are less than 1.0, there is some uncertainly about the level of the stock price at option expiration. From the definition of d_1, d_2 must be smaller than d_1. Assume that we know that $N(d_1)$ is 0.75 and $N(d_2)$ is 0.25. Then the Black–Scholes model becomes

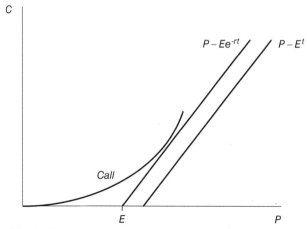

Figure 11.9 Black–Scholes model.

equation (11.19). The Black–Scholes function is shown in Figure 11.9.

$$C = (0.75)\, P - (0.25)\, Ee^{-rt} \qquad\qquad (11.19)$$

Since the Black–Scholes model requires no cash payments and interest rate certainty, it cannot be applied to debt instruments. However, the Black–Scholes models can be applied to common stocks without dividends. The model can be adapted for common stocks that pay dividends.

One of the attractions of the Black–Scholes model is that most of the inputs are readily observable. The standard deviation of the return on the underlying asset is not directly observable. However, this can be estimated from past data, if the standard deviation is relatively stable over time.

12

The new economic paradigm: how does it affect the valuation of financial markets?

During the 1990s, strong economic growth in the United States, combined with low inflation and a pick-up in labour productivity growth, led many people to label the phenomenon a 'new economy'. But there is really little consensus on what is different about the US economy nor on what the term means. In this chapter we examine the components that would be included in a general discussion of the new economy.

The new economy defined

Definitions of the 'new economy' are not precise but typically include one or more of the following characteristics.

1. A higher rate of productivity growth

The higher rate of productivity growth is largely related to investment in information technology (IT). This has resulted in what economists refer to as 'capital deepening', the process whereby the quantity of capital per worker increases over time (the capital/labour ratio). Recent examples of this are the investment in information technologies reflecting falling computer prices and new ways computers can help accomplish old tasks with fewer inputs. The microprocessor lies at the heart of these technological developments. The microprocessor's ability to manipulate, store and move vast amounts of information has, it is argued, shifted the US economy's centre of gravity, creating the era of smaller, faster, smarter, better, cheaper. To gain an appreciation of the implications of these technological developments it is instructive to look back in history (see McTeer, 1999).

From 1895 to 1915, a great burst of inventiveness ushered in an era of rapid technological change and economic growth. Americans saw the arrival of one marvel after another – automobiles, aeroplanes, telephones, phonographs, radios, elevators, refrigeration, and much more. These new inventions barely registered as a blip in a GDP dominated by farming, shopkeeping and small-scale production. In time, though, the industries that grew out of them formed the economic backbone of the 20th century. The advances of this long-ago era would have been impossible without a technology that arrived just after the Civil War: electricity. Thomas Edison created the light bulb in 1879 for the simple task of illuminating a room. To build a market for his invention, Edison harnessed electricity, building the world's first generating plant and a distribution network in New York City. As it spread through the economy, electricity recast the economic paradigm. Without electricity, there would be no spark for internal combustion engines, no power for telephones, radios, refrigerators and air conditioners. Electricity provided an ever-ready energy source for factories, with mass production driving down the cost of making just about everything.

Like electricity, the microprocesor is an important invention in its own right and one that shook the world as it touched off a rapid-fire proliferation of spillovers. In 1958 Jack Kilby of Texas Instruments fashioned the first integrated circuit, a bundle of transistors on a piece of silicon. Thus began the grand theme of modern electronics – ever smaller, ever more powerful. Thirteen years later, Ted Hoff of Intel developed the silicon-etching process that produced the first true microprocessors. Initial applications centred on number crunching and rapid data entry. Handheld calculators arrived in 1972, bar code scanners in 1974 and the personal computer in 1975.

Over the next decade or so, American industry applied microprocessors to other tasks. Whole new products, progeny of the digital electronic revolution, burst onto the marketplace, e.g. cellular telephones, robotic factory hands, air traffic control systems, global positioning satellites, laser surgery tools, camcorders, palm-size personal organizers, to name a few.

Microprocessors made existing products better, cheaper and more efficient. Starting in the early 1980s, 'smart' features helped fine-tune televisions, cut energy use by refrigerators, control cooking in microwave ovens, memorize programme schedules in VCRs and generate diagnostic reports for automobiles.

Universities were the first to hook computers into networks, but it wasn't long before everyday Americans began to connect via electronic mail. The Internet entered the 1990s as an obscure communications network for educators and scientists. It ended the decade as the library, shopping mall and playground of the masses. The Internet is creating spillovers making existing industries more efficient and spawning entirely new ones, including web page design and Internet service.

Computer processing power leapt 7000 fold in three decades. Number crunching tasks that took a week in the early 1970s now require but a minute. The Pentium chip, released by Intel in May 1993, crowds 3.1 million flawless transistors on a square of silicon 16 by 17 mm. It can churn out calculations at up to 112 million instructions per second (mips).

Data storage capacity and transmission speeds surged right along with the more powerful microprocessors. A single memory chip now holds 250 000 times as much data as one from the early 1970s – the difference between one page of text and 1600 books. Transmission speeds increased by a factor of nearly 200 000. Sending the 32-volume *Encyclopaedia Britannica* on the then equivalent to the Internet from New York to San Francisco would have taken 97 minutes in 1970. Today's trunk lines can move the equivalent of eight full sets in just one second.

Great leaps of power, capacity and speed led to even greater reductions in the cost of managing information. Intel's vintage 1970 chips sold for $7600 per megahertz. Today's Pentium III chip supplies its computing power for 17¢ per megahertz. The cost of storing one megabit of information, enough for a 320-page book, fell from $5257 in 1975 to 17¢ in 1999. Sending the *Encyclopaedia Britannica* coast to coast would have cost $187 in 1970, largely because of slow data-transmission speeds and the expense of a long-distance telephone call. Today, the entire Library of Congress could move across the nation on fibre-optic networks for just $40.

As the new technology became better and cheaper, American businesses and households embraced it. Only a few thousand homes had a PC in 1980. Now more than half of US families own computers, the newest of them 200 times more powerful than

IBM's first PC, introduced in 1981. Three-fifths of US households are connected to the Internet, a mode of instant communication scarcely heard of even at the start of the 1990s. This growth in technology provides the underpinning to the idea that the old rules of economics have been dramatically changed.

2. A rise in total factor productivity growth

Total factor productivity growth refers to the growth in output that is not explained by the physical increase in either capital or labour. Its contribution to economic growth is not easy to identify and measure but nevertheless it is an important source of economic growth. This phenomenon is due to the increased utilization of information technology across the economy resulting in spillover effects. Total factor productivity growth depends on:

● technological change
● other advances in knowledge, e.g. just-in-time manufacturing
● economies of scale.

Spillover effects occur when returns to an investment increase because others make similar investments. Examples here would be networking and the returns to an Internet capable computer as more consumers and businesses connect to the Internet.

The effect of the Internet has been to intensify product market competition with associated efficiency. The potential impact of the Internet gains can be seen from Figure 12.1. It took 36 years to achieve 50 million users for radio, 13 years for TV, 16 years for PCs but for the Internet it has taken fewer than five years.

Technology spillovers: increasing returns and decreasing costs

Even when individual industries face decreasing returns to scale, the economy as a whole may enjoy increasing returns when technology spillovers from one industry benefit others. Technology spillovers are especially abundant with inventions, whose applications spread far and wide. Innovation in one company, although intended solely for internal benefit, can spark innovation in others, triggering a powerful, economy-wide cascading effect. Revolutionary technologies can take decades to spawn all their spillovers, during which, for all practical purposes, aggregate returns to scale increase. Examples of this would include the following.

- Texas Instruments was trying to reduce the size of electronic circuitry when engineer Jack Kilby developed the integrated circuit in 1958. The benefits of that innovation far exceeded what Texas Instruments could internalize, opening a whole new science in which electronic circuitry would shrink to sizes once thought unachievable.
- Intel was pursuing circuitry small enough for a pocket calculator when Ted Hoff developed the silicon-etching process that ultimately led to the microprocessor. A 1971 advertisement in *Electronic News* heralded the 'computer on a chip' and signalled the start of the digital age.
- In seeking to make microprocessors ever smaller, IBM developed the scanning tunnelling microscope. The benefits of that research, however, went far beyond what was envisioned. The microscope enabled an entirely new industry, i.e., nano-technology, that promises to deliver molecularly-engineered materials that will reshape our world.

Gordon (1998a), a leading new economy sceptic, argues that computers pale in comparison to earlier technological advances, such as electricity, the internal combustion engine, or bio-technology. He also argues that computers may not be exceptionally productive since they primarily redistribute output, not create it. By this Gordon means that computers may increase the utility of workers by providing better working conditions, which would include computer games, or they create output which is unvalued by customers, e.g. fancy fonts.

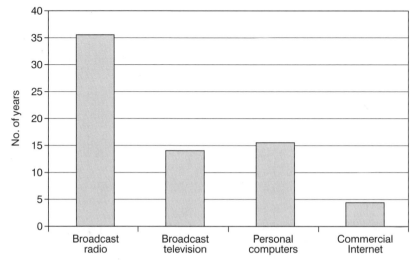

Figure 12.1 Years to achieve 50 million users. (Source: US Commerce Department.)

3. An increase in factor utilization

This is seen most clearly in the decline in the Non-Accelerating Inflation Rate of Unemployment (NAIRU), a concept first defined by Modigliani and Papademos (1975). Many economists (e.g. Meyer, 1997) subscribe to the view that there is some threshold level of the unemployment rate at which supply and demand are balanced in the labour market (and perhaps in the product market as well). This balance yields a constant inflation rate. So NAIRU is that rate of unemployment which can be sustained without a change in the inflation rate. If the unemployment rate falls below this threshold level (NAIRU), inflation tends to rise progressively over time. The US unemployment rate throughout the late 1990s and early 2000s was widely believed to be below this threshold; hence the puzzlement at the low inflation rate.

A possible explanation of the recent failure of inflation to rise in the face of strong GDP growth and low unemployment is that the NAIRU has declined, i.e., the level of the unemployment rate at which the supply of and demand for labour are in balance may be lower than it used to be. The argument, expressed, for example, by Federal Reserve Chairman Alan Greenspan (1997), that technological change has added to workers' insecurity in recent years and made them less willing to push for higher wages, may be thought of as one version of this explanation. Greater insecurity might reduce the upward pressure on wage rates at any unemployment rate and so lower the threshold rate at which wages (and prices) would begin to move upward. The reason why intensification of product market competition should lower the level of NAIRU is due to the effect of the Internet and to the globalization of world markets (discussed below).

Wadhwani (2000) has demonstrated that the effect of the Internet in the retail market should be to lower prices. This is because:

- lower search costs should lead to lower prices
- lower market entry costs will limit the price premiums sustainable by existing market participants, by increasing actual or potential competition
- shortening the supply chain will lower distribution and inventory cost.

Estimates of NAIRU suggest that the low level of unemployment during the late 1990s and early 2000s should have produced a fairly significant acceleration in prices, yet inflation continued to decline. Some like Robert Gordon (1997) and Staiger, Stock, and Watson (1997), took this occurrence as evidence that the NAIRU has declined. Others argued that special factors, such as recent movements of employee health coverage to health maintenance organizations, had temporarily masked the increase in inflation. Another often cited explanation for the surprisingly good inflation performance of the late 1990s concerns the increasing sensitivity of the US economy to foreign economic conditions. Since capacity utilization outside the US has been slack in recent years, it is argued, US inflation has remained mild. The reasoning behind this lies in the globalization of the world economy, discussed below.

4. Globalization of the world economy

'Globalization' in its economic aspect refers to the increasing integration of economies around the world, particularly through trade and financial flows. The term sometimes also refers to the movement of people (labour) and knowledge (technology) across international borders.

Increasing and unprecedented globalization, driven partly by technological change and partly by the deliberate removal of government-created barriers to the international movement of goods, services, people, financial capital, enterprises and ideas has transformed the international and domestic competitive environments.

At its most basic, there is nothing mysterious about globalization. The term has come into common usage since the 1980s, reflecting technological advances that have made it easier and quicker to complete international transactions, both trade and financial flows. It refers to an extension beyond national borders of the same market forces that have operated for centuries at all levels of human economic activity, e.g. village markets, urban industries, or financial centres.

Markets promote efficiency through competition and the division of labour – the specialization that allows people and economies to focus on what they do best. Global markets offer greater opportunity for people to tap into more and larger markets around the world. It means that they can have access to more capital flows, technology, cheaper imports, and larger export markets.

Critics of the view that globalization can raise productivity and contain inflation, particularly Krugman (1997), point out that about 85 per cent of the US economy, primarily services, is not subject to the intense pressure of the market place.

So what is the new economic paradigm?

The new economic paradigm may be summarized as the view that globalization and information technology has led to a surge in the productivity of US workers. This, in turn, has produced a sharp increase in the rate of growth that the US economy can achieve without running up against inflationary capacity limits. At the heart of the new economic paradigm is the belief that the US economy is in a phase of structural, rather than cyclical, improvement.

The essence of the new paradigm (and of its followers, the new paradigmatics, as the proponents of this idea are known) is the claim that the changes everyone can see in the US economy – the rise of digital technology, the growing volume of international trade and investment – have qualitatively altered the economic rules as represented by standard economic theories. Rapid technological change means that the economy can grow much faster than it used to. One implication being put forward by the new paradigmatics is that the US Federal Reserve should adopt higher economic growth targets in its monetary targeting.

There is no doubt that there has been a revolution in information technology. It is all around us, e.g. fax machines, WAP cellular phones, personal computers, modems, the Internet, to name just a small sample of the changes taking place. The changes taking place are in fact deeper than a cursory examination would indicate.

Information has now been digitized – words, pictures, data and so on. Digitization refers to a process whereby information is processed by manipulating numerical digits. The alternative way of processing information, analog, relies on visual information, e.g. the figures on a clock. The crudest data representation is binary: every fact to be represented must be distilled to a yes or a no, a 1 or a 0. The corresponding measure is the binary information unit, or bit. A yes or a no is a bit. A mixture of 20 yesses and noes represents 20 bits, which actually allows over a million combinations. Digital information technology usually works internally with two voltage levels, representing 0 and 1 respectively. Digitization enables information to be given a quantitative dimension. This digital technology is creating new companies and new industries.

Housing and cars used to drive the US economy. Now information technology accounts for a quarter to a third of economic growth. Information technology affects every other industry. It boosts productivity, reduces costs, cuts inventories, and facilitates electronic commerce. It is, in short, a transcendent technology, like railroads in the nineteenth century and automobiles in the twentieth.

The new paradigmatics argue that productivity growth has accelerated, which means that the acceptable rate of economic growth taking place without inflationary pressures building up, has been repealed. Here the statistics are clear. Annual labour productivity growth for the US non-farm business sector averaged 2.8 per cent over the 1995–2000 period, double its average annual rate of growth for 1973–95 and just short of its 2.9 average for 1959–73. As Robert Solow (1987), Nobel Prize winner for Economics, famously commented 'The computer is everywhere except in the productivity statistics', a comment which is now seen to be premature.

A second theme of the new paradigmatics is that global competition has the effect that the economy does not need to fear overheating and the subsequent inflation. The implication being propounded here is that because of globalization monetary expansion can now be pursued without the risk of inflation.

The globalization of business refers to the fact that capitalism is spreading around the world. This may not be full-blown capitalism but at least we are seeing the widespread introduction of market forces, freer trade and widespread deregulation. It is happening in the former communist countries, in the developing world of Latin America, and Asia.

These two trends, information technology and globalization, are undermining the old order, forcing business to restructure. If you want to compete in global markets or take advantage of rapid technological change, so the argument goes, you have to move quickly, and that often means getting rid of layers of technology. The effect is a radical restructuring that makes business more efficient.

Critics, particularly Krugman (1997), contend that there are conceptual and empirical holes in the new paradigm which mean that we have not entered a new world of higher economic growth without the undesirable effects of inflation.

Moving on to the next aspect of the new paradigm thinking, the argument claims that the happy combination of low unemployment and low inflation proves the pay-off from higher productivity growth. There is no doubt that higher productivity growth does mean lower inflation for any given rate of wage increase.

Turning now to the new importance of global competition. Unlike in the past, the story goes, US companies now have to face actual or potential competition from rivals in Europe and Asia; thus even in the face of strong demand they will not dare raise prices, for fear that these rivals will seize the market.

It is possible to question this assertion on the facts. There are without question many American firms facing international competition to an unprecedented degree. However, such global competition mainly occurs in the goods-producing sector (very few services are traded on international markets) and even within manufacturing there are many industries that remain largely isolated from foreign competitors (as Krugman comments, 'seen any Chinese refrigerators lately?'). Since the US is mainly a service economy, this means that no more than 25 per cent and probably less than 15 per cent of employment and value-added are actually subjected to the kind of global market discipline that the new paradigm emphasizes.

Why has the post-1991 US economic expansion not resulted in rising inflation?

A novel method for understanding the recent behaviour of US inflation has been propounded by Rich and Rissmiller (2000) and this has attracted the attention of financial market analysts. The longevity of the recent US business cycle expansionary phase has not resulted in the standard textbook effect of rising inflation. Two major explanations have been offered for this. The first attributes the low rates to conventional economic forces and, in particular, to a series of 'positive supply shocks'. These shocks include periodic declines in commodity and energy prices, intervals of dollar appreciation, and dramatically slower growth in medical costs. Such shocks are transitory in nature and so can be reversed at any time. The second explanation for the behaviour of inflation during the last decade holds that heightened competition among producers and the productivity advances made possible by the new information technology, have fundamentally altered the relationship between economic growth and inflation. According to this explanation, the low inflation rates reflect a permanent change in the dynamics of the inflation process.

The triangle model

To understand the behaviour of inflation during the current expansion, Rich and Rissmiller use a formulation of the Philips curve known as the triangle model of inflation (see Figure 12.2). Developed principally by Robert Gordon of North Western University, the triangle model takes its name from the specified dependence of the inflation rate on a set of three determinants: inertia, demand, and supply. How do these determinants affect inflation?

Inertia

Inertia describes the tendency of inflation to deviate only gradually from its own past values. When the economy is buffeted by a shock, inflation responds slowly, with changes occurring over a number of quarters or years. Various explanations for the persistence of inflation have been proposed. Some economists argue that the sluggish adjustment of inflation expectations keep the rate of increase in the general price level on a steady course. Others contend that the presence of wage and price contracts in the economy acts as a significant restraint on rapid changes in inflation. But whatever its sources, this slow adjustment means that past inflation will help to determine the current level of inflation.

Demand

Understanding how demand affects inflation is a bit more complicated. The relationship requires some familiarity with

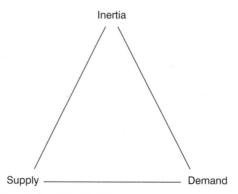

Figure 12.2 The triangle model of inflation.

the notion of output trends. The amount of output produced in the economy tends to grow over time because of increases in labour and capital and advances in technology. Although the utilization of these resources varies over the business cycle, their long-run movements can be thought of as generating a smooth underlying trend for output. When demand is above the trend level of output, there is excess demand in the economy and inflation will begin to rise. When demand is below the trend level of output, there is slack in the economy and inflation will begin to fall. Economists assume that there are unique levels of unemployment and capacity utilization that correspond to this trend growth in output. To gauge excess demand pressures in the economy, economists construct proxies measuring the current deviation of a demand variable, such as unemployment or capacity utilization from the level at which there would be no tendency for inflation to accelerate or decelerate.

Supply

Supply factors, the third determinant in the triangle model, influence inflation through sharp changes in business costs. In the 1970s, large increases in the price of imported inputs raised producers' costs dramatically and contributed to acceleration in inflation. Such supply shocks may take on greater relevance as the increased openness of the US economy exposes domestic producers and consumers more fully to shifts in the prices of imported inputs and final goods. Variables intended to capture supply shocks include the price of imports as well as food and energy prices. All three of these items can affect inflation directly because they are components of the domestic price index. In addition, import prices may have an indirect effect on inflation because changes in import prices can induce domestic firms to alter the prices of competing goods.

Does the model work?

Rich and Rissmiller found that conventional economic forces, particularly the decline in import prices explained a large proportion of the decline in inflation. Supply shocks and other conventional economic factors, rather than a change in the inflation process itself, underline the low rates of inflation of the 1990s.

The new paradigm and the price earnings ratio

The changing structure of the US economy, it can be argued, has radically altered the business environment in a manner not yet fully accounted for by accounting conventions. Newly developed products, widely used, have necessitated large-scale investment in what accountants call intangible assets, raising the value of copyrights and patents.

Microsoft's Windows 98, Paramount's movie 'Titanic', Pfizer's Viagra, and Gillette's Mach3 razor blades are four prominent examples of this. Developing each product required its corporate sponsor to invest hundreds of millions of dollars. For example, Gillette invested $700 million to develop the Mach3 razor blade in an effort begun in 1990. Paramount spent over $200 million to bring director James Cameron's vision of 'Titanic' to the screen.

These investment expenditures gave rise to economically valuable, legally recognized intangible assets, including copyrights ('Titanic' and Windows 98) and patents (Viagra and Mach3) that give the investing firms the exclusive right for a certain period to sell the newly developed products. Pfizer sold over $700 million worth of Viagra in 1998 after its introduction in April of that year; 'Titanic' sold $1 billion in cinema tickets before it entered video sales; and Gillette's Mach3 razor blade was the top seller in the US by the end of 1998, having secured more than 10 per cent of the razor blade replacement market in less than a full year.

Patents and copyrights on new consumer products are not the only types of intangible assets. New processes for making existing goods, such as the process for coating cookie wafers with chocolate, and new producer goods, such as PC servers and fibre-optic telephone cables, can also be patented or copyrighted or, perhaps, protected as trade secrets. Other intangible assets are brand names and trademarks, which can help a firm to certify the quality of an existing product or introduce new products to potential purchasers. Not only can a reputation for quality persuade shoppers to try an item for the first time, but a clever use of advertisements can go a long way toward targeting precisely those who will gain the most from the product and thereafter become loyal, repeat customers.

Yet, because they are not investments in tangible assets, most expenditures on intangible assets are not fully recognized as investments in either US companies' financial accounts or the US national income and product accounts. This practice may have been reasonable when investment in such assets was a negligible portion of US total investment, but that is no longer the case.

The effect of this lack of recognition is that corporate profits are understated because corporations are investing more of their cash flow in intangible assets. As a result price/earnings ratios are overstated, making comparison between differing time periods and different companies difficult to use as bases for deciding whether markets or individual companies are overvalued or undervalued.

Other things being equal, the price/earnings ratio should be high when the expected growth rate of profits (and thus of earnings per share) is high relative to the rate of return that stockholders require on the shares they own. That can happen when profits are temporarily low and expected to bounce back, as was the case during the 1990–91 recession in the United States. It can also happen when profits are high, as during the second half of the 1990s, if they are expected to grow rapidly in the future.

But in the long run, profits have tended to grow at the same rate as the economy as a whole. It is therefore legitimate to ask if there is any rational reason to believe that profits should grow strongly in the future and thereby justify the, until recently, high valuations placed on stocks. In fact, as Nakamura (1999) has shown, there is. As Nakamura shows, rising investment in intangible assets reduces measured current profits and raises expected future profits. Thus, rising new product development can help to explain the current high price/earnings ratio.

The accurate measurement of profits is fundamental to financial accounting. Profit tells us two things: how much revenue exceeded costs (a measure of the economic value of current operations of the firm), and how much the assets of the corporation have increased (before any cash distributions to shareholders). Accountants formally define profit as 'The excess of revenues over all expenses'. Expenses are 'the costs of goods, services, and facilities used in the production of current revenue' (Estes, 1981). To the extent that a firm buys things that are not used up in production, those additional costs are investments, not expenses, and are capitalized, i.e., considered as assets. A capital asset gives rise to an expense only to the extent that the capital asset's value falls while in use, a process called depreciation or capital consumption.

Research and Development costs are treated as part of the current expenses of the firm, and this treatment reduces reported profits. If R&D expenditure was treated as investment and capitalized and depreciated accordingly, the profitability of US non-financial corporations would have been much higher. Thus the high P/E ratios of the 1990s become easier to understand.

13

Bubbleology and financial markets

'How do we know when irrational exuberance has unduly escalated asset values?' (Alan Greenspan, 1996)

Introduction

The above quote by Alan Greenspan, Chairman of the US Federal Reserve, provoked a large fall in the US stock market and opened up the debate as to whether or not stock markets are prone to speculative bubbles and, if so, as to how financial economists can identify them?

Movements in prices in any market which are thought to be self-fulfilling prophecies are often called 'bubbles' to denote their dependence on events that come from outside the market being studied. Proponents of the idea that bubbles in financial markets occur are usually referred to as 'bubbleologists'. The idea that bubbles exist is often traced to John Maynard Keynes.

'Professional investment may be likened to those newspaper competitions in which the competitors have to pick out the six prettiest faces from a hundred photographs, the prize being awarded to the competitor whose choice most nearly corresponds to the average preferences of the competitors as a whole; so that each competitor has to pick, not those faces which he himself finds prettiest, but those which he thinks likeliest to catch the fancy of other competitors, all of whom are looking at the problem from the same point of view. It is not a case of choosing those which, to the best of one's judgement, are really the prettiest, nor even those which average opinion genuinely thinks the prettiest. We have reached the third degree where we devote our intelligences to anticipating what average opinion expects the average opinion to be. And there are some, I believe, who practice the fourth, fifth and higher degrees.' (Keynes, 1936)

The stock market Keynes (1936) wrote, 'is a game of musical chairs, of Snap, where the winner is the one who makes his move fractionally ahead of everyone else'. So the equity market, in Keynes's view, is an environment in which speculators anticipate 'what average opinion expects average opinion to be', rather than focusing on factors fundamental to the market itself, including expected future dividends etc. The implication here is that if bubbles exist in asset markets prices will differ from their long-term fundamental values.

It is only recently that serious research has taken place on the existence of bubbles. Economic theory, until recently, placed essentially no restrictions on how agents formed expectations of future prices. Thus a folklore of bubbles grew up. These would include the tulip bubbles in seventeenth century Holland, the South Sea bubble in eighteenth century England, and the increase in equity prices during the 1920s in the United States. All these events, when followed by subsequent collapses in asset values have been labelled as bubbles. However, the widespread adoption of rational expectations, discussed below, provides a model amenable to the empirical study of bubbles. But first of all we need to describe the terminology used by 'bubbleologists'.

The bubble terminology

Following the technical language of economics, a 'bubble' is any deviation from 'fundamental values' whether up or down. Fundamental values are a concept easier to define in theory than in practice. This refers to the prices stocks ought to sell for based on business's real economic value, speculation apart. The assumption is that stock prices will ultimately (whenever that is) return to their fundamental values, however much extraneous factors may be influencing them at any one moment.

A bubble is an upward price movement over an extended range that then implodes. An extended negative bubble is a crash. 'Noise' refers to small price variations about fundamental values. So a bubble is a situation in which the price of an asset differs from its fundamental market value. With a rational bubble, as discussed below, investors can have rational expectations that a bubble is occurring because the asset price is above its fundamental value but continue to hold the asset anyway. They might do this because they believe that someone else will buy the asset for a higher price in the future. In a rational bubble, asset prices can therefore deviate from their fundamental value for a long time because the bursting of the bubble cannot be predicted and so there are no unexploited profit opportunities.

The role of expectations in analysing bubbles

Beliefs about the future are an important determinant of behaviour today. Important disagreements between differing views of how expectations are formed lie at the centre of the discussion as to the existence or otherwise of bubbles. Different views about expectations can be usefully broken down into three groups: exogenous expectations, extrapolative expectations, and rational expectations. We will discuss these three groups in turn.

Exogenous expectations

Some economists remain almost completely agnostic on the vital question of how expectations are formed. When analysing the behaviour of the economy they simply treat expectations as exogenous or given. Expectations are one of the inputs to the analysis. The analysis can display the consequences of a change in expectations. For example, an increase in expected future profits might increase the share price of a firm. But this assumption of exogenous expectations means that the analysis does not investigate the cause of the change in expectations. In particular, it is unrelated to other parts of the analysis. With given expectations, there is no automatic feedback from rising output to expectations of higher profits in the future.

Thus, at best, economists using exogenous expectations in their analysis give an incomplete account of how the economy works. At worst they completely neglect some inevitable feedback from the variables they are analysing to the expectations that were an input to the analysis. On the other hand, since modelling expectations remains a contentious issue, proponents of this approach might argue that the various types of possible feedback on expectations can be explored in an ad hoc manner.

Extrapolative expectations

One simple way to make expectations endogenous, or determined by what is going on elsewhere in the analysis, when discussing the existence or otherwise of bubbles, is to assume that people forecast some variable, for example future profits, by extrapolating the behaviour of profits in the recent past, or extrapolate past inflation in order to form expectations of inflation in the near future. Proponents of this approach suggest that it offers a simple rule of thumb and corresponds to what many people seem to do in the real world.

Rational expectations

Suppose the rate of money growth is steadily increasing and inflation is steadily accelerating. If forecasting inflation then extrapolating past inflation rates will persistently under-forecast future inflation. Many economists believe that it is implausible that people will continue to use a forecasting rule that makes the same mistake (under-forecasting of future inflation, say) period after period. The hypothesis of rational expectations makes the opposite assumption: on average, people guess the future correctly. They do not use forecasting systems that systematically give too low a forecast or too high a forecast. Any tendency for expectations to be systematically wrong will quickly be detected and put right.

This in no way says that everybody gets everything exactly right all the time. We live in a risky world where unforeseeable things are always happening. Expectations will be fulfilled only rarely. Rational expectations says that people make good use of the information that is available today and do not make forecasts that are already knowably incorrect. Only genuinely unforeseeable things cause present forecasts to go wrong. Sometimes people will under-predict and sometimes they will over-predict. But any systematic tendency to do one or other will be noticed and the basis of expectations formation will be amended until guesses are on average correct.

Bubbles and the formation of expectations

The existence or otherwise of bubbles depends on which one of these models of expectations one applies. The adoption of the rational expectations assumption has clarified considerably the nature of price bubbles. With rational expectations a researcher can specify a model of bubbles, which can then be tested. If the expected rate of market price change influences the current market price the researcher has a model to work with. This is not to say that this is straightforward. There is an indeterminacy in the model as a researcher is in fact faced with something to explain, the market equilibrium price, with two variables, the market price and the expected rate of market price change, both of which are interrelated within the economic system.

A bubble can arise when the actual market price depends positively on its own expected rate of change, as normally occurs in asset markets. Since agents forming rational expectations do not make systematic prediction errors, the positive relationship between price and its expected rate of change implies a similar relationship between price and its actual rate of change. In such conditions, the arbitrary, self-fulfilling expectation of price changes may drive actual price changes independently of market fundamentals. This situation is referred to as a price bubble.

An explicit definition of market fundamentals depends on a particular model's structure; indeed, the very notion of a bubble can make no sense in the absence of a precise model detailing a markets operation. Without such a model, it is impossible both to define market fundamentals and to then isolate them from the presence, or otherwise, of a bubble.

Bubbles and the efficient market hypothesis

Efficient market theory (EMH) applies the theory of rational expectations to the pricing of securities. The EMH comes in three versions: the weak form, the semi-strong form, and the strong form.

- The weak form of the (EMH) asserts that prices fully reflect the information contained in the historical sequence of prices. Thus, investors cannot devise an investment strategy to yield abnormal profits on the basis of an analysis of past price patterns.

- The semi-strong form of the EMH asserts that current stock prices reflect not only historical price information but also all publicly available information relevant to a company's securities. If markets are efficient in this sense, then an analysis of balance sheets, income statements, announcements of dividend changes or stock splits or any other public information about a company (the technique of fundamental analysis) will not yield abnormal economic profits.
- The strong form of the EMH asserts that all information that is known to any market participant about a company, is fully reflected in market prices. Hence, not even those with privileged inside information can make use of it to secure superior investment results. There is perfect revelation of all private information in market prices.

The theory of rational expectations states that expectations will not differ from optimal forecasts (the best guesses of the future) using all available information. Rational expectations theory makes sense because it is costly for people not to have the best forecast of the future. The theory has two important implications:

- if there is a change in the way a variable moves, there will be a change in the way expectations of this variable are formed, too
- the forecast errors of expectations are unpredictable.

The lessons of the EMH are that bubbles are impossible because markets are 'efficient', i.e., prices reflect all available information about an asset. Adherents of EMH, believing that stocks are always correctly priced, tend to deny a connection between excessive speculation and subsequent economic crises. However, the necessary assumptions underlying the EMH must be simultaneously held. Thus it is necessary to examine the extent to which they do hold.

The stock market crash on 19 October 1987 should make us question the validity of efficient markets and rational expectations. EMH critics do not believe that a rational market place could have produced such a massive swing in share prices. To what degree should the stock market crash make us doubt the validity of rational expectations and efficient markets theory?

Nothing in rational expectations theory rules out large one-day changes in stock prices. A large change in stock prices can result from new information that produces a dramatic change in optimal forecasts of the future valuation of firms. Some financial economists have pointed out that there are many possible explanations for why rational explanations of the future value of firms dropped dramatically on 19 October 1987: moves in Congress to restrict corporate take-overs, the disappointing performance of the trade deficit, congressional failure to reduce the budget deficit substantially, increased fears of inflation, the decline of the dollar, and increased fears of financial stress in the banking industry. Other financial economists doubt whether these explanations are enough to explain the stock market drop because none of these market fundamentals seems important enough.

One lesson from the 1987 Black Monday stock market crash appears to be that factors other than market fundamentals may have had an effect on stock prices. The crash of 1987 has therefore convinced many financial economists that the stronger version of efficient markets theory, which states that asset prices reflect the true fundamental (intrinsic) value of securities, is in fact incorrect. They attribute a large role in the determination of stock prices to market psychology and to the institutional nature of the market place. However, nothing in this view contradicts the basic reasoning behind rational expectations of efficient markets theory, i.e., that market participants eliminate unexploited profit opportunities. Even though stock market prices may not always solely reflect market fundamentals, this does not mean that rational expectations do not hold. As long as the stock market crash was unpredictable, the basic lessons of the theory of rational expectations hold.

Rational bubbles

Famous documented 'first' bubbles (Garber, 1990) include the South Sea share price bubble of the 1720s and the Tulipmania bubble. In the latter case, the price of tulip bulbs rocketed between November 1636 and January 1637 only to collapse suddenly in February 1637, and by 1639 the price had fallen to around 1/200th of 1 per cent of its peak value. The increase in stock prices in the 1920s and subsequent 'crash' in 1929, the stock market crash of 1987, and the rise of the dollar between

1982 and 1985 and its subsequent fall, have also been interpreted in terms of a self-fulfilling bubble.

Keynes (1936), as mentioned earlier, is noted for his observation that stock prices may not be governed by an objective view of 'fundamentals' but by what 'average opinion expects average opinion to be'. His analogy for the forecasting of stock prices was that of trying to forecast the winner of a beauty contest. Objective beauty is not necessarily the issue; what is important is how one thinks the other judges' perception of beauty will be reflected in their voting patterns.

Rational bubbles arise because of the indeterminate aspect of solutions to rational expectations models, which for stocks is implicitly reflected in what is known as the Euler equation for stock prices. The Euler equation states that the price you are prepared to pay today for a stock depends on the price you think you can obtain at some point in the future. The standard form of the Euler equation determines a sequence of prices but does not 'pin down' a unique price level. However, in general the Euler equation does not rule out the possibility that the price may contain an explosive bubble.

While one can certainly try and explain prolonged rises or falls in stock prices as due to some kind of irrational behaviour such as 'herding', or 'market psychology', nevertheless recent work emphasizes that such sharp movements or 'bubbles' may be consistent with the assumption of rational behaviour. Even if traders are perfectly rational, the actual stock price may contain a 'bubble element' and therefore there can be a divergence between the stock price and its fundamental value.

So proponents of rational bubbles attempt to demonstrate how the market prices of stocks may deviate, possibly substantially from their fundamental values even when agents are homogenous, rational, and the market is informationally efficient. To do this they must show that the market price may equal its fundamental value plus a 'bubble term', and yet the stock will be willingly held by rational agents and no supernormal profits can be made.

It must be stressed that firm conclusions about the existence or otherwise of speculative bubbles are difficult to establish. There are severe econometric difficulties in testing for rational bubbles. Such tests critically depend on the correct specification for asset returns. Rejection of the no-bubble hypothesis may well be due to mis-specifying the underlying model of the fundamentals.

Some bubbles in history

It is instructive to examine some of the most famous 'bubbles' in history that have ended in speculative collapses. The most analysed have been the Tulipmania in Holland in 1636, the South Sea Bubble in England 1711–1720, and the 1929 Wall Street Crash. Recent empirical work, particularly on Tulipmania and the South Sea Bubble (Garber, 1998), has cast doubts on whether these could be classified as 'bubbles'. But it is still useful to paint the picture.

Tulipmania – Holland in 1636

The first account of tulips in Europe is from 1559 when a collector of exotic flora, Councillor Hewart, received a consignment of tulip bulbs from a friend in Constantinople, which he planted in his garden in Augsberg, Germany. His tulips drew a good deal of attention and in the following years this flower became more and more popular among the upper classes, particularly in Germany and Holland, where it became the custom to order bulbs at exorbitant prices directly from Constantinople. Up to 1634 this custom became increasingly common, and from that year affluent society in Holland considered a lack of a tulip collection to be proof of poor taste.

Year by year tulip bulb prices rose, finally reaching astronomic heights. According to original accounts of the peak of the tulip mania, in one deal the following price was paid for one tulip bulb of the rare *Semper Augustus* variety: 4600 florins, a new carriage, two gray mares and a complete bridle and harness. As a fatted ox at that time cost 120 florins, 4600 florins was an awful lot of money! One single bulb of another rare variety, *Viceroy*, was sold for 24 carriage loads of grain, eight fat hogs, four cows, four barrels of ale, 1000 pounds of butter, and a few tons of cheese.

In early 1636 demand for tulip bulbs had risen so drastically that people started to trade them on exchanges in a number of Dutch towns. Tulips were no longer bought only by well-to-do collectors but also by agents and speculators. At the smallest price drop they bought up, to sell later at a profit. To facilitate trading on margin, tulip options were introduced, requiring a margin deposit of only 10–20 per cent. Ordinary people in all business sectors started to sell off assets to invest in this attractive market.

The Dutch tulip boom also drew attention from abroad and capital began to stream into the market. This capital forced up prices for land, property and luxury goods, as well as tulips, to new record heights. Fortunes grew and a growing nouveau riche group was added to the old upper classes. This new affluent class had earned its money from, and reinvested in, tulip bulbs. The story is told of a brewer in Utrecht who went so far as to exchange his brewery for three valuable tulip bulbs.

In September and October of 1636 market psychology began to alter and doubts began to emerge. How could one be sure that three tulip bulbs were worth as much as a brewery? Suppressed mirth began to be heard. Who said a tulip bulb was worth anything at all? The market was seized by panic and prices began to plummet.

Many of the nouveau riche had to face the fact that they owned a fortune consisting only of tulip bulbs which nobody wanted, less broker cash loans which they could not repay. The government tried to find a compromise by declaring all tulip contracts from before November 1636 as being invalid, while all subsequent contracts would be honoured at 10 per cent of the original value. But prices dropped below this 10 per cent and the number of bankruptcies increased day by day. The Dutch tulip mania was followed by a depression from which it took the country many years to recover.

Garber (1989) points out that the standard version of tulipmania neglects discussion about what the market fundamental price of bulbs should have been. To form an expectation about the price of tulip bulbs, Garber collected data on bulb price patterns for various highly valued tulip bulbs. He found that the extremely high prices reported for rare bulbs and their rapid decline, reflected normal pricing behaviour in bulb markets and cannot be interpreted as evidence of market irrationality. Garber points out that serious traders ignored the market and participants in the market had almost no wealth anyway. Garber concludes that tulip prices at the time could be explained by market fundamentals and that tulipmania does not qualify as being a bubble. It must be stressed that his findings have been hotly disputed.

The South Sea Bubble

A second instructive example of bubbles was the speculation in England at the beginning of the eighteenth century. A company, later known under the name 'The South Sea Bubble', started in

1711 when the Earl of Oxford founded the South Sea Company, financed by a number of the merchants of that time. The company's full name was 'The Governor and Company of the Merchants of Great Britain to the South Seas and other parts of America for the encouragement of the Fishing'. The company acquired almost 10 million pounds of the British national debt, against a guaranteed annuity of 6 per cent, and the monopoly of all trading with Latin America.

A short time after the company's founding, rumours of incredible profits from the South Sea trading arose, where English goods could be bartered for gold and silver from the 'inexhaustible' mines of Peru and Mexico. In fact, the Spanish colonial power allowed only one English ship to call per year, for which it charged one quarter of all profits and 5 per cent of turnover. On the stock exchange the South Sea stock led a quiet existence, the price often moving only two or three points over a month.

In 1717 the King of England recommended that the national debt be 'privatized' once more. The country's two large financial institutions, the Bank of England and the South Sea Company, each submitted a proposed solution and, after heated parliamentary debate, it was resolved to allow the South Sea Company to acquire a further debt liability at an interest rate of 5 per cent per year.

But in 1719 an event took place in France that was to be of great significance for the English company. A well-to-do man named John Law had founded a company in Paris, 'Compagnie d'Occident', to trade with, and colonize, the American State of Mississippi. By a series of manipulations John Law succeeded in starting a massive wave of speculation in this company's stock, the price rising from 466 francs on 9 August to 1705 francs on 2 December 1719. Buyers were French and foreigners alike, which caused the British Ambassador to request His Majesty's Government to do something to stop the massive flow of English capital to the 'Mississippi Bubble' on the French stock exchange. The Mississippi Bubble collapsed on 2 December 1719, and in the ensuing crash investors, seeking profitable opportunities, moved their funds from France to England.

The opportunity to privatize the UK national debt provided an interesting opportunity for the principal stockholders in the British South Sea Company, who now offered to take over the entire debt of the English State. On 22 January 1720 the House of Commons appointed a committee to consider the proposal.

Despite many warnings, on 2 February the decision was taken to submit a bill to Parliament. Investors were delighted at this prospect of further capitalization of the company and over a few days the price rose to £176, supported by the inflow of funds from France by investors who were seeking new profitable opportunities. During further readings of the bill new rumours started to circulate on the unbelievable profits which could be made and stocks rose further to a price of £317.

Even at this price the company's original founders and co-directors could reap a capital gain that was enormous by the standards of that time, and in a virtually inactive company. This whetted their appetites for more, and new positive rumours were circulated on 12 April and fresh stock was subscribed to for one million pounds at a price of £300. The issue was subscribed twice over and a few days later stock was traded at £340. The company then declared that a 10 per cent dividend would be paid on all new and old stock and a further new subscription was invited for one million pounds at a price of £400. This was also over-subscribed. The company was still almost totally inactive.

Many other companies jumped on this speculative band-wagon issuing their own shares. However on 11 June 1720 the King proclaimed a number of these companies to be 'public nuisances' and trading in their stocks was prohibited on penalty of a fine. A list of 104 prohibited companies, described by Mackay (1841) below, were banned.

Despite the government's endeavours new bubbles appeared every single day and the speculation fever continued to rise. Figure 13.1 charts the progress of the South Sea bubble. The South Sea Company was traded at a price of £550 on 28 May 1720. From this already impressive level, during June the price rose above £700. In this period price movements were extremely nervous, with great periodic shifts. On a single day, 3 June, the price thus dropped before noon to £650, to rise again in the afternoon to £750. Many large investors used the high prices to take profits, which were reinvested in anything from land and commodities to real estate and other stocks. However, others bought the South Sea Company's stock, one of them the physicist, Isaac Newton. During the stock's early rises he had sold all his South Sea stock, cashing a profit of £7000. In midsummer he bought again, a transaction which would come to cost him £20 000.

At the beginning of June, South Sea stock rose again and for a short enchanted moment, on 24 June 1720, the security was

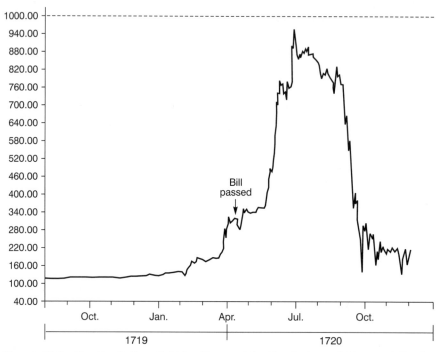

Figure 13.1 The South Sea Bubble. (Source: The Psychology of Finance & Trade. John Wiley & Sons Ltd.)

traded at £1050. As only few were aware, the time was running out for investors. Those in the know were the company's original founders and its Board Chairman, who had used the earlier high prices to get rid of their own stock. At the beginning of August this ominous fact began to leak to the general public and the stock price began to fall slowly and steadily.

On 31 August the South Sea Management announced that an annual dividend of 50 per cent would be paid for the following 12 years. This would have completely drained the company of cash and the news did not stop the investors' increasing unease. On 1 September the stock continued to fall and when it reached £725 two days later, panic broke out. The security went through the floor over the rest of the month and when the company's bank was declared bankrupt on 24 September the fall accelerated. On the last day of the month the share could be bought at a price of £150. In only three months it had fallen by 85 per cent.

The company was finally dissolved in 1855 and its stock converted to bonds. In its 140 years of existence the company never succeeded in trading in the South Seas on any note-worthy scale.

The Wall Street Crash of 1929

The 1929 Wall Street Crash was the conclusion of one of history's largest episodes of mad speculation. For a number of years up to 1924 the American Dow Jones Industrial Index fluctuated within a relatively narrow price interval with strong selling pressure whenever it reached 110. From 1921, when the stock market was very depressed, to 1928, industrial output rose by 4 per cent annually and by 15 per cent from 1928 to 1929. Inflation was low and new industries sprouted forth everywhere.

This rising optimism, combined with easy access to cheap money, stimulated stock investors and after a temporary reversal in 1926 almost no month passed without a rise in stocks creating a new generation of rich investors. Investment trusts increased in number as stock investments rose in popularity. From around 40 companies before 1921, the number rose to 160 at the beginning of 1927 and 300 at the end of the same year. From the beginning of 1927 to the autumn of 1929 the total assets of investment trusts increased more than 10-fold and there was almost unlimited confidence in these companies.

On 24 October 1929, trading reached 12 million stocks. Nervousness, however, had set in and a panic was evident. As the situation was clearly getting out of hand, on 25 October President Hoover made the following statement: 'The fundamental business of the country, that is, production and distribution of commodities, is on a sound and prosperous basis'.

Hoover's declaration had the same reassuring effect as a pilot announcing that the engine was not on fire. Panic grew and in the next few days prices continued to fall. This culminated on 29 October when, in a wave of enforced sales, 16 million stocks were realized at any price going. The story goes that a messenger at the exchange got the idea of bidding a dollar per share for a lot without buyers – and got his deal. Prices did not start to stabilize until the index reached 224, on 13 November, as shown in Figure 13.2. In 1930 prices started to fall once more, continuing to a bottom of 58 on 8 July 1932.

Speculative bubbles theory

Applying the speculative bubbles theory, stock market investment is more about inflating and bursting speculative bubbles than about investors making rational long-term forecasts.

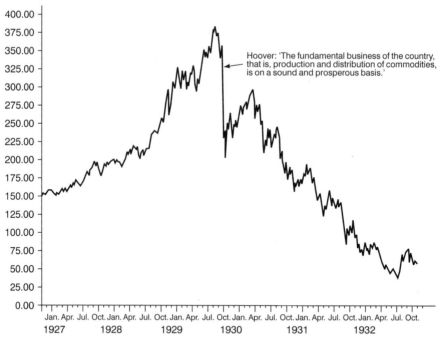

Figure 13.2   The 1929 stock market crash. (Source: The Psychology of Finance & Trade. John Wiley & Sons Ltd.)

Under the speculative bubble theory an asset's price can be bid up above its intrinsic value because some market participants believe that others will be willing to pay still more for it tomorrow. For a while this belief is self-sustaining and the market booms, but eventually participants lose faith that prices can rise further and the market crashes.

   This theory, also named by Malkiel (2000) the 'Castles in the Air' Theory, based upon the thrills of making a killing by selling castles in the air, has long antecedents. Examples in history abound. Two, of its best known examples are the Tulip Bulb Mania and the South Sea Bubble, discussed earlier. Under the Tulip Bulb Theory of 1593, the price of tulips rose to the extent that, prior to its collapse, one tulip would have fed a ship's crew for a year. The South Sea Bubble of 1711 offered the rights to monopolies in the South Sea enabling fortunes to be made and lost.

   MacKay (1841) provides an impressive list of South Sea Bubble emulators. Companies were created to:

- design a wheel of perpetual motion
- build hospitals for bastard children
- build ships to defeat pirates

- improve the art of making soap
- extract silver from lead.

One of the most outrageous companies was one which was designed to be 'a company for carrying on an undertaking of great advantage but nobody knew what it was'. The propagator of this company took £2000 in one afternoon and was never seen again! The shares of all these companies had the characteristics of speculative bubbles.

Rational speculative bubbles

Hardouvelis (1988) has argued that speculative bubbles may be triggered by an extraneous event that is unrelated to funda-mental economic conditions. For example, one group of invest-ors buys with the expectation of a large capital gain, and others follow suit, without paying proper attention to economic factors, such as future dividends or interest rates. If such behaviour persists, it may feed on itself as consecutive waves of buying increase prices. Speculative bubbles may subsequently burst very suddenly. An overvalued market is fragile and a relatively unimportant piece of 'bad' news may easily create pessimism and set off a selling wave.

The traditional method of searching for market overvaluation or speculative bubbles counts the number of unusually high returns during the suspected bubble period and assesses the likelihood that the total number of these high returns could have arisen from chance (Blanchard and Watson, 1982). An unusually high return (or a positive 'abnormal' return) is a return higher than the risk-free rate plus the usual risk premium necessary to compensate risk-averse shareholders for the uncertainty associated with their security returns. In the absence of a speculative bubble, a very large number of unusually high returns would normally occur by chance only with a small probability. Hence, a large number of unusually high returns constitutes evidence consistent with the presence of speculative bubbles.

Unfortunately, although simple, the traditional test has low statistical power to detect speculative bubbles; share prices are very volatile and their swings generate both large positive and large negative returns. The latter tend to mask any existing bubble evidence.

In order to construct a more powerful test for bubbles, it is necessary to formulate a more precise economic account of the development of the bubble. One can imagine many different scenarios of market overvaluation, but analysis restricts the possible scenarios to those in which investors know that the market is overvalued yet show no special desire to liquidate their positions and continue to buy or sell as they would in the absence of bubbles. This is a realistic working assumption for the period before October 1987. Robert Schiller (1987) provides survey evidence indicting that, before October 1987, 71.7 per cent of individual investors and 84.3 per cent of institutional investors thought that the market was overvalued at the time. Schiller argued that the crash was generated by what he calls a 'feedback loop'. After a first price decline investors sold, not based on fundamentals, but because they were worried about what was going on and about market irrationality. The drop did not stop until enough people started to have opposing feelings.

Explaining why investors did not get out of an overvalued market is more difficult. One could argue that the presence of highly liquid futures markets and associated trading strategies, such as portfolio insurance, led investors to the false belief that they could enjoy large positive returns in an upward market yet still avoid suffering a large loss if the market took a big plunge.

An alternative explanation outlined above by Hardouvelis (1988) is one that does not depend on some sort of collective irrationality. Within the economics literature this is known as the 'rational speculative bubble hypothesis'.

The 'bubble premium'

In the case of a rational speculative bubble, investors know that the bubble may crash and that they will not be able to get out once the crash starts, but they remain in the market because they believe (for whatever reason) that there is a good probability that the bubble will continue to grow, bringing them large positive returns. These returns are expected to be higher than the risk-free rate plus the usual risk premium in the absence of bubbles, and large enough to compensate them exactly for the probability of the bubble crash and a large one-time negative return. Hence, it is rational for investors to stay in the market.

The expected extra return when no bubble crash occurs can be called the 'bubble premium'. The theory implies that the bubble premium is not only positive, but also increases during the lifetime of the bubble. The time trend in the bubble premium derives from the explosive nature of the bubble component of the share price. As time goes on, the bubble component of the share price grows larger and larger relative to the fundamental components. This growth implies that with the passage of time, the expected drop in the share price in the case of a bubble crash grows larger too, necessitating a larger and larger bubble premium.

Diffusion indexes: their construction and interpretation

Burns and Mitchell (1946) observed that a business cycle expansion does not imply that every underlying economic activity is expanding, nor does a business cycle contraction mean that every business cycle firm has declining sales. They further observed that economic activity has two types of cycles: seen and unseen. One cycle is in the fluctuation of the aggregate measure itself and consequently is seen. But a second cycle – the unseen or diffusion cycle – exists in the distribution of components within that aggregate based on the number of expanding or contracting segments. This unseen cycle is important because it helps to monitor and forecast the path of the cycle. In particular, cyclical expansions or contractions diminish in scope before they come to an end and contractions that ultimately become severe are widespread in their early stages.

The concept of diffusion is made operational by defining it as a time series representing the percentage of components within an aggregate that are expanding. An index of diffusion is calculated from the percentage of components expanding (E), the percentage of components that are unchanged (U), and the percentage of components that are contracting (C) as $E + (\frac{1}{2} \times U)$, where $E + U + C = 100\%$. A related concept is the net per cent rising (NPR), which is defined as $E - C$.

About 15 regional purchasing manager surveys, including the Business Outlook Survey of the Philadelphia Fed, are taken around the country and many of those surveys report their results using the NPR formula, which can range between +100 and –100. Since NPR simply takes the difference between the percentage of the responses reporting 'higher' and the percentage reporting 'lower' (higher–lower), the bounds are clear. If all the responses are higher, then 100 – 0 per cent, or +100, is the upper bound, while if all the responses are lower, then 0–100 per cent, or –100, determines the lower bound. This is the format in which the Philadelphia Fed diffusion index, discussed in Chapter 7, is reported.

On the other hand, the National Association of Purchasing Management's survey results (discussed in Chapter 7) are compiled into a diffusion index (DI) that is bounded by 0 and 100 per cent. The DI is calculated as $100 \times (\text{higher} + (\text{same}/2))$, where higher represents the percentage of the sample reporting an increase, and same represents the percentage of the total reporting no change. Note that those reporting lower responses are excluded. The relationship between these two summary measures, the NPR and the DI, is illustrated below.

How do you compare the two methods?

Consider the basic information used to calculate both measures, that is, the share of the sample that is higher, lower, and unchanged. For example, assume that the Philly Fed reported a NPR reading for their new orders series of +20 based on the following responses: higher, 30 per cent; same, 60 per cent; lower, 10 per cent. Then the NPR equals the percentage of the sample reporting higher minus the percentage reporting lower, that is, 30 – 10 per cent, or 20 per cent, and that is expressed as a +20 reading. The DI, however, is 30 + (60/2) per cent, or 60 per cent. The relationship between the two measures is:

$$NPR + 2 \times (DI - 50)$$

where NPR is the net percentage rising (e.g. +20) and DI is the NAPM-type diffusion index (e.g. 60 per cent). Alternatively, the identity can be expressed as:

$$DI = 50 + (NPR/2)$$

The relationship between the aggregate time series and the diffusion index is shown in Figure A.1. There are four stages of the diffusion index and its corresponding phase in the aggregate cycle. Stage 1 occurs when the diffusion index moves up from 50 to 100 per cent (or simply when the index is above 50 per cent and rising), which implies that the aggregate series is increasing at an increasing rate. In stage 2, the diffusion index is declining from its upper bound of 100 to 50 per cent (or simply the index moves from a higher to a lower number above 50 per cent); this implies that the aggregate series is increasing at a decreasing rate. At stage 3, the diffusion index is below 50 per cent and declining, which implies that aggregate series is decreasing at an increasing rate. Finally, stage 4 takes place when the diffusion index is moving up from its lower bound of 0 to 50 per cent; this implies that the aggregate series is declining at a decreasing rate.

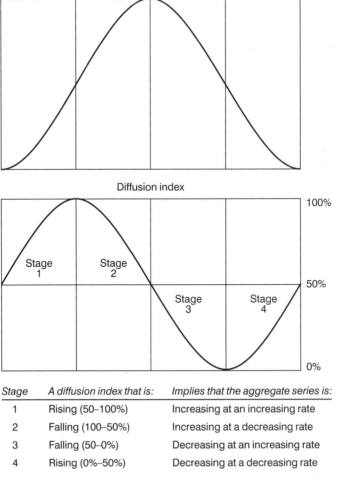

Stage	A diffusion index that is:	Implies that the aggregate series is:
1	Rising (50–100%)	Increasing at an increasing rate
2	Falling (100–50%)	Increasing at a decreasing rate
3	Falling (50–0%)	Decreasing at an increasing rate
4	Rising (0%–50%)	Decreasing at a decreasing rate

Figure A.1 The relationship between the aggregate series and the diffusion index. (Source: Economic Review, 1971, Federal Reserve Bank of Cleveland.)

The construction and interpretation of price indices

This appendix provides additional details about the GNP deflator and the consumer price index. Knowing how the indexes are actually put together makes it easier to understand the differences between the two and how to best interpret them.

The GNP deflator for a simplified economy

A much simpler economy than that of the United States will serve to illustrate the computation of price indexes. Table B.1

Table B.1 Nominal GNP in selected years for a simple economy

1992	Quantity	Price	Value
Movies	50	$2.00	$100
Apples	1000	.20	200
Shirts	10	10.00	100
1992 Nominal GNP			$400
2002			
Movies	100	$4.00	$400
Apples	500	.60	300
Shirts	20	15.00	300
2002 Nominal GNP			$1000

shows price and quantity data for 2 years for an economy in which only three goods are produced: movies, apples and shirts. The exhibit indicates that nominal GNP grew from $400 in 1992 to $1000 in 2002. But how are these figures to be interpreted? Do they mean that people really had more of the things they wanted in 2002 than in 1992? More exactly, do they mean that people had 2.5 times as much? These questions are not easy to answer from an inspection of Table B.1 as it stands.

In this simple economy, where only three goods are produced, nominal national income grew from $400 in 1992 to $1000 in 2002. Prices also went up in that time, though, so people did not really have 2.5 times as many goods as in 1992.

A line-by-line comparison of the 2 years shows that the figures on nominal income do not tell the whole story. Clearly, prices went up sharply between 1992 and 2002. Movies cost twice what they used to, apples three times as much, and shirts half again as much. We notice also that the quantities of goods produced have changed. Twice as many movies and shirts were produced in 2002 as 1992, but only half as many apples.

If we want to know how much better off people were in 2002 than in 1992, we need a way to separate the quantity changes that have taken place from the price changes. One way to do this is to ask how much the total value of output would have changed from 1992 to 2002 if prices had not changed. This approach gives the results shown in Table B.2. There, we see that the 2002 output of 100 movies, 500 apples, and 20 shirts, which had a value of $1000 in terms of the prices at which the goods were actually sold, would have had a value of only $500 in terms of the prices that prevailed in 1992. The $500 is thus a measure of real GNP for 2002. It is this measure that should be compared to the 1992 GNP of $400 if we want to know what really happened to output between the two years. Instead of having 250 per cent more output in 2002 than in 1992, as indicated by the change in nominal GNP from $400 to $1000, the people in this simple economy really had only about 25 per cent more, indicated by the change in real GNP from $400 to $500.

Table B.2 shows how the figures from Table B.1 can be adjusted to take changing prices into account. The 2002 quantities are multiplied by 1992 prices to get the value of the 2002 GNP as it would have been if prices had not changed. The total of 2002 quantities valued at 1992 prices is a measure of real GNP for 2002, stated in constant 1992 dollars. The implicit

Table B.2 Nominal and real GNP in 2002 for a simple economy

	2002 Quantity	2002 Price	Value at 2002 price	1992 Price	Value of 2002 Output at 1992 price
Movies	100	$4.00	$400	$2.00	$200
Apples	500	0.60	300	0.20	100
Shirts	20	15.00	300	10.00	200
Totals		2002 nominal GNP = $1000		2002 real GNP = $500	

GNP deflator for 2002, calculated as the ratio of 2002 nominal GNP to 2002 real GNP, has a value of 200.

We have now seen how to compute real and nominal GNP for 2002 directly from price and quantity data, without using a price index to convert nominal to real values. But although we have not explicitly used a price index, we have created one implicitly. This implicit index, or implicit GNP deflator, is the ratio of current-year nominal GNP to current-year real GNP times 100, as expressed by the formula:

$$\text{GNP deflator} = \frac{\text{Current year output valued at current year prices}}{\text{Current year output valued at base year prices}} \times 100$$

Applying the formula to the data in Tables B.1 and B.2 gives a value of 200 for the 2002 deflator.

The consumer price index for a simplified economy

The consumer price index differs from the GNP deflator in two ways. First, as mentioned in Chapter 5, it takes into account only the prices of goods and services typically consumed by urban households. Second, it is calculated according to a formula that uses base-year quantities rather than current-year quantities. The first difference does not matter for this simple economy in which all goods are consumer goods, but the second difference does matter, as Table B.3 demonstrates.

The consumer price index can be calculated as the base-year market basket of goods valued at current-year prices divided by the base-year market basket valued at base-year prices,

Table B.3 Calculation of a consumer price index for a simplified economy

Good	1992 Quantity	1992 Price	Value of 1992 Quantity at 1992 price	2002 Price	Value of 1992 Output at 2002 price
Movies	50	$2.00	$100	$4.00	$200
Apples	100	0.20	200	0.60	600
Shirts	10	10.00	100	15.00	150
Totals			$400		$950

$$CPI = \frac{\$950}{\$400} \times 100 = 237.5$$

multiplied by 100. Table B.3 shows how such an index can be calculated for the simple economy used in Tables B.1 and B.2. The 1992 output cost $400 at the prices at which it was actually sold. If it had been sold at 2002 prices, it would have cost $950. The CPI for 2002 is thus 237.5.

To calculate the CPI for this simplified economy, instead of asking how much current-year output would have cost at base-year prices, we begin by asking how much base-year quantity would have cost at current-year prices. The index is then calculated as the ratio of the two different valuations of base-year quantities.

Consumer price index

$$= \frac{\text{Base-year market basket valued at current-year prices}}{\text{Base-year market basket valued at base-year prices}} \times 100$$

The CPI is calculated using base-year quantities in part because current price data are easier to collect than are current output data. This index can thus be announced each month with a minimum of delay.

Comparing the CPI and GNP deflator

As Table B.3 shows, the CPI for 1992 in our simple economy had a value of 237.5, whereas the GNP deflator for 2002 was only 200. Both indexes were calculated using the same underlying data, and both used 1992 as a base year. Which, if either, is the true measure of the change in the price level between the two years?

The reply is that neither the CPI nor the GNP deflator is the only correct measure of change in the price level. Instead, each is the answer to a different question. The GNP deflator is the answer to the question: How much more did the 2002 output cost at the prices at which it was actually sold than it would have cost if it had been sold at 1992 prices instead? The CPI, in contrast, is the answer to the question: How much more would the 1992 output have cost if it had been sold at 2002 prices instead of its actual 1992 prices?

Careful inspection of the data shows why the answers to the two questions are not the same. In 1992 lots of apples and not very many shirts were produced in comparison to 2002. Yet, between the two years, the price of apples increased 200 per cent while the price of shirts increased only 50 per cent. Because the CPI uses base-year quantities, it gives a heavy weight to apples, which experienced relatively the greatest price increase, and not much weight to shirts, which experienced only a modest price increase. In contrast, the GNP deflator uses current-year quantities, thereby downplaying the importance of apples and emphasizing that of shirts.

We see now why it is that the CPI tends to have what is referred to as an upward substitution bias relative to the GNP deflator. But that does not make the GNP deflator a true measure of change in the cost of living. It could just as well be said that the GNP deflator has a downward substitution bias relative to the CPI or that each has an opposite bias from some 'true' price index lying between them.

Appendix C

Title, Announcement Time, and Reporting Entities for Macroeconomic Announcements

Time	Short Title	Full Title	Reporting Entity
8.30 a.m.	Consumer Price Index (CPI)	Consumer Price Index	Bureau of Labor Statistics
8.30 a.m.	Durable Goods Orders	Advance Report on Durable Goods Manufacturers' Shipments and Orders	Bureau of the Census
8.30 a.m.	Employment	The Employment Situation	Bureau of Labor Statistics
8.30 a.m.	Gross Domestic Product (GDP)	Gross Domestic Product	Bureau of Economic Analysis
8.30 a.m.	Housing Starts	Housing Starts and Building Permits	Bureau of the Census
8.30 a.m.	Initial Jobless Claims	Initial Jobless Claims	Bureau of Labor Statistics
8.30 a.m.	Leading Indicators	Composite Indexes of Leading, Coincident, and Lagging Indicators	Bureau of Economic Analysis
8.30 a.m.	Personal Income	Personal Income and Outlays	Bureau of Economic Analysis
8.30 a.m.	Producer Price Index (PPI)	Producer Price Indexes	Bureau of Labor Statistics
8.30 a.m.	Retail Sales	Advance Retail Sales	Bureau of the Census
8.30 a.m.	Trade Balance	US International Trade in Goods and Services	Bureau of the Census. Bureau of Economic Analysis
9.15 a.m.	Industrial Production and Capacity Utilization	Industrial Production and Capacity Utilization	Federal Reserve Board
10:00 a.m.	Business Inventories	Manufacturing and Trade: Inventories and Sales	Bureau of the Census
10:00 a.m.	Consumer Confidence	Consumer Confidence Index	Conference Board
10:00 a.m.	Construction Spending	Value of New Construction Put in Place	Bureau of the Census
10:00 a.m.	Factory Inventories	Manufacturers' Shipments, Inventories and Orders	Bureau of the Census
10:00 a.m.	NAPM Survey	National Association of Purchasing Management Index	National Association of Purchasing Management
14:00 p.m.	New Single-Family Home Sales	New One-Family Houses Sold and For Sale	Bureau of the Census

Consumer and Business Confidence Surveys

(a) Business Surveys

Performed by	Since	Frequency	Sectors	Sample Size	Form of Publication
National Association of Purchasing Management Tempe, AZ	1931	Monthly	Purchasing Managers	300	'Report on Business'
Dun & Bradstreet New York	1947	Quarterly	Manufacturing, wholesale, retail non-financial services	3000	'Dun & Bradstreet Looks at Business'
	1987	Quarterly	Business executives in 14 countries	9000	'Dun & Bradstreet Looks at Business'
	1990	Monthly	Manufacturers	1000	Press Releases
Federal Reserve Bank Philadelphia, PA	1967	Monthly	Regional manufacturers		'Business Outlook Survey'

Organization	Year	Frequency	Coverage	Sample	Publication
Manpower Temporary Services, Inc. Milwaukee, WI	1977	Quarterly	Public and private industries in all regions	15 000	Hiring intentions survey; in-press release
National Federation of Independent Business (NFIB) Washington, DC	1973	Quarterly	Small business in manufacturing, wholesale, retail trade, services, construction, and transportation	2000	Quarterly press release
The Conference Board New York	1976	Quarterly	All industries	1600	'Report on Business Expectations'

(b) Investment Surveys

Organization	Year	Frequency	Coverage	Sample	Publication
US Department of Commerce Washington, DC	1947	Quarterly	All industries	13 000	'Survey of Current Business'

(c) Consumer Surveys

Organization	Year	Frequency	Coverage	Sample	Publication
ABC News/Money Magazine New York	1985	Weekly		1000	Consumer Comfort Index report to clients
Sindlinger & Co. Wallingford, PA	1957	Weekly		2000	Reports to clients
Conference Board New York	1968	Monthly		5000	Reports to clients; press releases
University of Michigan Survey Research Institute Ann Arbor, MI	1946	Monthly		500	Reports to clients

Useful web addresses

Search engines

Alta Vista	www.altavista.com
MSN	www.msn.com
Yahoo	www.yahoo.com
Netscape	www.netscape.com
AOL	www.aol.com
Hotbot	www.hotbot.com
Excite	www.excite.com
Infoseek	www.infoseek.com
Lycos	www.lycos.com
Euroseek	www.euroseek.com
Copernic	www.copernic.com
Ukplus	www.ukplus.com
Google	www.google.com

Newspapers

The Financial Times	www.ft.com
The Times	www.the-times.co.uk
The Independent	www.independent.co.uk
The Telegraph	www.telegraph.co.uk
The Sunday Times	www.sunday-times.co.uk

Journals

The Economist	www.economist.com
Risk	www.risk.com
Securities Data	www.secdata.com
Capital Data	www.capitaldata.com

International Financing Review	www.ifr.com
Euroweek	www.euroweek.com
Euromoney	www.euromoney.com
Futures and Options World	www.fow.com
The Banker	www.banker.com
Investors Chronicle	www.investors.chronicle.co.uk
The Wall Street Journal	www.wsj.com
Institutional Investor Journals	www.iijournals.com
Waters	www.watersinfo.com
Risk Publications	www.riskpublications.com
Futuresmag	www.futuresmag.com
International Financing Review	www.ifrpub.com
Stocks and Commodities	www.traders.com
Numa Web	www.numa.com

Information service providers

Bloomberg	www.bloomberg.com
Electronic Share Information	www.esi.com
Datastream	www.datastream.com
Market-eye	www.market-eye.com
CNBC	www.cnbc.com
Knight Rider	www.rider.com
Bridge	www.bridge.com
Reuters	www.reuters.com
Telekurs	www.telkurs-financial.com
Extel	www.info.ft.com

Investment banks

J P Morgan	www.jpmorgan.com
Lehman Brothers	www.lehman.com
Banque Paribas	www.paribas.com
Warburg Dillon Read	www.wdr.com
Salomon Smith Barney	www.ssb.com
Merrill Lynch	www.ml.com
Commerzbank	www.commerzbank.de
Killik & Co	www.killickco.co.uk.

Cazenove	www.cazenove.co.uk.
GNI	www.gni.co.uk
Bankers Trust	www.bankerstrust.com
Schroders	www.schroders.com
Natwest Global Financial Market	www.natwestgfm.com
Goldman Sachs	www.gs.com
Rabobank	www.rabobank.com
The Bank of New York	www.bankofny.com
HSBC	www.hsbc.co.uk
Chase Manhattan	www.chase.com
Fleming Asset Management	www.flemings.com
Charles Stanley	www.charles-stanley.com
Bank of America	www.bankamerica.com
ABN AMRO Hoare Govett	www.abn.com
Nomura	www.nomura.jp
Societe Generale	www.socgen.com
Morgan Stanley Dean Witter	www.ms.com
Deutsche Morgan Grenfell	www.deutsche-bank.de/global
Dresdner Kleinwort Benson	www.dresdner.com
Citibank	www.citibank.com
Charles Schwab	www.schwab-europe.com
Barclays Capital	www.barcap.com

Regulators and associations

The Bond Market Association	www.bondmarket.com
British Bankers Association	www.bba.org.uk
ACI	www.aci.org.uk
European Bond Commission	www.ukbe.org.uk
IMRO	www.imro.org
LAUTRO	www.lautro.org
Securities Industry Association	www.sia.com
Securities and Exchange Commission	www.sec.gov
International Organisation of Securities Commission	www.iosco.org
International Swaps and Derivatives Association	www.isda.org
International Securities Market Association	www.isma.org
Financial Services Authority	www.fsa.gov

International exchanges

New York Stock Exchange	www.nyse.com
New York Mercantile Exchange	www.nyme.com
NASDAQ	www.nasdaq.com
AMEX	www.amex.com
LIFFE	www.liffe.com
LSE	www.lse.com
LME	www.lme.com
FTSE	www.ftse.com
CREST Co	www.crestco.co.uk
MATIF	www.matif.fr
SIMEX	www.simex.com
Chicago Mercantile Exchange	www.cme.com
Chicago Board of Trade	www.cbot.com
Chicago Board Option Exchange	www.cboe.com
Deutsche Term Bourse	www.dtb.de
Dow Jones	www.dowjones.com
Philadelphia Stock Exchange	www.phlx.com

Ratings agencies

Standard and Poors	www.spglobal.com
Moody's	www.moodys.com
Fitch IBCA	www.fitchibca.com

Financial software

Artisan Analytics	www.artisananalytics.com
Risk Manager	www.riskmanager.com
Fast	www.fastweb.gsia.cmu.edu
Trader Trainer	www.tradertrainer.dk

International government organizations

European Commission	http://europa.eu.int
European Investment Bank	www.eib.eu
European Bank of Reconstruction and Development	www.ebrd.org

European Central Bank	www.ecb.int
Bank for International Settlements	www.bis.org
Bank of England	www.bankofengland.co.uk
HM Treasury	www.hm-treasury.gov.uk
UK Office for National Statistics	www.ons.org
Department of Trade and Industry	www.dti.org
Organisation for Economic Co-operation and Development	www.oecd.org
National Bureau of Economic Research	www.nber.gov
The World Bank	www.worldbank.org
United Nations	www.un.int
United Nations Conference on Trade and Development	www.unctad.org
US Federal Reserve	www.bog.frb.fed.us
World Trade Organisation	www.wto.org
International Monetary Fund	www.imf.org

UK institutions

Bank of England	www.bankofengland.co.uk
Bank of England: Euro	www.bankofengland.co.uk/euro.htm
Bank of England: Practical Issues	www.bankofengland.co.uk/euro/piq.htm
Bank of England: Practical Preparations Q&A	www.bankofengland.co.uk/euro/qanda.htm
HM Treasury	www.hm-treasury.gov.uk
HM Treasury: Euro	www.euro.gov.uk
The Financial Services Authority	www.fsa.gov.uk
Investment Management Regulatory Organisation (IMRO)	www.imro.co.uk
The Securities and Futures Authority (SFA)	www.sfa.org.uk
Corporation of London	www.cityoflondon.gov.uk

European Union institutions

European Institutions (General)	europa.eu.int/index.htm
European Commission	europa.eu.int/comm/index_ en.htm
European Parliament	europa.europarl.eu.int
Economic and Financial Committee	europa.eu.int/comm/ economy_finance/

Member states' euro information

Austria	www.bmwa.gv.at
Belgium	euro.fgov.be
Finland	www.bof.fi
France	www.finances.gouv.fr/euro
Germany	www.bundesfinanzministerium. de
Ireland	www.irlgov.ie/finance
Italy	www.tesoro.it
Luxembourg	www.etat.lu/Fl/
The Netherlands	www.euro.nl or www.minfin.nl

Central banks

Banca d'Italia	www.bancaditalia.it
Banco de Espana	www.bde.es
Banco de Portugal	www.bportugal.pt
Banque Centrale du Luxembourg	www.bcl.lu
Banque de France	www.banque-france.fr
Banque Nationale de Belgique	www.bnb.be
Danmarks Nationalbank	www.nationalbanken.dk
De Nederlandsche Bank	www.bnb.nl
Deutsche Bundesbank	www.bundesbank.de
European Central Bank (ECB)	www.ecb.int
Central Bank of Ireland	www.centralbank.ie
National Bank of Greece	www.bankofgreece.gr
Oesterreichische Nationalbank	www.oenb.co.at
Suomen Pankki	www.bof.fi
Sveriges Riksbank	www.riksbank.se
Swiss National Bank	www.snb.ch

US Federal Reserve

The Board of Governors and each of the 12 Reserve banks have their own sites. The sites offer a variety of materials, including basic information about the economy, money, and banking; regional and economic data; upcoming conferences and events; tour information; text of speeches, publications, articles, reports, and other research; and economic education materials.

Board of Governors website	www.federalreserve.gov
Atlanta website	www.frbatlanta.org
Boston website	www.bos.frb.org
Chicago website	www.frbchi.org
Cleveland website	www.clev.frb.org
Dallas website	www.dallasfed.org
Kansas City website	www.kc.frb.org
Minneapolis website	woodrow.mpls.frb.fed.us
New York website	www.ny.frb.org
Philadelphia website	www.phil.frb.org
Richmond website	www.rich.frb.org
St Louis website	www.stls.frb.org
San Francisco website	www.frbsf.org

Economics on the net

Nouriel Roubini	www.stern.nyu.edu/~nroubini/asia/AsiaHomepage.html
Paul Krugman	web.mit.edu/krugman/www
National Bureau of Economic Research	www.nber.org
Nicholas Economides	raven.stern.nyu.edu/networks
Hal Varian	sims.berkeley.edu/resources/infoecon

US economic indicators

CPI	stats.bls.gov/news.release/cpi.toc.htm
Durable Goods	www.census.gov/ftp/pub/indicator
Employment	stats.bls.gov:80/newsrels.htm

GDP	www.bea.doc.gov/
Housing Starts	www.census.gov/pub/const/ www/c20index.html
Industrial Production	www.borg.frb/fed.us/releases/ G17
US International Trade	www.census.gov/foreign-trade/
NAPM	www.napm.org/public/rob/ index2.html
PPI	stats.bls.gov/news.release/ ppi.toc.htm
Retail Sales	www.census.gov/svsd/www/ advtable.html
Unemployment Insurance Claims	www.dol.gov/dol/public/ media/main.html
Personal Income and Wages and Salaries Bureau of Economic Analysis	www.bea.doc.gov
Initial Claims for Unemployment Insurance	www.itsc.state.md.us/data_ stats/data_stats.html
Help Wanted and Consumer Confidence Conference Board	www.conference-board.org
Construction Contracts F W Dodge	www.mag.fwdodge.com
Housing Permits Bureau of the Census	www.census.gov/pub/const/ Building_Permits/

Bibliography

Ariel, R.A. High stock returns before holidays: existence and evidence on possible causes. *Journal of Finance* 1990; 45:1611–26.

Bachelier, L. Théorie de la Spéculation. In *Annales de l'Ecole Normale Supérieure*, vol. 3. Paris: Gauthier-Villars, 1900. (English translation in Cooter, P.H. (ed.), *The Random Character of Stock Market Prices*. Cambridge: MIT Press, 1964.)

Banz, R. The Relationship between return and market value of common stocks. *Journal of Financial Economics* 1981; 3–18.

Bayes, T. An essay toward solving a problem in the doctrine of chances. *Philosophical Transactions*, Essay LII, 1763: 370–418.

Baxter, M. and Jermann, U. The International Diversification Puzzle is worse than you think. *American Economic Review* 1997; 87:177–80.

Benartzi, S. and Thaler, R.H. Myopic loss aversion and the equity premium puzzle. *Quarterly Journal of Economics* 1995; 110:73–92.

Black, F. The pricing of commodity contracts. *Journal of Financial Economics* 1976;3:167–79.

Black, F. How we came up with the option formula. *Journal of Portfolio Management* 1989.

Black, F. and Scholes, M.S. The valuation of options contracts and a test of market efficiency. *Journal of Finance* 1972; 27: 399–417.

Black, F. and Scholes, M.S. The pricing of options and corporate liabilities. *Journal of Political Economy* 1973; 81: 637–54.

Black, F., Jensen, M.C. and Scholes, M. S. The capital asset pricing model: some empirical tests. In: Jensen, M. (ed.) *Studies in the Theory of Capital Markets*. New York: Praeger, 1972.

Blake, D. *Financial Market Analysis*. John Wiley, 2000.

Blanchard, O.J. Speculative bubbles, crashes and rational expectations. *Economic Letters* 1979; 3:387–89.

Blanchard, O.J. and Watson, M.W. Bubbles, rational expectations and financial markets. In: Wachtel, P. (ed.) *Crisis in the Economic and Financial System*. Lexington, Massachusetts: Lexington Books, 1982: 295–315.

Blinder, A. *Central Banking in Theory and Practice*. MIT Press, 1998.

Bookstaber, R.M. *Option Pricing and Strategies in Investing*. Reading, MA: Addison-Wesley, 1982.

Brown, P., Kiem, D., Kleidon, A. and Marsh, T. Stock return seasonalities and the tax loss selling hypothesis: analysis of the arguments and Australian evidence. *Journal of Financial Economics* 1983.

Burns, A. and Mitchell, W. *Measuring Business Cycles* 1946.

Campbell, J.Y. and Shiller, R. Stock prices earnings and expected dividends. *Journal of Finance* 1988; 43:661–76.

Canner, N., Mankiw, N.G. and Weil, D.N. An asset allocation puzzle. *American Economic Review* 1997; 181–91.

Chen, N., Ross, S.A. and Roll, R. Economic forces and the stock market. *Journal of Business* 1986.

Cochrane, J. New facts in finance. Economic perspectives. *Federal Reserve Bank of Chicago,* 1997; 21:3–37.

Cochrane, J. *Portfolio Advice For a MultiFactor World*. NBER Working Paper no. 7170, 1999.

Constantinides, G.M., Donaldson, J.B. and Mehra, R. *Junior can't borrow: a new perspective on the equity premium puzzle*. NBER Working Paper no. 6617, 1998.

Cox, J.S., Ross, S.A. and Rubinstein, M. Option pricing: a simplified approach. *Journal of Financial Economics* 1979.

Cox, J.S. and Rubinstein, M. A survey of alternative option pricing models. In: Brenner, M. (ed.), *Option Pricing*. Cambridge, MA: Heath, 1993.

Cutler, D., Poterba, J. and Summers, L. What moves stock prices? *Journal of Portfolio Management* 1989;15:4–12.

David, P. The dynamo and the computer: an historical perspective on the productivity paradox. *American Economic Review Papers and Proceedings* 1990; 80:355–61.

David, P. Understanding digital technology's evolution and the path of measured productivity growth: present and future in the mirror of the past. In: Brynolfson, E. and Kahin, B. (eds), *Understanding the Digital Economy*. MIT Press, 2000.

Davis, S.J., Haltwinger, J.C. and Schuh, S. *Job Creation and Destruction*. Cambridge, Mass.: MIT Press, 1996.

DeBondt, W.F.M. and Thaler, R.H. Does the stock market overreact? *Journal of Finance* 1985; 40:793–805.

De Long, J.B., Shleifer, A., Summers, L.H. and Waldmann, R.J. Noise trader risk in financial markets. *Journal of Political Economy* 1990; 98:703–38.

Dewing, A., (1953) *The Financial Policy of Corporations*. New York: The Ronald Press, 1953.

Dumas, A. and Solnick, B. *The world price of exchange rate risk*. HEC School of Management Working Paper, 1993.

Estes, R. *Dictionary of Accounting*. Cambridge, MA: MIT Press, 1981:81–105.

Fama, E.F. The behavior of stock market prices. *Journal of Business* 1965; 38:34–105.

Fama, E.F. Efficient capital markets: a review of theory and empirical work. *Journal of Finance* 1970; 25:383–417.

Fama, E.F. Term-structure forecasts of interest rates, inflation, and real returns. *Journal of Monetary Economics* 1990a; 25:59–76.

Fama, E.F. Efficient capital markets: a review of theory and empirical work. *Journal of Finance* 1990b; 25: 383–423.

Fama, E.F. Efficient capital markets II. *Journal of Finance* 1991; 46:1575–617.

Fama, E.F. Market efficiency, long term returns, and behavioural finance. *Journal of Financial Economics* 1998.

Fama, E.F. and French, K.R. The cross section of expected stock returns. *Journal of Finance* 1992;47:427–66.

Fama, E.F. and French, K.R. Multifactor explanations of asset pricing anomalies. *Journal of Finance* 1996.

Fama, E.F., Fisher, L., Jensen, M.C. and Roll, R. The adjustment of stock prices to new information. *International Economic Review* 1969;10:1–21.

Fosler, G. and Stiroh, K.J. A sectoral perspective on economic stability. *Business Economics* 1998; 33:46–52.

French, K.R. Stock returns and the weekend effect. *Journal of Financial Economics*, 1980;8, pp. 55–69.

French, K. and Poterba, J. International diversification and international equity markets. *American Economic Review* 1991; 81:222–26.

Fisher, I. Appreciation and interest. *Publications of the American Economic Association* 1896:23–9, 91–2.

Fisher, I. *The Rate of Interest.* New York: Macmillan, 1907.

Fisher, I. *The Theory of Interest.* New York: Macmillan, 1930.

Friedman, M. The role of monetary policy. *American Economic Review* 1968; 58:1–17.

Garber, P.M. Who put the mania in tulipmania? *The Journal of Portfolio Management* 1989; 16:53–60.

Garber, P.M. Tulipmania. *Journal of Political Economy* 1989; 97:535–60.

Garber, P.M. Famous first bubbles. *Journal of Economic Perspectives* 1990; 4.

Garber, P.M. *Famous First Bubbles: The Fundamentals of Early Manias.* Cambridge, Mass.: MIT Press, 2000.

Gordon, R.J. Inflation, flexible exchange rates, and the natural rate of unemployment. In: Baily, M.N. (ed.), *Workers, Jobs and Inflation.*Washington, D.C.: Brookings Institution, 1982: 88–152.

Gordon, R.J. Can the inflation of the 1970s be explained? *Brookings Papers on Economic Activity* 1997; 8:253–77.

Gordon, R.J. The time varying NAIRU and its implications for economic policy. *Journal of Economic Perspectives* 1997; 11:11–32.

Gordon, R.J. Monetary policy in the age of information and technology: computers and the Solow paradox. 1998a.

Gordon, R.J. Foundations of the Goldilocks economy: supply shocks and the time-varying NAIRU. *Brookings Papers on Economic Activity* 1998b:297–346.

Gordon, R.J. Has the 'new economy' rendered the productivity slowdown obsolete? Working Paper, Northwestern University, 1999.

Graham, B, and Dodd, D. *Securities Analysis.* New York: McGraw-Hill, 1934.

Greenspan, A. *The Challenge of Central Banking in a Democratic Society.* Remarks at The Annual Dinner and Francis Boyer Lecture at the American Enterprise Institute for Public Policy Research, Washington, D.C. 1996.

Greenspan, A. *Monetary Policy Testimony and Report to Congress.* Subcommittee on Domestic and International Monetary

Policy on Banking and Financial Services, U.S. House of Representatives, 1997.

Griliches, Z. Productivity, R&D, and the data constraint. *American Economic Review* 1994; 84:1–23.

Hall, R. E. The Stock Market and Capital Accumulation. http://www.stanford. edu/~rehall/ SMCA-d%205–12–00.pdf. (2000).

Hardouvelis, G.A. *Evidence on stock market speculative bubbles: Japan, United States and Great Britain.* Federal Reserve Bank of New York, Research Paper no. 8810, 1988.

Harris, L. How to profit from intradaily stock returns. *Journal of Portfolio Management* 1986; 12:61–4.

Haugen, R.A. *The Inefficient Stock Market.* Prentice Hall, 1999a.

Haugen, R.A. *The New Finance.* Prentice Hall, 1999b.

Holstrom, B. and Tirole, J. *LAPM: a liquidity-based asset pricing model.* NBER Working Paper no. 6673, 1998.

Jacquillat, A. and Solnik, B. Multinationals are poor tools for diversification. *Journal of Portfolio Management* 1978; 4:3–12.

Jensen, M.C. Some anomalous evidence regarding market efficiency. *Journal of Financial Economics* 1978; 6:95–101.

Jorion, P. and Goetzmann, W.N. Global stock markets in the twentieth century. *Journal of Finance* 1999; 54:953–80.

Jorgenson, D. and Stiroh, K. Information technology and growth. *American Economic Review Papers and Proceedings* 1999; 89:109–22.

Kahneman, D. and Tversky, A. Choices, values, and frames. *American Psychologist,* 1994; 39:342–47.

Kahneman, D., Knetsch, J.L. and Thaler, R.H. Experimental tests of the endowment effect and the Coase theorem. *Journal of Political Economy* 1990; 98:1325–48.

Keim, D.B. and Stambaugh, R.F. Predicting returns in the stock and bond markets. *Journal of Financial Economics* 1986; 17:357–90.

Kettell, B. *What Drives Financial Markets?* Financial Times-Prentice Hall, 1998.

Kettell, B. *Fed Watching.* Financial Times-Prentice Hall, 1999.

Kettell, B. *What Drives Currency Markets?* Financial Times-Prentice Hall, 2000.

Keynes, J.M. *The General Theory of Employment, Interest and Money.* New York: Harcourt, Brace and Co., 1936.

Krugman, P. How fast can the U.S. economy grow? *Harvard Business Review* 1997; 75:123–29.

Krugman, P. *The Accidental Theorist*. W.W. Norton, 1998.

Krugman, P. and Obstfeld, M. *International Economics*. Addison Wesley, 1998.

Lakonishok, J. and Smidt, S. Are seasonal anomalies real? A ninety-year perspective. *Review of Financial Studies* 1988; 1:403–25.

Lehman, M. B. *The Business One Guide to Using the Wall Street Journal*. Business One, 1990.

Levis, M. Are small firms big performs? *The Investment Analyst* 1985.

Lintner, J. The aggregation of investors, diverse judgements and preferences in purely competitive security markets. *Journal of Financial and Quantitative Analysis* 1971; 4:327–450.

Livingston, M. *Money and Capital Markets*. Blackwell Business, 1995.

Lo, A.W. and Mackinlay, A.C. *A Non-Random Walk Down Wall Street*. Princeton: Princeton University Press, 1999.

Lucas, R.E. Understanding business cycles. In: Brunner, K. and Meltzer, A.H. (eds), *Carnegie-Rochester Conference Series on Public Policy*, 1977; 5:10.

Lucas, R.E. On the mechanics of economic development. *Journal of Monetary Economics* 1986; 3–42.

Macaulay, F. *Some Theoretical Problems Suggested by The Movements of Interest Rates, Bond Yields and Stock Prices in the United States Since 1856*. New York: National Bureau for Economic Research, 1938.

Mackay, C. *Memoirs of Extraordinary Popular Delusions and the Madness of Crowds*. London: Bentley, 1841.

Malkiel, B.G. Expectations, bond prices and the term structure of interest rates. *Quarterly Journal of Economics* 1962.

Malkiel, B.G. *A Random Walk Down Wall Street*, 10th edn. W.W. Norton and Company, 2000.

Malkiel, B.G. and Cragg, J.G. Expectations and the structure of share prices. *American Economic Review* 1970.

Mandelbrot, B. *Fractals and Scaling in Finance; Discontinuity, Concentration, Risk*. New York: Springer-Verlag, 1997.

Markowitz, H.M. Portfolio selection. *Journal of Finance* 1952; 7:13–37.

Markowitz, H.M. *Portfolio Selection*. New Haven Connecticut: Yale University Press, 1959.

McTeer, R.D. *The New Paradigm*. Annual Report of the Federal Reserve Bank of Dallas, 1999.

Mehra, R. and Prescott, E.C. The equity premium puzzle. *Journal of Monetary Economics* 1985; 15:145–61.

Mehra, R. and Prescott, E.C. The equity premium puzzle. *Journal of Monetary Economics* 1988; 22:133–36.

Merton, R.C. The theory of rational option pricing. *Bell Journal of Economics and Management Science* 1973; 4:141–83.

Merton, R.C. *Continuous Time Finance.* Cambridge: Cambridge University Press, 1990.

Merton, R.C. Influence of mathematical models in finance on practice: past present and future. *Financial Practice and Education* 1995; 5:7–15.

Meyer, L.H. *Statement on Monetary Policy.* Committee on Banking and Financial Services, U.S. House of Representatives, 1997.

Modigliani, F. and Miller, M. The cost capital, corporation finance and the theory of investment. *The American Economic Review* 1958; 48:261–97.

Modigliani, F. and Papademos, L. Targets for monetary policy in the coming year. *Brookings Papers on Economic Activity* 1975;1:141–63.

Modigliani, F. and Cohn, R.A. Inflation, rational valuation, and the market. *Financial Analysts' Journal* 1979; 35:22–44. (Reprinted in Johnson, S. (ed.), *The Collected Papers of Franco Modigliani,* Vol. 5. Cambridge, Mass.: MIT Press, 1989.)

Mossin, J. Equilibrium in a capital assets market. *Econometrica* 1966; 34:768–83.

Nakamura, L. Intangibles: what put the new in the new economy? *Federal Reserve Bank of Philadelphia Business Review* 1999.

Niemira, M.P. and Zukowski, G. *Trading the Fundamentals: The Trader's Complete Guide to Interpreting Economic Indicators and Monetary Policy.* Chicago: Probus Publishing Company, Inc., 1994.

Obstfeld, M. and Rogoff, K. The six major puzzles in international macroeconomics: is there a common cause? *National Bureau of Economic Research Working Paper* 7777, 2000.

Oliver, S. and Sichel, D. *The resurgence of growth in the late 1990s: is information technology the story?* Paper given at the conference on Structural Change and Monetary Policy at the Federal Reserve Bank of San Francisco, 2000.

Phelps, E.S. Money wage dynamics and labour market equilibrium. *Journal of Political Economy* 1968; 76:678–711.

Phillips, A.W. The relation between Uunemployment and the rate of change of money wage rates in the United Kingdom, 1861–1957. *Economica* 1958; 25:283–99.

Poterba, J. and Summers, L. Mean reversion in stock prices: evidence and implications. *Journal of Financial Economics* 1988; 22:27–59.

Rich, R.W. and Rissmiller, D. Understanding the recent behaviour of US inflation. *Current Issues in Economics and Finance*, Federal Reserve Bank of New York, 2000.

Ritter, J. and Warr, R.S. *Decline of inflation and the bull markets of 1982–1997*. University of Florida, Gainesville, 1999.

Roberts, H.V. Stock market patterns and financial analysis: methodological suggestions. *Journal of Finance* 1959.

Roll, R. A critique of the asset pricing theory's tests. Part 1: on past and potential testability of the theory. *Journal of Financial Economics* 1977; 129–76.

Ross, S.A. The arbitrage theory of capital asset pricing. *Journal of Economic Theory* 1976;13:342–60.

Ross, S.A. The current status of the capital asset pricing model (CAPM). *Journal of Finance* 1978.

Roll, R. and Ross, S.A. An empirical investigation of the arbitrage pricing theory. *Journal of Finance* 1980; 35: 1073–103.

Romer, P. Increasing returns and long-run growth. *Journal of Political Economy* 1986; 1002–37.

Romer, P. The origins of endogenous growth. *Journal of Economic Perspectives* 1994; 3–22.

Rozeff, M. and Kinney, W. Capital market seasonality; the case of stock returns. *Journal of Financial Economics* 1976; 3:379–402.

Samuelson, P.A. and Solow, R.M. Analytical aspects of anti-inflation policy. *American Economic Review* 1960; 40:174–94.

Samuelson, P.A. *Economics*, 10th edn. New York: McGraw-Hill, 1976.

Schiller, R.J. *Investor behaviour in the October 1987 stock market crash*. National Bureau of Economic Research Working Paper no. 2446, 1987.

Schiller, R.J. *Market Volatility*. Cambridge, Massachusetts: Cambridge University Press, 1989.

Schiller, R.J. *Irrational Exuberance*. Princeton: Princeton University Press, 2000a.

Schiller, R.J. Measuring bubble expectations and investor confidence. *Journal of Psychology and Market,* 2000b; 1:49–60.

Sharpe, W.F. Capital asset prices: a theory of market equilibrium under condition of risk. *Journal of Finance* 1964.

Sharpe, W.F. Mutual fund performance. *Journal of Business* 1966.

Sharpe, W.F. Portfolio analysis. *Journal of Financial and Quantitative Analysis* 1967; 2:425–39.

Sharpe, W.F. Investor wealth measures and expected return. In: Sharpe, W. F. (ed.), *Quantifying the Market Risk Premium Phenomenon for Investment Decision-Making*. Charlottesville, Virginia: The Institute of Chartered Financial Analysts, 1990:29–37.

Sharpe, W.F., Alexander, G.J. and Bailey, J.V. *Investments*. Prentice Hall, 1995.

Siegel, J. The real rate of interest from 1800–1990: A study of the US and UK. Working Paper, Wharton School, 1991.

Siegel, J. The equity premium: stock and bond returns since 1802. *Financial Analysts Journal* 1992; 48:28–38.

Siegel, J. *Stocks for the Long Run: A Guide to Selecting Markets for Long-Term Growth*. Burr Ridge, Illinois: Irwin Professional Publishing, 1995.

Solow, R.M. A contribution to the theory of economic growth. *Quarterly Journal of Economics* 1956; 65–94.

Solow, R.M. We'd better watch out. *New York Times Book Review* 1987; July 12th: p.36.

Smithers, A. and Wright, S. *Valuing Wall Street: Protecting Wealth in Turbulent Markets*. McGraw Hill, 2000.

Staiger, D., Stock, J.H. and Watson, M.W. The NAIRU, unemployment and monetary policy. *Journal of Economic Perspectives* 1997; 11:33–50.

Taylor, J.B. Discretion versus policy rules in practice. *Carnegie-Rochester Conference Series on Public Policy* 1993; 39:195–214.

Taylor, J.B. The inflation/output variability tradeoff revisited. In: *Goals, Guidelines, and Constraints Facing Monetary Policymakers*. Federal Reserve Bank of Boston, 1994.

Thaler, R.H. *Advances in Behavioural Finance*. New York: Russell Sage Foundation, 1993.

Thaler, R.H. Behavioural economics. *NBER Reporter, National Bureau of Economic Research* 1995; 9–13.

Thaler, R.H. and Shefin, H. An economic theory of self-control. *Journal of Political Economy* 1981; 89:392–406.

Thaler, R.H., Tversky, D. and Knetsch, J.L. Experimental tests of the endowment effect. *Journal of Political Economy* 1990; 98:1325–48.

Thaler, R.H., Tversky, D. and Knetsch, J.L. Endowment effect, loss aversion, and status quo bias. *Journal of Economic Perspectives* 1991; 5:193–206.

Tobin, J. Liquidity preference as behaviour toward risk. *Review of Economic Studies* 1958; 65–85.

Treynor, J.L. How to rate management investment funds. *Harvard Business Review* 1965.

Treynor, J.L. Information-based investing. *Financial Analysts Journal* 1989; 6–7.

Treynor, J.L. The 10 most important questions to ask in selecting a money manager. *Financial Analysts Journal*, 1990; 4–5.

Tversky, A. and Kahnemann, D. Judgement under uncertainty: heuristics and biases. *Science* 1974; 1124–31.

Wadhwani, S. The US stock and the global economic crisis. *National Institute Economic Review* 1999; 86–105.

Wadhwani, S. Monetary challenges in a 'new economy'. *Bank of England Quarterly Bulletin* 2000; 40:411–22.

Zarnowitz, V. *Business Cycles: Theory, History, Indicators and Forecasting.* Chicago: The University of Chicago Press, 1992.

Zarnowitz, V. Theory and history behind business cycles: are the 1990s the onset of a golden age? *Journal of Economic Perspectives* 1999; 13:69–90.

Zeeman, E.C. On the unstable behaviour of stock exchanges. *Journal of Mathematical Economics* 1974; 1:39–49.

Index

Training in Financial Markets

Brian Kettell, author of *Economics for Financial Markets*, runs training courses on financial markets for banks, financial institutions, investment banks and for institutional and retail investors.

The courses are taught in-house and can be modified according to the needs of the client. Courses currently being taught range from graduate trainee programmes to courses on specific instruments and markets.

Among the courses offered are:

- economics of financial markets – what lies behind all this volatility?
- graduate training programme for newcomers to financial markets
- financial markets for dealers/fund managers/investors
- US economic indicators – which ones should you watch?
- foreign exchange market fundamentals for dealers/fund managers/investors
- portfolio management and investment analysis: the basics
- Fed-watching for dealers/fund managers/investors
- finance for non-financial managers
- statistics and mathematics for financial markets: what you really need to know.

For further information on in-house training, please contact:
Brian Kettell at bkettell@hotmail.com